Developing Leisure Time Skills

for People with

Autism Spectrum Disorders

Practical Strategies

for Home, School

& Community

Phyllis Coyne,
Mary Lou Klagge &
Colleen Nyberg

REVISED & EXPANDED SECOND EDITION

Developing Leisure Time Skills for People with Autism Spectrum Disorders

All marketing and publishing rights guaranteed to and reserved by:

FUTURE HORIZONS INC.

721 W Abram St, Arlington, TX 76013

800-489-0727 (toll free)

817-277-0727 (local)

817-277-2270 (fax)

E-mail: *info@fhautism.com*

www.fhautism.com

ISBN: 9781941765036

Contents

Preface

Leisure represents time free of obligations, when an individual can choose to pursue activities of interest. For most of us, leisure is enjoyable and something that we eagerly anticipate. We may choose to use leisure time to challenge ourselves, relax, express ourselves creatively, be entertained, or socialize.

For individuals with Autism Spectrum Disorder (ASD) unstructured or free time is often very challenging. Family members and service providers who support them may wish that they could entertain themselves safely, even for just a few minutes.

When individuals with ASD are engaged in personally meaningful activities, challenging behavior often decreases. Satisfying leisure engagement increases the quality of life for everyone involved, so parents, caregivers, teachers, and service providers want to know how to assist them to be more independent and self-directing in leisure.

This book provides a comprehensive, structured process which addresses what to do to engage individuals in activities, help them discover new leisure interests, and teach them the skills for preferred leisure activities at home, school, work, and in the community. The useful strategies, guidelines, and tools will assist individuals with ASD of all ages and abilities to increase leisure satisfaction. The methods of leisure assessment and the Components of Leisure Development focus on the unique needs of each individual with ASD. Real life examples of one adult and two children with differing severity levels of ASD in real life settings illustrate practical aspects of applying the principles and techniques.

This book is a valuable resource for the wide range of people who support individuals with ASD, including family members, caregivers, babysitters, teachers, recreation service providers, certified therapeutic recreation specialists (CTRS), physical education teachers, adaptive physical education specialists, occupational therapists (OTRS), university students in the previous professions, program directors, residential staff, youth service workers, camp staff, and autism consultants. Different sections of this book may be more useful depending on your role with individuals with ASD. For instance, family members, babysitters, respite care providers, and others who support individuals with ASD can employ the user friendly Activity Cards to facilitate exposure to new activities, while some of the more technical aspects of assessment and training may be used more frequently by professionals, such as teachers, recreation specialists, and occupational therapists (OTRs).

Contents of This Book

The six chapters and four appendices in this book cover subjects and provide resources vital to leisure engagement for individuals with ASD.

- Chapter 1 provides the foundation for understanding the importance of leisure engagement and the impact of ASD on leisure engagement.
- Chapter 2 introduces the three components of leisure development. These include the *Immediate Component, Exposure Component,* and *Training Component.*
- Chapter 3 describes a variety of methods and tools for gathering the necessary information to facilitate decision making for developing leisure interests and skills. Use of the tools is illustrated through sample completed assessment forms.
- Chapter 4 explains and provides examples for the elements of the *Immediate Component.* This component provides appealing materials that generate immediate interest because of their sensory features and/or relationship to special interests.
- Chapter 5 explains and provides examples for the elements of the *Exposure Component,* including guidelines for activity selection and evidence-based support strategies. This component provides structured, repeated exposure to new activities with preferred sensory features and/ or inclusion of special interests to develop new interests.
- Chapter 6 explains and provides examples for the elements of the *Training Component,* including recommendations for evidence-based practices. This component provides training in the skills necessary for choosing and participating in preferred activities in the home, school or work, and community.
- Appendix A provides lists of typical and age appropriate behaviors and activities for use with some of the assessment tools and to help generate ideas for leisure activities.
- Appendix B contains 10 reproducible blank forms with directions for the methods of assessment introduced in Chapters 3, 4, and 6 in a large-size format for easy photocopying.
- Appendix C provides a checklist of support strategies, as well as glossaries of terms for support and training strategies to aid in the use of evidence-based practices in the *Exposure* and *Training Components.*
- Appendix D provides easy to use Activity Cards for 48 activities in a large-size format for easy photocopying.

Revisions and Additions in the Second Edition

The understanding of ASD and leisure engagement has grown, since the first edition of this book was published in 2000 as *Developing Leisure Time Skills for Persons with Autism*. As a result, a number of revisions and additions have been made in the second edition. This revised and expanded edition provides the most up-to-date information on ASD and leisure pursuits and reflects some of the major changes in the field. The following provides a sample of the new information contained in this edition:

- up-to-date review of the literature on leisure and individuals with ASD;
- expanded information on how to apply the three Components of Leisure Development;
- latest evidence-based practices;
- more real life examples for the three individuals featured in this book, who span childhood to adulthood and the full autism spectrum;
- new and expanded appendices;
- more assessment tools;
- revised Activity Cards.

How to Use This Book

If you do not have the time to read this book from beginning to end, we recommend that you begin with the review of the Table of Contents to familiarize yourself with what it covers. Then carefully read Chapters 1 and 2 so that you understand the foundational concepts of this book. Once you have the foundation, you can focus on parts of the book that are most relevant to your situation and the individual(s) with ASD that you support. This book is designed as a resource for you to return to again and again, as you need more information or tools.

The approach and information in this book are based on our 90 plus years of collective experience working with individuals with ASD and providing training for the families members and professionals who support them. We hope that the practical and comprehensive information in this book will help you feel more confident and rewarded as you increase the quality of life of individuals with ASD and their families.

Leisure and Autism Spectrum Disorder

Chapter 1

utism Spectrum Disorder (ASD) is a complex and pervasive neurodevelopmental disability. This disorder has recently grown to an estimated 1 in 68 children in the United States (Centers for Disease Control and Prevention, 2014). As the number of individuals with ASD increases, so does the need to focus on their quality of life. Quality of life for people with ASD consists of the same aspects of life for all of us, including leisure engagement.

Leisure represents time free from obligations when we can choose to pursue activities of interest. Participation in leisure activities fills an important need in our lives and enhances our quality of life. We are all different in our leisure pursuits. Some of us like doing things primarily by ourselves while others are more group-oriented. However, most of us do a variety of activities alone and with others in our home, school, work, and community. Conversely, unstructured or free time may be one of the most challenging times for an individual on the autism spectrum and those who support him.

Importance of Leisure Engagement

Leisure engagement can increase our quality of life (García-Villamisar 2007; Hutchinson et al, 2008; Garcia-Villamisar & Dattilo, 2010). The importance of leisure participation has been recognized in international and federal laws, including the United Nation's Convention on the Rights of the Child (1989), the No Child Left Behind Act (2001), the Individuals with Disabilities Education Improvement Act (2004), the Rehabilitation Act Amendments (2003), and the Americans with Disabilities Act (2010).

When taught to enjoy their free time by engaging in personally satisfying, age appropriate leisure activities, individuals with ASD experience many benefits. Participation in leisure activities enhances quality of life in the following ways:

- Can increase life and leisure satisfaction.
- Can provide a sense of accomplishment or achievement.
- Can provide enjoyment.
- Can improve physical health.
- Can reduce stress and depression.
- Can increase choice and control (self-determination).
- Can increase participation in the community.
- Can enhance the quality of life of families and staff by easing some stress and reducing the need for constant, intense supervision.

Because of its importance to quality of life, leisure is being included more and more in individual support plans (ISPs), individualized educational plans (IEPs), and other formal plans for individuals with ASD. To ensure success, the approach to meeting these goals must be systematic and well planned. However, family members, caregivers, teachers, and service providers often have little guidance on how to assist individuals with ASD to have personally meaningful and satisfying leisure pursuits.

Nature of Autism Spectrum Disorder

Understanding the nature of ASD is vital, if the goal is to enable individuals with ASD to actively choose and engage in a variety of leisure activities in a variety of environments. The core characteristics of ASD, can seriously impact leisure engagement both positively and negatively (Potvin, Prelock, Snider, & Savard, 2013). These characteristics include:

- impairments in social communication and social interaction;
- restricted, repetitive patterns of behavior, interests, or activities (APA, 2013).

Despite their limitations, individuals with ASD are able to develop leisure interests and skills that they can choose and enjoy during unstructured time. However, to develop their interests and skills, they need a comprehensive, structured approach, such as the one promoted in this book, which focuses on using the characteristics as strengths as much as possible, and to accommodate for them where necessary. Some characteristics, such as adherence to routine and seeking sensory input, can be used as strengths in developing leisure competence.

Social Interactions

By definition, individuals with ASD have impairments in social communication and social interaction (APA, 2013) and these individuals often express concern about their difficulties with relationships and social interaction during leisure (Brewster & Coleyshaw, 2011; Fullerton & Rake, 2014). This aspect of ASD may lead to challenges with leisure activities because many leisure activities include social interactions that are cooperative or competitive in nature. This can range from sharing materials and waiting for a turn to all the social complexities of being part of a sports team or the intricate and vague demands of social gatherings (e.g., parties).

Furthermore, the social requirements in leisure activities can be demotivating for individuals with ASD and potentially anxiety provoking (Brown and Murray, 2001). Therefore, individuals on the spectrum tend to engage in solitary activities that do not require social interaction (Badia, Orgaz,

Verdugo, & Ullán, 2013; Buttimer & Tierney, 2005, Orsmond, Krauss, & Seltzer, 2004). These solitary activities may include leisure pastimes like watching television, listening to music, going for walks, and building models. In addition, individuals with ASD also participate in fewer casual social activities (e.g., socializing with relatives, neighbors, schoolmates, or work friends) than those both with and without other disabilities (Orsmond et al. 2004).

The social demands of a leisure activity significantly affect the enjoyment and success of individuals with ASD. Depending on the activity and skills of an individual, an activity can either be a major challenge or a way to meet others and form friendships around mutual interests and shared activities. Often individuals on the spectrum have difficulty with an activity or refuse to participate because the social skills required are too demanding given their current skills.

Individuals with ASD are more apt to enjoy leisure experiences that have a low demand for social interaction (e.g., swimming, photography, and collections) or very clear rules that govern interaction (e.g., board games and ping pong). Sometimes an activity can be done at different levels of social difficulty to match an individual's social skills and comfort level. For instance, if playing basketball as part of a team is too complex, a person may enjoy shooting baskets alone or with one or two people instead.

Restricted, Repetitive Behavior Patterns, Interests, or Activities

The restricted, repetitive patterns of behavior, interests, or activities that are inherent to ASD negatively impact and limit leisure engagement. These patterns may include any combination of the following:

- stereotyped or repetitive use of objects;
- excessive adherence to routines or excessive resistance to change;
- highly restricted, fixated interests;
- hyper or hypo-reactivity to sensory input or unusual interest in sensory aspects of objects and the environment (APA, 2013).

Stereotyped or Repetitive Use of Objects

When left on their own, individuals with ASD tend to spend inordinate amounts of time in repetitive and persistent activities, such as turning on/off lights or electronics, hand or object flapping, and body rocking. They may get stuck on one or a few activities reflecting earlier stages of development, including simple exploration and manipulation of objects (e.g., mouthing, banging, and twisting). Additional repetitive actions include stacking, lining up, sorting, matching, sequencing, fitting objects into spaces, or putting objects in order.

Leisure activities that incorporate stereotyped or repetitive actions can be used positively to motivate engagement during unstructured times. For instance, certain card games (e.g., Yugio and Magik) and many other video games involve ordering objects in some manner over and over again.

Adherence to Routines and Resistance to Change

Individuals on the spectrum develop and seek routine. They may engage in elaborate routines and rituals, such as lining up objects according to size or insistence on the same route. Once routines are established, it can be very difficult to alter them.

However, adherence to routines can also be recognized as a positive when individuals learn routines as part of activities. For instance, individuals with ASD tend to learn long routines in activities quickly and persist in completing activities that have a clear routine. In fact, consistent routines and structure helps an activity to become fun and personally meaningful for individuals with ASD. Structured classes, such as Taekwondo or yoga tend to have consistent routines and some activities, such as line dances or making key chains with gimp have specific routines.

Individuals on the spectrum often resist change of any kind. They like consistency and predictability in the environment and may insist on the same activities. They often resist or avoid new activities, because of their aversion to novelty and preference for familiar actions or objects. Even if they are looking forward to an activity, they may have difficulty coping with aspects of new activities (e.g., new materials, actions, environments, and people). Wearing different clothes for an activity, substitute instructors, and cancellations can all be very stressful.

Preparing individuals for change ahead of time, so they can anticipate what will occur can help reduce the stress associated with change. In addition, certain features can help make activities more predictable, such as:

- regularly scheduled, e.g., music class;
- consistent routine, e.g., line dance;
- clear, static rules, e.g., play checkers;
- reliable structure and organization, e.g., art class;
- well-defined beginning and end, e.g., complete puzzle;
- clear visual representation of what to do, e.g., Legos with diagram.

Restricted Interests and Obsessions

Individuals on the spectrum may pursue particular obsessions or narrowly focused interests, such as fixating on train schedules, weather, geography, electrical supplies, or a particular movie. All of these fixated interests can make it difficult for others to get the individuals involved in traditional leisure activities, which in turn, decreases opportunities for leisure skill development. On the other hand, their intense focus on specific interests may allow individuals with ASD to develop a unique perspective, a specific skill, or a depth of understanding, which may lead to meaningful leisure activities. They may have a noticeably long attention span for activities related to their area of intense focus. Incorporating these passions into activities can promote interest and sustained engagement in leisure activities (Baker, 2000; Boyd, Conroy, Mancil, Nakao, & Alter, 2007; Charlop-Christy & Haymes, 1998).

Individuals who have a special interest in a subject or object are often attracted to catalogs, magazines, books, videos, maps, and objects depicting an element of that subject. They may also seek to depict their special interest through drawing, clay modeling, or other creative mediums.

Unusual Responses to Sensory Experiences

The sensory issues related to ASD can have a tremendous positive or negative impact on participation in leisure activities. Most individuals with ASD have either hyper or hypo-sensitivity to sensory input or unusual interest in sensory aspects of objects and the environment (e.g., excessive smelling or touching of objects, fascination with lights or spinning objects). They may seek out or avoid sensory input from one or more sensory systems, including taste, smell, hearing, vision, touch, and where one's body is in space (i.e., vestibular and proprioceptive).

Individuals with ASD tend to seek out and sustain interaction more with leisure materials that provide favored sensory input and avoid those that are related to sensory sensitivities (Gutierrez-Griep, 1984; Hilton et al, 2008; Hochhauser & Engel-Yeger, 2010; Little, 2012; Potvin et al., 2013). Therefore, it is vital to understand the sensory issues of individuals with ASD.

A variety of types of sensory stimulation may cause extreme discomfort and avoidance, if appropriate supports are not in place (e.g., loud sounds, bright lights, textures, quick movements, and close physical proximity to people). Individuals on the spectrum may try to escape the lighting, movement, crowding, reverberation of sound in a theater, multi-purpose room, or gymnasium.

On the other hand, they may seek sensations through actions, such as jumping, touching objects with attractive textures, rocking, lifting heavy objects, swinging, wearing tight clothes, or hugging. In addition, studies indicate that leisure engagement in individuals with ASD is stimulated by the use of cause and effect toys or objects. Cause and effect materials in which an object does something in response to an action, such as provide lights, sounds, movements, or tactile sensation, often promotes interest. A number of individuals on the spectrum are attracted to electronic and computer games, in part, because of their reactive features.

In conclusion, leisure activities that contain preferred sensory features generate interest and motivate sustained involvement. Consideration needs to be given to individual preferences for sensory feedback and the intensity of sensory stimulation desired.

Three Individuals Featured in this Book

Individuals with ASD may have the same diagnosis, but their abilities and levels of functioning vary widely both across and within individuals over time. They can exhibit any combination of the characteristics described in the previous section in any degree of severity. Each person has his or her own unique strengths, interests, and needs. The adage, "If you've met one person with autism, you've met one person with autism" is a gentle reminder that each person with ASD has a unique personality with a unique combination of interests, strengths, and challenges.

The following section introduces one young adult and two children with different severity levels of ASD to illustrate how abilities and levels of functioning vary widely across and within individuals. Additionally, these three individuals are featured throughout this book to show how principles and methods are applied.

Young Adult: Dan

Dan is a handsome 23-year-old man who lives in a group home and is involved in supported employment 15 hours a week. He uses a few two – three word functional phrases for requests, such as "I want music" and, also, points to line drawings to make requests and choices. He follows basic one step directions and uses a visual schedule of line drawing for activities throughout the day. He appears to enjoy being with people he knows well one-on-one or in a small group of up to four people, but does not initiate interaction other than to make a request.

Dan still demonstrates a variety of restricted and repetitive behaviors, although the behaviors are much less `than when he was younger. For instance, he enjoys listening to contemporary music, but left to his own devices, he would endlessly and exclusively replay his favorite song, "Little Drummer Boy." He records voices of favorite people and then listens to the same recordings over and over again while he simultaneously flaps his hands, laughs boisterously, and sometimes jumps up and down.

Dan has always sought out a variety of sensory input. For instance, he seeks out blowing air, particularly warm air, and frequently lies over heat registers for extended periods. He rubs soft material on parts of his body and walks directly through the clothes hanging on the racks in department stores, if not redirected. He has dropped, hit or thrown objects that result in loud sounds for most of his life. He is fascinated by lights and used to break light bulbs to alter lighting and perhaps create sound. He smells objects and identified his cassette tapes by smelling them, when he was younger. If not supervised, he may gorge on food. He enjoys jumping and other vestibular activities. He retreats from crowded and noisy places.

A great deal is known about Dan's interests and what works for him, due to his age and long history of intervention. At this point, many of his behaviors and interests have been directed to enjoyable leisure activities that are described later in this book.

Preteen: Julie

Julie is an 11-year-old girl who lives at home and attends her local school. She is primarily in a self-contained academic classroom, but is included with general education peers for lunch, recess, specialists, and science classes. She primarily uses verbal language to communicate; however, she does not engage in social conversation. Instead, she almost exclusively makes requests, directs other people, and monologues on her favorite topic, snakes. She has a difficult time communicating her desires and needs when she is anxious or upset. She understands much more when given pictures and written words rather than verbal information. She relies on a written schedule to make the transition from one activity to another and written instructions to complete a sequence of tasks.

Julie enjoys visual input. Currently, her preferred leisure activity is drawing her special interest, snakes. She has significant difficulty with tactile input. When given adequate structure, she will play a board game with one peer. Parents report that it is difficult to introduce Julie to new leisure activities.

Young Child: John

John is an energetic four-year-old boy who lives at home with his mother, father, and older sister. He is enrolled in early childhood special education services. In addition, his mother takes him to an indoor playground at a nearby church basement.

Communication is difficult for John. He makes requests by reaching and grabbing desired objects and protests by screaming, hitting, and kicking. He has recently begun to follow several pictures to complete an activity; however, he does not make requests with pictures.

Most of John's leisure interests are centered on strong sensory feedback. He prefers repetitive motor movements, such as swinging, rocking, bouncing, and jumping. He gets stuck on bouncing or dropping a variety of objects on the floor. He is drawn to hard plastic objects, especially a plastic phone which he bangs on himself, and hard, reverberating surfaces. He quickly establishes unbreakable repetitive routines with new toys. Meanwhile, the rest of his family enjoys a wide variety of activities, especially outdoor pursuits, such as biking, hiking, and camping.

Pattern of Leisure Engagement

Individuals with ASD of all ages and abilities have a significantly limited range of leisure activities. They engage in fewer leisure activities than both those with and without disabilities. Their leisure pursuits are more passive, mostly solitary, and mainly at home (Badia et al., 2013; Buttimer & Tierney, 2005, Hochhauser & Engel-Yeger, 2010; Orsmond et al., 2004; Reynolds, Bendixen, Lawrence, & Lane, 2011).

There is no one leisure activity that will suit every person with ASD. Individuals with ASD have varying strengths, interests, preferences, and challenges. There is a world of possible leisure activities that they could enjoy, such as hobbies, sports, fitness activities, aquatics and water-related activities, arts and crafts, music, dance, art, drama, nature experiences, and games. In addition, there is a wide range of leisure experiences or events, such as spectating and appreciating (e.g., sports, museums, and concerts), community service, relaxation and meditation, self-care (e.g., spa visits and massages), religious events or rituals, studying areas of interest, eating, food preparation, shopping, home improvement, caring for pets and plants, computer and Internet activities, travel, sightseeing, vacations, interacting with family and friends, telephone and e-mail conversations, and watching television (Stumbo & Peterson, 2009).

In fact, individuals with ASD, who did not also have an intellectual disability, have expressed interest in a similar range of activities as their peers, although they actually participated in appreciably fewer activities (Brewster & Coleyshaw, 2010; Potvin et al., 2013). The only type of leisure activity for which children with ASD expressed less interest than peers is physical activities (Potvin et al., 2013). Many individuals with ASD have motor challenges that may cause them to avoid physical activities.

Within this world of leisure possibilities, children with ASD, who do not also have an intellectual disability, engage in some activities more than their neurotypical peers. These activities include:

- transportation vehicles;
- construction activities;

- video games;
- computers;
- science and nature activities (Reynolds et al., 2011);
- swimming (Orsmond & Kuo, 2011; Schleien & Ray, 1997);
- collections.

Individuals on the spectrum tend to have a strong visual-spatial ability related to how objects and figures relate in three-dimensional space, which may, in part, account for their more frequent engagement in construction and other activities that involve putting objects together. Individuals who like assembling often like materials, such as puzzles, Qubits, Rubik's Cube, and puzzle lock toys; individuals who like building often like materials, such as blocks, Legos, and K'Nex. The use of computers also frequently involves putting objects together, as well as a cause and effect reaction. For instance, a number of apps for mobile devices (e.g., tablets, smart phones, and iPod Touch) involve putting something together or actions that cause a reaction.

In contrast, children with ASD participate in some activities less than their typically developing peers (Reynolds et al., 2011). Fewer children with ASD played with dolls or action figures, or engaged in arts and craft activities (e.g., painting or model building). A smaller number of children with ASD than typically developing children participated in music, while about the same number played board and card games (Reynolds et al., 2011).

As adolescents and adults, their leisure pattern tends to become even more restricted. They are often preoccupied with screen based media, such as television, computers, and video games (Hilton et al., 2008; Brewster & Coleyshaw, 2011; Orsmond, & Kuo, 2011; Mazurek et al., 2012). Parents and others who support them are concerned about this pattern of isolation and lack of engagement (Fox, Vaughn, Wyatte, & Dunlap, 2002; Thompson & Emira, 2011).

The patterns described above are not intended to direct the reader to specific activities. Rather, it is provided to inform the reader of noteworthy trends in participation. The reasons for participation in some activities over others may relate to strengths or challenges related to ASD, abilities, opportunities, or other factors. Regardless of the reasons, individuals with ASD need to be systematically exposed to a wide variety of experiences and activities to develop broader interests.

Summary

Leisure engagement contributes to quality of life and life satisfaction. By definition, leisure is a time to participate in activities that one likes to do. The nature of ASD can affect engagement both positively and negatively. This book focuses on using the strengths related to the characteristics of ASD, whenever possible, and accommodating them, where necessary.

The range of leisure engagement is significantly limited for individuals with ASD of all ages and abilities. Through the systematic methods in this book, individuals with ASD can develop leisure interests and skills to actively choose and partake in diverse activities in a variety of environments.

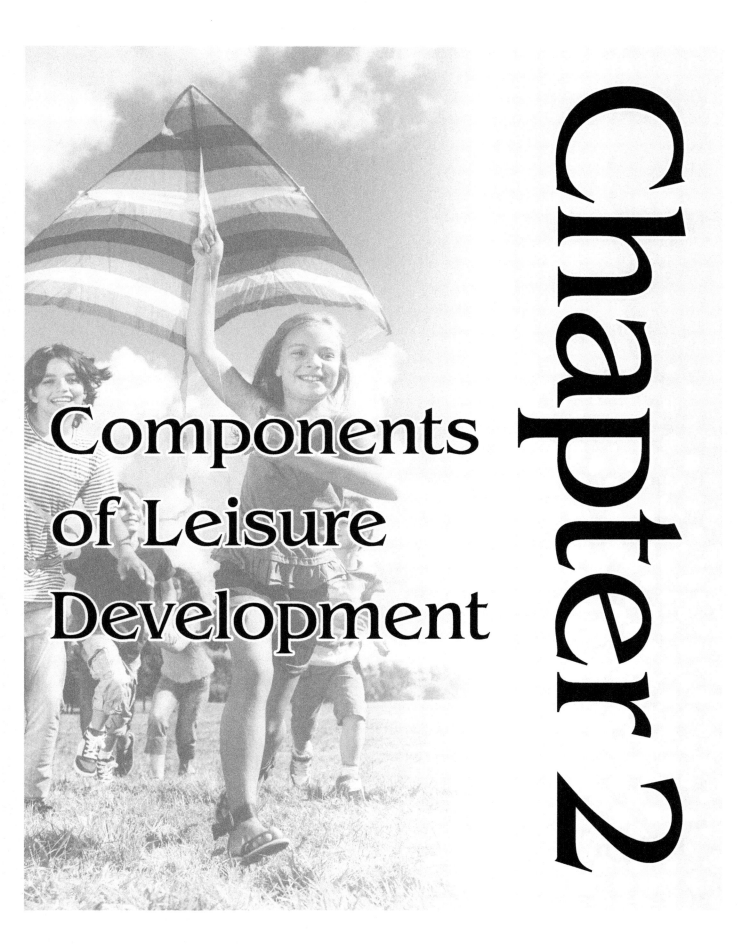

Components of Leisure Development

Chapter 2

Many family members, caregivers, and service providers want to help individuals with Autism Spectrum Disorder (ASD) develop meaningful leisure interests and skills, but do not know an effective, systematic approach. This book provides a comprehensive method to develop leisure skills and interests in the home, school, work, and community for individuals with ASD of all ages and severity of ASD. It presents practical guidelines for three critical Components of Leisure Development for individuals with ASD:

- using untaught activities with sensory features and/or special interests that provide immediate, meaningful engagement during unstructured time (*Immediate Component*);
- repeated and structured exposure to carefully selected leisure activities to develop new interests (*Exposure Component*);
- systematic development of leisure activity and related skills for independent as possible engagement in activities of interest in the home, school, work, and community (*Training Component*).

The ultimate goal of the Components of Leisure Development is for the individual with ASD to have interests and skills to actively choose and engage in meaningful activities of sufficient variety to enhance his quality of life. Each component contributes to this goal in a different manner and has its own essential elements as can be seen below. The first line of the comparison of the Components of Leisure Development reveals the main focus of each component and is followed by its essential elements.

Figure 2.1: Components of Leisure Development		
Immediate	**Exposure**	**Training**
Key Elements:	Key Elements:	Key Elements:
• meaningful engagement during unstructured time; • sensory preferences and special interest; • untaught materials and minimal supervision; • formative assessment.	• discovery of new leisure interests; • guidelines for activity selection; • supported, repeated exposure to new activities; • formative assessment.	• development of leisure activity and related skills; • guidelines for prioritizing activities; • systematic training; • formative assessment.

The Immediate Component

Many individuals with ASD cannot entertain themselves safely for even short periods of unstructured time (Brewster & Coleyshaw, 2010; Fox, Vaughn, Wyatte, & Dunlap, 2002). In this component, toys, games, and other materials that provide preferred sensory input and/or incorporate a special interest are utilized to help individuals with ASD to be meaningfully and safely engaged for a brief time. In addition, it offers relief from the need for constant supervision during unstructured times. The benefits of this approach go beyond a positive way to independently entertain themselves minimizing the need for supervision during free time. It can, also, reduce challenging behaviors the individual may engage in during unstructured times.

This component is referred to as "immediate" because the toys, games, and other materials generate interest right away, do not require instruction, and do not require set-up or preparation. Individuals with ASD are drawn to the materials right away, because they provide the sensory input that they seek and/or depict their special interests. The reason these materials and activities do not need to be taught is that the objects themselves dictate what to do with them or only require a brief demonstration. The need for any instruction is further reduced, because the individual can use the materials in any way desired, as long as it is safe and not destructive.

This component has potential application for unstructured times in all settings (e.g., home, school, work, and community) and with all ages and abilities of individuals on the spectrum. It is particularly effective in the home (e.g., when caregivers need to do chores, or take care of their own personal hygiene) and during short, unstructured times in the community (e.g., waiting for a bus or in a doctor's office and riding in a car or bus). However, it is also useful during brief periods between structured activities at school and during breaks at work.

Materials used in this component may be included in an Individualized Family Service Plan (IFSP), Individualized Education Plan (IEP), Transition Plan, or Individual Support Plan (ISP) under accommodations or supports.

The *Immediate Component* is explained in more detail in Chapter 4.

The Exposure Component

The restricted, repetitive patterns of behavior, interests, or activities that are inherent to ASD negatively impact and limit leisure engagement. Individuals with ASD of all ages engage in fewer leisure activities than both those with and without other disabilities (Badia et al., 2013; Buttimer & Tierney,

2005, Hochhauser & Engel-Yeger, 2010; Orsmond et al., 2004; Reynolds et al., 2011). They tend to resist or be reluctant to try out new activities, so they may not be exposed to the range of leisure experiences available to their peers. Without experience with leisure activities, they, in turn, cannot make informed choices about their leisure involvement.

To offset these challenges, individuals with ASD need to be exposed to a variety of experiences and activities at home, school, work, and in the community in a manner that accommodates their difficulties. Therefore, the *Exposure Component* is designed to broaden leisure interests and pursuits through structured and supported try outs of new leisure activities with a high likelihood of becoming desired activities.

A range of leisure experiences needs to be carefully provided over time for individuals on the spectrum to discover new desired activities. Reality dictates that any of us can only try out a limited number of activities at a time, so it is judicious to choose activities carefully. To be most efficient and avoid frustration for everyone involved, activities for the *Exposure Component* are thoughtfully chosen based on preferences and/or special interests, factors that effect whether the activity can be done regularly and over time, gaps in leisure engagement in settings (e.g., home, school, work, and community), and balance of interests (e.g., solitary or social activities, and active or passive activities). Figure 5.1 titled Guidelines for Activity Selection in Chapter 5 steers the selection of activities.

Once activities are chosen, individuals try out activities in carefully planned leisure experiences. This exposure needs to be structured, supportive, and carefully guided so that the individual can experience what it is like to appropriately and successfully engage in the activity. The process includes planning for the activity, preparing the individual prior to the activity, developing and providing supports, and supporting and guiding participation in the activity.

The user-friendly Activity Cards in Appendix D provide specific tips for exposure to a variety of activities. These Activity Cards can be used by a variety of people who help individuals with ASD. For instance, a parent, babysitter, or respite care provider can readily use them at home or in the community. They can also be used in a school setting to prepare for and help structure field trips and special classes, such as art. In addition, day program and residential facility staff will find them useful in structuring leisure time in the community.

Because individuals with ASD may be reluctant with new activities or have difficulty understanding them, it is important to provide multiple opportunities to experience an activity to ensure that individuals have adequate exposure to an activity to discover if it is meaningful and enjoyable for them. Initially, an individual may refuse to participate, but the structure and repetition of the *Exposure Component* enables individuals with ASD to discover and engage in new interests. Not all activities chosen for exposure will necessarily become an interest. It is important to remember that interests change over time and that an individual may like something better later on in life.

Trying out new activities to develop leisure interests may be included in an Individualized Family Service Plan (IFSP), Individualized Education Plan (IEP), Transition Plan (section of IEP), or Individual Support Plan (ISP).

This component is explained thoroughly in Chapter 5: *Exposure Component*.

The Training Component

Individuals with ASD often require intense support to learn preferred leisure activities. Having a few leisure activities an individual can do independently or semi-independently with visual or other supports, can outweigh having a dozen activities that might require intense support from others.

Generally, people learn leisure activities and related leisure skills from friends or family members, through classes, clubs or organizations, or by reading. It may involve informal training (e.g., imitating what another person does) or formal instruction (e.g., taking a class). Due to the limited ability of many individuals with ASD to imitate behavior, systematic instruction is needed. The *Training Component* is designed to develop the necessary skills and knowledge for the individual to participate, as independently and successfully as possible, in preferred activities in home, school, work, and community settings.

Because individuals with ASD can learn only a limited number of activities at any one time, few activities, and sometimes only one activity, are prioritized for training. This means that it is vital that careful consideration is given to prioritizing activities before training begins. Activities are prioritized based on favorites, activities that can be done alone regularly and alone over time, gaps in leisure engagement in settings (e.g., home, school, work, and community), and a balance of solitary or social activities, as well as active or passive activities that require training.

The *Training Component* emphasizes the simultaneous development of activity skills and a variety of related skills, because all of these skills are necessary for successful and independent functioning in a leisure activity. In addition to the skills required to do the activity itself, it includes related skills, including an awareness of leisure and free time, identification of community and personal resources, choice-making skills, the ability to initiate activities, social interaction skills, and problem-solving skills.

Once an activity or activities are chosen, the skills and supports that need to be taught for each activity are identified. Then the individual is prepared for the activity and given instruction. This component involves direct teaching, and, therefore, includes the use of evidenced-based practices (EBP). Those implementing this component need to have some knowledge of instructional techniques for individuals with ASD. As a result, primarily professionals who teach leisure skills as part of their job responsibilities implement this component. However, most of us whether parents or service providers end up teaching leisure skills from time to time. To assist everyone in applying EBP, a list of websites that provide free learning modules on how to implement EBP is provided in Chapter 6 and Appendix C provides other resources on EBP.

Training in leisure activity and related skills may be included in an Individualized Family Service Plan (IFSP), Individualized Education Plan (IEP), Transition Plan, or Individual Support Plan (ISP).

More information on increasing independence through training is provided in Chapter 6: *Training Component*.

Interrelationship of the Components of Leisure Development

Since there are three components to the Components of Leisure Development, it may not be clear where to start. Figure 2.2 (on the next page) provides a flow chart to help you decide where to begin.

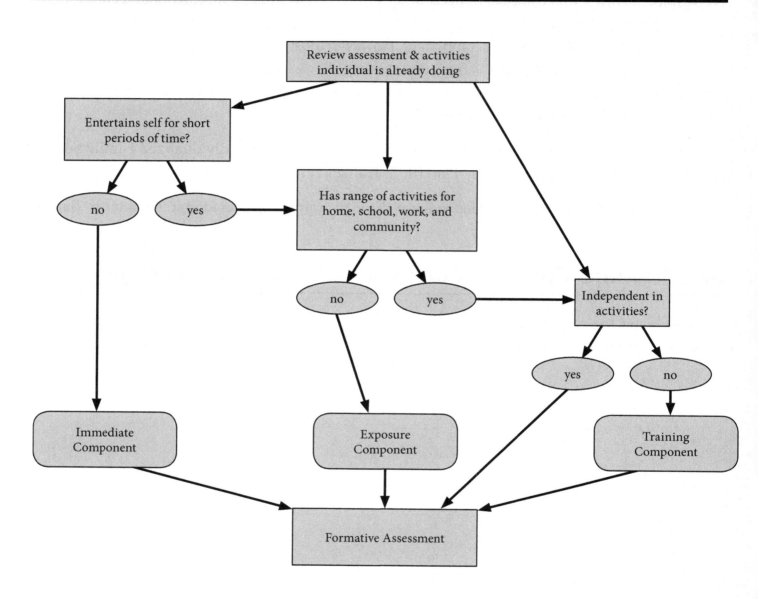

Figure 2.2: Decision Tree for Components of Leisure Development

Chapter 2: Components of Leisure Development

It is prudent to begin with one component. When an individual's present leisure engagement is examined, it may become apparent that further development is needed in a particular area. The initial focus will be the *Immediate Component* for an individual who cannot safely entertain himself for even short periods of time. The focus for an individual with restricted interests may be developing leisure interests through the *Exposure Component*. When an individual has an interest, but lacks the skills to be able to pursue the activity as independently as possible, he may be engaged in the *Training Component* for activity and related skills for that activity.

Individuals with ASD are complex and, in reality, deciding where to begin is often not so straight forward. They are likely to have challenges related to all three components, so the team may need to prioritize where to begin based on what individuals and those closest to them want. Although the Components of Leisure Development are presented separately in this chapter and each component has a chapter dedicated to it in this book, the components are not designed to be offered in a sequence.

More than one component may be used with an individual to accomplish different goals. Most of us are in an ongoing process of developing new interests and getting better at the things that interest us.

Which component or components are used at any one time with an individual is based on the unique and changing needs and interests of the individual with ASD. An individual who is not entertaining himself for even five minutes is likely to need *Immediate Component* leisure materials, as well as *Exposure Component* to potential activities of interest to develop interests. Another individual, who has only a few interests that are limited to home could benefit from developing skills in at least one of those interests (*Training Component*), while having leisure experiences in the community to broaden interests (*Exposure Component*). Yet, another individual, who has a favorite activity he does at home, could benefit from *Training Component* to do that activity in other settings with other people. An individual may still benefit from the portable leisure materials (*Immediate Component*) that provide sensory input for unstructured and waiting times while involved in the *Exposure Component* and/or *Training Component*.

In some instances, all the components may be important to an individual's development of leisure interests and skills.

CASE EXAMPLE: Julie

For instance, leisure development for preteen Julie, who was introduced in Chapter 1, might include:

- Playing with a hand-held game (*Immediate Component*) while waiting for the bus to school, during breaks at school, or while waiting for dinner at home.
- Being exposed to new activities through art or other elective classes at school, through neighborhood friends, or through a youth organization like the Girl Scouts (*Exposure Component*).
- Taking animation class through the local recreation department (*Training Component*).

Summary

Individuals with ASD need assistance to develop satisfying leisure. The three Components of Leisure Development provides a comprehensive approach and comprehensive method to develop leisure skills and interests in the home, school, work, and community for individuals with ASD of all ages and severity of ASD. The ultimate goal is for individuals with ASD to acquire interests and skills to actively choose and engage in meaningful activities of sufficient variety to enhance his quality of life. To accomplish this goal, each of the three components focuses on different areas of leisure development. The *Immediate Component* focuses on using untaught activities with sensory features and/or special interests that provides immediate, meaningful engagement during unstructured time; the *Exposure Component* focuses on repeated and structured exposure to carefully selected leisure activities to develop new interests; and the *Training Component* focuses on the systematic development of leisure activity and related skills for as independent as possible engagement in activities of interest in the home, school, work, and community. Developing leisure satisfaction is an ongoing process, which may require any or all of the three components over time.

Leisure Assessment

Chapter 3

n order to determine how to assist a person in leisure development, it is important to learn as much as possible about the person. Therefore, assessment of the individual's preferences, interests, strengths, challenges, and needs related to meaningful leisure engagement both precedes use of the Components of Leisure Development and is an ongoing process that provides feedback on the development of leisure competencies. Gathering the necessary information saves time and frustration for both individuals with ASD and the people who are concerned about their leisure development.

To effectively implement the three Components of Leisure Development, a variety of information is required. This includes identifying the person's:

- preferences and interests, including sensory preferences, special and leisure interests;
- dislikes in activities and environments;
- past and present participation in leisure activities at home school, work, and in the community;
- knowledge and skills related to leisure activities;
- present leisure partners and interests of family members and friends.

Such knowledge is critical to the selection of leisure materials and activities, environments for activities, as well as supports and strategies for the *Exposure Component* and *Training Component*. In addition, it provides the foundation for identifying a satisfying and meaningful leisure.

This chapter focuses on several methods and a variety of tools for gathering and recording valuable information about an individual with ASD, as well as his family and friends. The methods of assessment discussed in this chapter include:

- interviews;
- direct observation;
- surveys;
- summary profile.

The methods and tools that will be most useful in a specific situation will vary depending on what is already know about an individual, the type of information needed, and who is doing the assessment. Gathering information does not need to be complicated. Much is often already known about an individual and can be reviewed in school or agency records. In some cases, the individual's leisure pattern and interests have already been identified and may be easily recorded on a summary profile. The summary profile can then be updated as further interests and skills develop. In other cases, the interests and skills of the individual will be less obvious and require more in-depth assessment.

Family members and caregivers may gather this information informally through conversations with others, while professionals may be mandated by government or agency regulations to conduct an assessment in a more systematic way. Although many methods and tools in this chapter are likely to be used more by professionals, the concepts are also useful for parents and caregivers. The reader is encouraged to select the methods and tools that are most useful in individual situations.

In order to choose one assessment method or tool over another for the initial assessment, the reader must consider what needs to be assessed. There may already be sufficient information to know which Component of Leisure Development will be addressed first. If the initial focus of leisure development is the *Immediate Component*, it may be adequate to begin by assessing sensory preferences and special interests. If the individual is going to try out new activities in the *Exposure Component*, it is important to know about the individual's sensory preferences and special interests, preferred environments, and current leisure interests at a minimum. If the individual will be developing leisure skills, in the *Training Component*, it is necessary to know current leisure interests, where activities are done, who are they done with, and present level of skills in activities for training. To assist in the selection of methods and tools, Figure 3.1 shows the purpose, methods, and tools described in this chapter.

Chapter 3: Leisure Assessment

Figure 3.1: Leisure Assessment for Individuals with ASD				
Purpose	**Methods**			**Tools**
Gather information about:	Interview*	Observation	Questionnaire+	
History of leisure engagement	X		X	Sample Interview Questions (Fig. 3.2)
Present leisure engagement	X	X	X	Sample Interview Questions (Fig. 3.2) Sample Requests (Fig. 3.3) Leisure Behavior Questionnaire (App. B) Leisure Interest Survey (Fig. 3.5 & App. B) Leisure Lifestyle Profile (Fig. 3.6 & App. B)
Competence in activity skills	X	X	X	Sample Interview Questions (Fig. 3.2) Leisure Behavior Questionnaire (App. B) Activity Assessment Form (App. B) Leisure Lifestyle Profile (Fig. 3.6 & App. B) Environmental Assessment (Fig. 6.5 & App. B) Environmental Inventory (Fig 6.6 & App. B)
Competence in related skills	X	X	X	Leisure Lifestyle Profile (Fig. 3.6 & App. B) Environmental Inventory (Fig 6.6 & App. B)
Sensory preferences	X	X	X	Sample Interview Questions (Fig. 3.2)
Interests	X	X	X	Sample Interview Questions (Fig. 3.2) Sample Requests (Fig. 3.3) Leisure Observation Form (App. B) Leisure Behavior Questionnaire (App. B) Leisure Interest Survey (Fig. 3.5 & App. B) Activity Assessment Form (App. B) Leisure Lifestyle Profile (Fig. 3.6 & App. B)
Potential leisure partners	X		X	Sample Interview Questions (Fig.3.2) Sample Requests (Fig. 3.3) Leisure Interest Survey (Fig. 3.4 & App. B) Leisure Interest Questionnaire for Friends & Family (Fig. 3.4 & App B)
Activities available in the individual's community				Settings and Resources for Activities (Fig. 5.3 & App. B).
Support strategies	X	X	X	Sample Interview Questions (Fig. 3.2) Environmental Assessment (Fig. 6.5 & App. B) Environmental Inventory (Fig 6.6 & App. B) Checklist for Supports (App. C)

* Interviews may be individual or group with individual with ASD and those who know him well.
\+ Questionnaires may also include checklists and surveys.

The ongoing assessment during the *Immediate, Exposure,* and *Training Components* will provide valuable information about the individual's interests, as well as the degree of support needed. It provides vital information to use in modifying the goals and strategies for leisure development.

Interviews

The individual with ASD and those who know the individual best all have important information about the individual's preferences, interests, strengths, challenges, and needs related to meaningful leisure participation. Therefore, individual or group interviews with these people are a primary means to acquire critical information. An advantage of interviews is the specificity of facts that can be learned about an individual, because it is natural to probe and ask follow-up questions for clarification or specific examples.

An interview is an informal assessment technique, but it must have a structure that focuses on the key questions. Specific questions should be prepared ahead of time. In addition, if any questionnaires are completed before the interviews, the interviewer will be able to use them to generate specific questions ahead of time. Since interviewees may have difficulty recalling important facts on the spot, it is beneficial if they have an opportunity to review these questions before the interview and to write notes to refer to during the interview.

A face-to-face interview is preferred. However, if a person is not available for a face-to-face interview, a telephone interview is another option.

Parent or Caregiver Interview

Because parents and caregivers generally know the most about the person, it is important to interview them. Structured interviews with those who know the individual best can efficiently draw out essential information in an hour or less. Some key topics for interviews are: sensory and activity preferences, frequency of participation, location of participation, assistance needed, and shared family interests.

The interviewer should ask open-ended questions that allow for broad answers, as much as possible. When more specific information is desired, the interviewer can ask follow up questions to expand and clarify responses (e.g., Can you tell me more about that? What exactly did he or she do?). Figure 3.2 provides some sample questions about interests and leisure pattern that is a good starting place for an interview.

Figure 3.2: Interview Questions Samples

What does this person do during unstructured time at home, school, work, or community settings?

What special interest does this person have?

Sensory input can be anything that a person sees, hears, touches, smells, or tastes. What sensory input does the person seek and avoid?

How does this person show or express interest?

What activities does this person enjoy?

Describe what this person does in that activity?

What teaching or supports were needed to make the activity successful for this person?

How often does this person do that activity?

How long does this person engage in the activity at one time?

Where does this person do that activity?

Who does this person do the activity with?

How does this person get involved in the activity?

Who else might enjoy doing activities with this person?

What new activities do you think this person would be interested in?

What has kept this person from being involved in this activity in the past?

Describe what this person does on a typical Saturday. Describe a typical day after school.

What activities has this person tried in the past but did not like?

What activities did this person do in the past that he enjoyed but is no longer doing?

Why is he no longer doing the activity?

What activities has this person expressed an interest in but has never tried?

What are your hopes and dreams for this person's future leisure participation?

Alternatively, you can structure your interview by using the categories in the Leisure Lifestyle Profile, which is described later in this chapter and in Appendix B, page 135.

The answers to each of these questions help guide decisions related to the Components of Leisure Development. For instance, knowing what an individual actually does in an activity is important because it reflects the type of interest and skill level. This, in turn, helps inform the selection of activities and skills to be taught.

Dan, a young man with ASD, is one of the three, featured individuals introduced in Chapter 1. Dan's mother says that he likes to play basketball, which could mean throwing a basketball in the air and catching it, bouncing it, shooting baskets alone, shooting baskets with one or more people, or playing a regular basketball game. When questioned further, she explains that he shoots baskets outside only and primarily alone, but tolerates playing with one other person. This information tells us a great deal about his preferences and skills, which, in turn, guides planning.

The mother of preschooler, John, says that he plays with toy trucks by spinning their wheels. John's interest is really in spinning objects rather than the truck as a toy, so the people who support him might look for other objects whose purpose is to spin, such as a top, rather than give him more cars.

The places where an individual does activities may indicate several factors, such as his or her knowledge of community and personal resources, the opportunities that he or she has been given, and preference for certain types of places. Such information is vital for making decisions about the locations of leisure activities.

Dan only likes to shoot baskets outside, because he does not like the lights and reverberating noise on a basketball court. Preteen Julie only likes to swim in lakes because she does not like the chlorine, crowds or limited space associated with an indoor pool.

The degree of interest and enjoyment in present and past activities is often overlooked in interviews. Knowing what an individual dislikes is every bit as important as knowing what he or she likes. Be careful not to assume that an activity is of interest simply because the person does it when told it is time to do it or when it is on the schedule. Many individuals with ASD have learned to follow their schedule whether a task or activity is enjoyable or not. Indications that an activity is not enjoyed may include that it is no longer pursued, is never chosen, or is protested. It is important to gather information that is as specific as possible to determine which conditions and or supports may have contributed to the positive and negative experiences the person has had.

Dan's mother provides extensive information about him in the interview. Dan has always enjoyed bicycling with his mother—first in a bike trailer, then on a tag-a-long bike and finally on a tandem bike as he grew older—but his mother has lost interest in bicycling. Due to the loss of his bicycling partner, he no longer has an opportunity to do this favored activity. On the other hand, Dan has an exercise bike at his group home that he peddles only because it is on his schedule rather than as a preference or choice. Certainly, peddling the exercise bike is good for his physical well-being, but it is not a choice. His mother figured out that what he likes about riding a tandem bike (e.g., the wind on his face, motion, vibration, being outside, and being with his mother) is absent in riding an exercise bike.

Dan's mother tells another revealing story about Dan and bowling. Dan and the rest of the students in his former transition program went bowling every Wednesday. Given some of his preferences (e.g., throwing objects, flashing lights, and creating crashing noise), his team thought he might like the lights and sounds associated with bowling pins being knocked down. He followed the picture schedule of the bowling routine and visual structure to keep track of how many balls to roll down the alley, so his team assumed that he liked the activity. In fact, the random noise, people moving around, having to wait his turn, wearing different shoes with a unique smell, and other aspects of bowling were barely tolerable. When he was younger, his discomfort would have been obvious from his behavior, but he has learned many coping skills over the years. After more than a year of enduring bowling every Wednesday, he emphatically said his first new phrase in years, "No more bowling." to his mother. Fortunately, this cooperative young man's mother was able to convey his comment to his service providers, since he only expressed his dislike to her at home.

It is crucial to ask about activities that an individual enjoyed in the past but no longer pursues. Past activities may still be desired by an individual but not engaged in because of lack of opportunity or barriers (e.g., lack of transportation, money, or activity partner).

Other questions are equally important. For instance, how an individual gets involved in an activity can help identify self-initiation, choice making skills, motivation, and awareness of resources that may need to be supported or taught. Identifying present leisure partners helps assess present social interaction skills for activities, preferred people, and who is presently available to do activities with the individual.

Individual with ASD Interview

Individuals with ASD are the ultimate source of information regarding their own preferences, interests, and participation in leisure activities. Even in cases where they lack a realistic assessment of their own skills and behaviors, the interview process itself can provide rich information about their knowledge and skills.

Answering questions is generally difficult even for the most verbal person with ASD. Even those who can answer questions usually do better when the interview has certain elements. These include:

- carefully structured interview;
- conducted by someone the individual with ASD knows;
- conducted in a familiar environment;
- opportunity to review questions and take notes before the interview;
- explanation, at the individual's level of comprehension, regarding the purpose of the interview, what will happen and how long it will take;
- ample, unpressured time to process and respond;
- alternative to verbal response (e.g., written or typed);
- visual supports (e.g., pictorial schedule, visual timer, or written list of questions that are checked off as questions are answered).

Many individuals on the spectrum have extreme difficulty responding to open-ended questions, because these types of questions usually require the ability to figure out the topic (i.e., translate the words into a concept), stay on the topic, and guess how much information is appropriate. However, some individuals on the spectrum may be able to answer open-ended questions similar to those in Figure 3.2.

Responding to a request that specifies what and how much information to provide, rather than a question, is easier for some verbal individuals with ASD. Requesting specific information is often particularly helpful for those who respond off topic or with too much information when asked an open-ended question. These types of requests invite a short focused answer. Figure 3.3 provides examples of requests for information that may be useful when interviewing verbal individuals with ASD, but even these requests may need to be modified depending on the individual's receptive and expressive language skills.

The anxiety of being "put on the spot" may make it difficult for some individuals with ASD to respond to these requests. Those who can write may respond better by writing or typing responses (e.g., email or text). The responses may be the most complete, if they are written during a time when they are accustomed to writing new information, such as language arts time at school.

Not everyone with ASD will be able to respond to either the open-ended questions or request for information, but there are ways that most can, at least, provide information on what activities they like. This includes:

Figure 3.3: Requests Samples
Tell me three things that you like to do.
Tell me one thing that you are good at.
Tell me one thing that is hard for you.
Tell me one thing that you like to do with your mother, father, brother; sister; and/or your friends, etc.
Tell me one thing that you do for fun at home; school; work; and in the community.
Tell me one thing that you would like to learn for fun.

- simple "yes" or "no" questions;
- written or pictorial list of activity options.

Closed questions, which can be answered by a simple "yes" or "no" are usually easier for individuals with ASD to answer. If the purpose of the interview is just to find out what activities individuals would like to do and they have a reliable response to yes and no questions, this type of question may be appropriate. For instance, although Dan communicates with limited two or three word phrases, he can answer basic "yes/no" questions. He said "Yes" when asked, "Do you want to go shoot baskets?" and "No" when asked, "Do you want to go bowling?"

Pictures of activities often help generate responses from individuals who cannot read, lose their ability to read when "put on the spot", or have minimal to no verbal language. Some of these individuals can point to pictures when asked about interests. For instance, pre-teen Julie can benefit from a written and pictorial list of activities. The Age-Appropriate Activities List on page 119 provides ideas regarding what activities are typical at different ages and can be used to develop a written list for those who can read. Individuals can indicate whether an activity is one that that they already do or would like to do in whatever way is easiest for him.

Some programs that work with a large number of individuals with ASD to develop leisure interests and skills create cards with pictures of leisure activities while others use commercially available leisure assessments with pictures. For instance, one recent leisure assessment, Preferences for Leisure Attributes (PLA) assessment is an interactive software program that uses a forced-choice presentation of photographs to assist 16–22 year olds in making and communicating choices regarding leisure interests and preferences. Burlingame and Blasko (2010) have reviewed many additional interest inventories.

There are some cautions with pictures. First, because of the nature of ASD, answers may be based on irrelevant details (e.g., color of a swimsuit) within the visual representation of the leisure activity. Next, the ability to respond may be hampered by limited knowledge of or experience with the activities depicted.

Finally, not everyone on the spectrum understands the meaning of pictures. Preschooler John does not understand the symbolic meaning of a picture of an activity yet. Individuals like John often "tell us" their interests by what they do with objects. Interviews with parents or caregivers and observation of behavior with objects generally yield the most information when an individual does not know what pictures represent.

Group Interview

A group interview can be both productive and efficient when the individual, parents, teachers, and others who support the individual with ASD have an opportunity to share together. It is also an excellent way to identify what an individual does in one setting but not another. Another benefit is that one person's description often triggers another person's memory.

For instance, Dan's mother did not remember the details of how he developed an interest in basketball. His high school teacher, who still supports Dan, remembered that Dan used to throw objects at lights that were turned on and later delighted in breaking the light bulbs as his aim improved. In an attempt to mimic the tinkling sound of glass breaking and change of lighting, she had put a glass wind chime and flashing lights on a lowered basketball hoop and taught him to shoot baskets, starting by standing on a rubberized mat with two footprints very close to the hoop. As his interest in throwing the ball into the hoop grew, she removed the wind chimes and lights from the basket. She then incrementally raised the hoop to standard height, moved the footprint mat farther and farther away over time, and placed the mat at different angles to the hoop. Eventually, Dan and one of his neurotypical peers shot baskets together after lunch at school.

It is highly recommended that person-centered planning, such as Personal Futures Planning (Mount & Zwernik, 1994), be used so that the individual with ASD creates a plan with persons concerned about his leisure. Person-centered planning, with its structured process and roles as well as use of visuals, helps the individual share his interests, choices, and needs. Furthermore, it can strengthen naturally occurring opportunities for support at home, school, work, and in the community.

Direct Observation

Observation is a critical method of gathering information, before and during the *Immediate, Exposure,* and *Training Components*. Observation can generate information about a number of important factors, such as:

- attraction to certain types of materials (e.g., seeks out specific sensory input; prefers round objects, objects that move, and/or realistic replicas);
- types of interactions with materials (e.g., prefers to spin objects, line up objects, or conventional object use);
- degree of interest in material and activities;
- choice of activities (e.g., prefers active, constructive, solitary);
- choice of leisure companions (e.g., prefers no one in particular, family members only, or one or more peers);
- choice of location (e.g., prefers inside or outdoors, large room or quiet corner);
- reactions to environmental conditions.

The times and places of observations depend on what is known about an individual with ASD and the type of information needed. Individuals on the spectrum may be observed during unstructured time at home, at school (e.g., arrival, recess, downtime, and lunch), at work (e.g., breaks, lunch, and downtime), and in the community (e.g., waiting times) to determine what they do, particularly if their interests and behaviors are unknown. In addition, they may be observed during structured leisure related activities at school (e.g., physical education, music, or art class). Observation may, also, take place in the community (e.g., summer parks program, class at crafts store, or fitness center), when they are already engaged in some leisure activities, but more information about interests, supports, and/or skills is needed for planning supports or further instruction.

Unstructured Time Observation

Individuals with ASD are more likely to engage with materials and pursue activities that they prefer. Therefore, observation during unstructured time to determine the individual's preferences (e.g., what sensory input, people, and location are sought), interests, and what is naturally reinforcing is an effective technique. Initially, it is important to know what materials and activities an individual shows interest in, even if the use of materials is unconventional.

It may be difficult to identify the interests of some individuals with ASD through observation, because they may express likes and dislikes in ways that are not readily understood. Generally, interest may be assumed when an individual moves towards, grabs, hugs, or otherwise manipulates an object. Similarly, disinterest may be assumed when an individual wanders away from leisure materials. However, individuals on the spectrum may show interest in subtler ways, such as several sidelong glances. It is important, therefore, to consult people who are familiar with how the individual expresses interest and enjoyment.

One approach to direct observation is to set up a variety of leisure materials that are age appropriate and representative of those commonly found in home, school, or other environments where the individual frequently spends time. You can use The Typical Leisure Play/Behaviors and Interests or the Age-Appropriate Activities List on page 119 to help you think of possible activities and materials. The Age-Appropriate Activities List divides the activities into the categories of media, physical activities, games/crafts, events, and other.

In this approach to direct observation, there should be at least six items that provide opportunity for different types of use and interaction. For example, a magazine would provide an opportunity for solitary activity, whereas a ball would provide the opportunity for solitary or social interaction. The area should be arranged so that different types of activities, such as table based activities and physical activities can occur. The facilitator should avoid direct participation in an activity, unless the individual directly requests participation.

The facilitator should explain, at the individual's level of understanding, that this is choice time and that the individual can use any of the materials and do what he or she wants in that area. It is important to know what materials the individual shows interest in now and what is done with the materials, even if he or she does not know how to use the materials. After an adjustment period of at least five minutes, observation of the individual's behavior can be recorded. The observer records which materials are used, how the materials are used, and how long the materials were used. Materials that the individual uses indicate some level of interest and the length of engagement in a leisure activity may reflect the degree of interest.

A structured means of recording what is observed provides the most complete information. The Leisure Observation Form provided in Appendix B, page 125 provides a structure for recording behaviors observed every 5 minutes during 20 minute sessions for four to six days. The individual's behaviors are coded under the categories of social level (e.g., alone, beside others), social interactions (e.g., with adults only, with peers) and activity involvement (e.g., object, behavior, place).

Observation in five-minute intervals is recommended to identify activity intent. It would be easy to assume an individual who picks up a game of checkers, takes it to the table, opens the box, and places the board next to a peer is going to play the game cooperatively or competitively with a peer.

However, during the five-minute period, the individual may ignore the peer and stack the game pieces in a repeated pattern alone.

One unique feature of the Components of Leisure Development is identifying and using an individual's preferences for specific types of sensory input. Individuals with ASD tend to interact more with leisure materials that give sensory feedback, such as lights, sounds, movements, and tactile sensation. Observing and recording how an individual commonly uses specific leisure materials, and then determining the sensory input provided, is important in assessing sensory preferences. A small number of leisure materials that provide different sensory stimuli, such as those in Figure 4.1. Sample Portable Leisure Materials in Chapter 4 can be presented to the individual with ASD and their response can be recorded.

Activity Participation Observation

Direct observation of the individual with ASD, during exposure to current or new activities, yields additional information on how the individual functions and the impact of environmental conditions on the ability to function. Some areas that may be assessed during observation during activity participation are:

- degree of interest in an activity;
- reactions to environmental conditions;
- if the activity is done with others;
- the type of cues and support needed to prepare for and participate in the activity;
- skills that the individual has for an activity (e.g., awareness of leisure time, identification of community and personal resources, choice making, initiation of activities, activity skills, social interaction skills, and problem-solving skills).

An individual should be observed a minimum of two or three different days so that variability in performance can be observed. Observations in more than one setting offer an opportunity to see how different conditions affect the individual and what conditions result in optimal functioning.

This information needs to be recorded so that it is not lost. Three tools for recording observations during an activity are provided in this book.

- Activity Assessment Form
- Environmental Assessment and Environmental Inventory

Activity Assessment Form

The easy to use Activity Assessment Form was designed to be used with the Activity Cards in Appendix D, page 163, but can be used effectively to record responses to any leisure activity. This form is used to document the individual's degree of interest, level of independence in an activity, type of assistance provided, and choices made during an activity. It can be filled out quickly by circling simple line drawings and writing brief responses. A unique feature of this tool is that some individuals with ASD may indicate their feelings toward an activity and how independent they were in an activity by circling line drawings. A blank reproducible copy of this tool can be found in Appendix B, page 127.

Environmental Assessment and Environmental Inventory

Environmental assessment, also referred to as situational assessment, measures an individual's interest and abilities while trying out an activity. The process of environmental assessment involves defining specific tasks or steps of activity (i.e., task analysis), then observing an individual engaged in the activity. Information from situational assessment may also track behaviors (e.g., on-task, following directions), affective information (e.g., person is happy, excited, frustrated, or bored), and reaction to environmental factors, (e.g., noise and crowding). A sample completed Environmental Assessment appears in Figure 6.5, while a completed sample Environmental Inventory appears in Figure 6.6 in Chapter 6. In addition, blank reproducible copies of these two tools can be found in Appendix B, pages 139 and 141.

Surveys

Surveys, such as questionnaires, inventories, and checklists, can generate a great deal of information about the preferences, interests, strengths, and challenges related to leisure participation of the individual, as well as family and friends in an organized format. Respondents can complete surveys in their own time and at their own pace, so that they can add to or revise answers for a thorough response.

Surveys can be used for different purposes. When a person is not available for an interview, a questionnaire may be used instead. Alternatively, a questionnaire can be completed previous to an interview and the responses can then be used to generate follow up questions for the interview, thus shortening the length of the interview.

Several surveys are presented in this section.

- Leisure Behavior Questionnaire
- Leisure Interest Questionnaire for Family and Friends
- Leisure Interest Survey

Leisure Behavior Questionnaire

The Leisure Behavior Questionnaire is comprised of open ended questions and rating scales that help parents and other caregivers provide a wide range of information about an individual with ASD related to leisure. The areas covered include:

- current activities enjoyed by individual with ASD;
- frequency of participation;
- location of participation;
- skills related to activity, social interaction and self initiation;
- challenges to participation;
- respondent's desired future activities for the individual;
- current activities enjoyed by respondent.

A reproducible blank for the Leisure Behavior Questionnaire can be found in Appendix B, page 128.

Leisure Interest Questionnaire for Family and Friends

Most of us do some activities with family and friends. One of the difficulties encountered by many individuals with ASD is depending on family and service providers for the opportunities to engage in leisure activities. To expand leisure options for individuals who may always need some level of support for participation, it is important to identify potential leisure partners, natural supports, and possible common interests with family and friends. This will expand the number of opportunities that individuals have to practice and continue to participate in activities that they enjoy.

One method of gathering information about leisure preferences of family and friends is a question-naire with open-ended questions. Leisure Interest Questionnaire for Family and Friends (Figure 3.4) was developed to help identify potential activities and leisure partners to expand opportunities for participation. Important people in the individual's life (e.g., family members and friends)—who are interested in doing activities with an individual—complete this questionnaire. The resulting questionnaires serve as a platform for creative discussion—as part of person-centered planning—regarding possible leisure involvement for the individual and how participation will be made possible. This includes identifying leisure partners, transportation sources, and leisure resources.

A reproducible blank copy of the Leisure Interest Questionnaire for Family and Friends can be found in Appendix B, page 131 and an example of the Leisure Interest Questionnaire completed by Dan's very active friend, Bert Smith, appears in Figure 3.4. This questionnaire provides important information regarding Bert's wide leisure interests. Some of his interests may match some of Dan's past, present, or potential interests. Dan and Bert may decide to do one or more of these activities together.

Chapter 3: Leisure Assessment

Figure 3.4: Leisure Interest Questionnaire for Family and Friends

Name: *Bert Smith* **Date:**

Directions: This purpose of this inventory is to determine the types of activities that you enjoy doing. Also, it will be used to identify possible leisure opportunities for your friend. Please take the time to think about your own leisure and complete this inventory.

1. List what you do for enjoyment or relaxation:
   - When you get home from school or work: *Sleep, workout, swim, play sports, hot tub/Jacuzzi, drive, run, walk, shop, visit with friends and family, eat*
   - After dinner: *Relax, sleep, talk to friends, go to or watch a movie at home, drive, visit with family, hot tub/Jacuzzi*
   - During break times at school or work: *Eat*
   - During lunch time: *Eat*

2. What do you like to do for exercise or fitness?

   Lift weights, play racquet sports, swim, walk, run, hike, snow ski, boating, jet ski, rollerblading, sports in general

3. List clubs or groups in which you participate:

   member ski-racing team

   member River Place Athletic club

4. List classes you have taken for fun in the last two years:

   woodworking

   weight training

5. List some activities you enjoy doing.
   - With your family:

     hiking

     camping

   - With your friends:

     partying

     sports

     going out

41

Leisure Interest Survey

Another approach to gathering information about leisure preferences of an individual or his family and friends is a forced-choice survey in which the possible leisure activities are predetermined. This type of survey takes time to develop and, therefore, is developed primarily by groups that serve a number of individuals on the spectrum (e.g., school districts, chapters of the Arc, chapters of the Autism Society, and other service organizations). Groups who develop this form frequently work on completing the Settings & Resources for Activities Form in Appendix B, page 137 at the same time.

The first step in developing a forced-choice survey for leisure is to prepare a list of age appropriate activities that are available in your local area. The Age-Appropriate Activities List in Appendix A, page 119 can be used as a reference in developing a list of activities for your area. This list does not include all possibilities of activities that may be available in your area, so it is important to determine other activities pursued by same-age peers in your community. In addition, be aware that some of the activities on the Age-Appropriate Activity List will not be available in your area.

Respondents are asked to answer the following questions for each activity.

- Do you enjoy this activity?
- Did you do this activity in the last month? How often?
- Does anyone else in the family enjoy this activity?
- Where do you do this activity?
- Who do you do this activity with?
- Would you like to do this activity with your special friend?

Dan's family and friends completed the Leisure Interest Survey that was developed for Dan's community. The first page of the Survey that Dan's friend, Bert Smith, completed is shown in Figure 3.5. Note that this first page is only on physical activities. The pages he completed on activities related to media, games/crafts, and events are not shown.

Chapter 3: Leisure Assessment

Figure 3.5: Completed Leisure Interest Survey Sample

Name:	Bert Smith			Date:				Age: 23

Activity	Do you enjoy it?	Did you do it in the last month?	How often?	Does anyone else in the family do it?	Where did you do it?	Who do you do it with?	Would you like to do it with your special friend?	Comments
Walking	Yes	Yes	Daily	Yes	Park/School	Friends	Yes	
Jogging	Yes	Yes		Yes	Park/School	Friends	Yes	
Riding a Bike	Yes	Yes	2x	No	Park/School	Myself	Yes	
Playing Catch	Yes	Yes	10x	Yes	Park/School	Friends	Yes	
Skill-Building Classes	So so	Yes	Daily	Yes	School	Friends/Classmates	Yes	
Swimming	Sometimes	Yes	10x	Yes	Club/River	Friends	Yes	
Aerobics/Slimnastic/Jazzercise	Sometimes	Yes	2x	No	Club/School	Friends	Yes	
Using Equipment	Yes	Yes	Everyday	No	Club/School	Friends/Classmates	Yes	
Weight Training	Yes	Yes	Everyday	No	Club/School	Friends/Classmates	Yes	I worked at the Riverplace Athletic Club and I like working out very much.
Playing Raquet Sports	Yes	Yes	15x	Yes	Club/Park	Friends	Yes	I love to play tennis, racquetball, and squash. I play sometimes in tournaments.
Skating/Rollerblading	Yes	Yes	2x	No	Park	Friends	Yes	
Skateboarding	No	No					Yes	
Dance Classes	No	No					Maybe	
Volleyball/Soccer	Yes	Yes	5x	No	Club/Park	Friends	Yes	
Being Team Manager	No							I don't like managing because I like to play.
Golfing	Yes	No	1x	No	Club	Friends	Yes	
Horseback Riding	No	No	5x	No				
Hiking/Backpacking	No						Maybe	
Snow Shoeing	Yes	Yes	1x	Yes	Desch. River	Friends	Yes	
Skiing	Yes	Yes	8x	No	Mt. Hood	Friends	Yes	I love snow skiing. I ski on a team/ we race / our team is sponsored by a ski shop in PDX.
Boating/Waterskiing	Yes	No	5x	Yes	River	Team/Friends	Yes	
Ping Pong	No					Friends	Maybe	

Comments: I would love to work with Dan in any of these categories.

The responses to the Leisure Interest Questionnaire and Leisure Interest Survey from Dan, his family and friends resulted in a lively discussion and many ideas in the ensuing meeting with Dan and his support team (his family, friends, and select service providers). Dan and his team were particularly excited about two opportunities that evolved.

- Dan and Bert both like swimming. Dan has the opportunity for a membership at the YMCA and can bring a leisure companion as an ADA accommodation. Bert and Dan both like the idea of Bert being that companion. Bert can support Dan while enjoying swimming. The hot tub at the Y is, also, appealing to both of them. They decide to go to the Y at the least busy time on Thursdays.

- Dan's sister, Sarah, enjoys bicycling and wants to ride local bike trails with Dan two Saturdays a month on the tandem bicycle that Dan and their mother used to ride together. Dan enthusiastically flaps his hands and exclaims, "Sarah bike" to express his approval of this idea. Sarah goes online to find a relaxed recreational bicycle group that they can join. She believes that the tandem bike will intrigue other members of the group and that Dan's contagious laughter will attract members also, so they will want to take turns on the tandem bike with Dan. She is looking forward to meeting new people and getting fitter while spending quality time with her only brother.

Recording Leisure Pattern and Skills

The information attained about the individual with ASD must be organized and recorded. Both a written summary of the information, as well as a means to keep all the information organized and available for review are important. This information should be clear and dated, because it will be used and expanded many times in the course of using the Components of Leisure Development. In addition, this information can help new caregivers and other service providers to understand an individual better.

Portfolio

A portfolio or file can keep interview or observation notes, questionnaires, checklists, and forms related to leisure engagement, sensory and other preferences, interests, and needed supports in a central location, so that the information can be accessed as needed. Parents, caregivers, teachers, and service providers may elect to utilize a web-based portfolio to track and store the key documents with this information. An example of a web-based portfolio that can store written documents with strengths, needs, interests, and accomplishments, as well as allow for the inclusion of pictures, and videos, is the Multimedia Transition Portfolio Guide http://blogs.4j.lane.edu/postsecondarytransi-tionportfolio). Although the Multimedia Transition Portfolio Guide was developed by a school district for early transition planning starting in the fifth grade, this personalized tool can be used to focus on developing satisfying and personally meaningful leisure at various ages. It includes a number of useful downloadable templates for individuals with ASD.

Summary Profile

The Leisure Lifestyle Profile is an effective summary profile for planning individualized leisure development and to monitor progress during the *Immediate, Exposure* and *Training Components*. It offers an overview of the individual's present leisure pattern, interests, and skills. Much of the information from the interviews, observations, and questionnaires described in this chapter can be consolidated on this form.

The Leisure Lifestyle Profile summarizes the following information about activities that an individual participates in a minimum of 15 minutes, at least 12 times a year:

- if the activity is of interest;
- the environment where an activity is done;
- if the activity is done with others;
- the type of cues and support needed to engage in the activity;
- the balance of activities in different settings.

This summary is unique, because the degree of independence and supports needed are identified for both the activity skill itself and six related skills for independent leisure participation for each activity. These skills include: identification of leisure and free time, identification of community and personal resources, choice-making, self-initiation of activities, and social interaction and problem-solving skills for activities. These leisure and related skills are described in Chapter 6. A blank reproducible Leisure Lifestyle Profile form is provided in Appendix B, page 135 for your use.

The rich information collected about an individual on the spectrum, such as information described in this chapter, provides a solid base for decision making about where more activities would be beneficial, as well as about what supports and skills for an activity need instruction. An initial goal is a minimum of one activity in each grid. For an individual without activities in each grid, initial planning usually includes expanding leisure interests for a better balance through exposure to age appropriate activities of potential interest (i.e., *Exposure Component*). Both solitary and activities with others is important. The majority of free time for all of us is generally spent at home, so a higher number of activities at home are appropriate. Once there are preferred activities in each grid, the development of activity and related skills necessary for independence becomes a major focus. The profile provides information for prioritizing necessary skills for instruction. Rather than adding more activities, many activities may also be expanded to other environments.

The completed Leisure Lifestyle Profile for Dan in Figure 3.6 reflects his leisure pattern and skills at the time of assessment.

Chapter 3: Leisure Assessment

		Figure 3.6: Leisure Lifestyle Profile							

Name:	Dan							Date:	

	Activity	Id time	Resources	Choice	Initiate	Skills	Interact	Problem Solve	Comments
HOME (Activity within property boundaries of home)									
Alone	0 Exercise Bike	IS	I	IS	IS	I	NA	TA	*Visual schedule & choice board.*
	+ Mini Trampoline	I	I	IS	IS	I	NA	TA	*Selects from picture of album cover. Help to check cords & recharge if not working*
	+ Listen to music (iPod with headphones)	I	IS	IS	I	I	NA	TA	*Visual for appropriate attire. Outside. Fenced yard.*
	+ Shoot baskets	IS	IS	IS	IS	I	NA	TA	
	+ Lay on heat register	I	NA	I	I	I	I	NA	
With Others	+ Listen to music with staff	IS	IS	IS	I	I	V	NA	*Visuals & structure for joint choices & ending.*
	+ Hang out with staff	I	NA	I	I	TA	TA	NA	*Very excited when focus is on him. Goes to quiet area when too excited.*
COMMUNITY (Activity beyond property boundaries of home)									
Alone									*Needs supervision so never alone in community*
With Others	0 Walk	IS	IS	IS	IS	V	V	TA	*Visuals for appropriate attire.*
	- Bowl	IS	IS	NA	IS	IS	TA	TA	*Schedule, Mini-schedule; preloaded wallet, 3 ball tracker*
	+ Concerts, family events, restaurant	IS	TA	NA	NA	V	V	TA	*With mother or sister*
SCHOOL OR WORK (Activity during recess, breaks, lunch, elective classes and extracurricular activities)									
Alone	+ Listen to music (iPod with headphones)	I	IS	I	I	V	IS	TA	*Makes choice with choice board of music or basketball*
	+ Set off fire alarm	I	I	I	I	I	NA		
With Others									*No activities*

- Record activities engaged in for at least 15 minutes, 12 times a year.
- Indicate interest with code: + = likes, 0 = neutral, - = not preferred
- Indicate level of independence or supports with code:
  - I = Independently completes without adaptations or supports.
  - IS = Independently completes predetermined adaptations or supports
  - V = Verbal cue or prompt require.
  - G = Gestural cue or prompt, such as point is required.
  - TA = Total assistance is needed.
  - NA = Not applicable; not required in activity or skill is not defined.

This profile clearly reflects that Dan has had the benefit of support and instruction for leisure pursuits for many years. Although it may look good at first glance, a closer examination reveals that he continues to have some gaps. In reality, developing meaningful and satisfactory leisure is an ongoing process for most of us. Some of the information that Dan's team learns from the profile and other information collected related to his present leisure engagement in the home, work, and community follows.

HOME: Like most of us, the majority of Dan's free time is spent at home and, since he only works part time, he does not have adequate pleasurable leisure activities to fill his time. Most of his leisure time at home is spent in sedentary and solitary activities—listening to music on his iPod, lying on a heat vent for hours on end, and being near group home staff without interacting. However, he gets some exercise by shooting baskets outside for about 20 minutes a day when the weather allows and briefly jumping on a mini trampoline inside. Unfortunately, he does not enjoy riding the stationary bike. He does not have the social interaction skills for the two passive activities that he does with staff, listening to music and hanging out. He could benefit from assistance to develop additional interests (*Exposure Component*) and skills for activities (*Training Component*) that he does at home by himself as well as with others. Decisions about specific activities for Dan at home are discussed in Chapters 5 and 6.

WORK: Most of us have activities that we do at work during breaks and lunch time. Dan's work is sedentary and he engages in a sedentary, solitary activity, listening to music, during breaks and lunch at work. He creates his own noise and excitement by occasionally setting off the fire alarm on the way to break or lunch. Dan, who likes to strike objects to make loud noises could benefit from developing an interest in a cause and effect activity that he can do at work. He could, also, benefit from an active activity that he could do with someone else, if he desires social interaction. Decisions about specific activities for Dan at work are discussed in Chapters 5 and 6.

COMMUNITY: Dan is not involved in community activities by himself at this point due to safety concerns, but he enjoys going to small music concerts, family gatherings, or small quiet restaurants with his mother or sister once or twice a month. He enjoys the concert as long as other people listen quietly, and he is in the front row or at a table with space from other people. At family gatherings, he is so excited to see his favorite people that he can only stay in the room with them for short periods of time. On shopping trips, he enjoys walking through the racks of clothes and touching the fabric. In restaurants, he loves to order with pictures and eat. He is mostly directed through the steps of these activities by his mother or sister. He participates less than enthusiastically in walking with staff in his neighborhood. He is doing fewer activities in the community than when he was younger, because of lack of opportunity. He could benefit from pursuing more activities in the community. This is likely to require both paid and natural supports. Identifying community activities that his family members and friends might do with him to expand participation in the community is vital. Decisions about specific activities for Dan in the community are discussed in Chapters 5 and 6.

Summary

Knowing the person with ASD provides the foundation for making decisions towards a satisfying and meaningful leisure. Before identifying leisure activities and materials, supports and training strategies, it is crucial to know the individual's preferences, interests, strengths, challenges, and needs related to meaningful leisure engagement. Taking the time to collect this information will save time and frustration for both individuals with ASD and the people who are concerned about their leisure.

There are many ways that an individual's leisure preferences, interests, needs, and strengths can be assessed. Possible methods include interviews, observations, questionnaires, and summary profiles. No single collection method can provide all the necessary information to support good decisions. Assessment methods need to be chosen based on what is already known about the individual with ASD and what information is needed.

Readers are encouraged to select from the methods and tools presented in this chapter based on their situation. This chapter is designed to be returned to again and again as the need for different information about individuals with ASD arise.

Chapter 4

The Immediate Component of Leisure Development

Parents, teachers, and service providers report that the inability of individuals with ASD to entertain themselves safely and to cope with unstructured time is often a challenge for all involved. The purpose of the *Immediate Component* is to engage individuals with ASD with appealing materials and activities that require little to no supervision for short periods of time. In this component, toys, games, and other materials that provide preferred sensory input and/or incorporate a special interest are utilized to help individuals with ASD to be meaningfully and safely engaged for a brief period of time. This component is referred to as "Immediate" because the materials generate interest right away, do not require instruction, and do not require set-up or preparation. This approach reduces the need for the constant supervision that occurs when individuals do not know how to entertain themselves. An additional benefit is that challenging behaviors that an individual may otherwise do during unstructured times are reduced while engaged with these leisure materials. The key elements of the *Immediate Component* are listed below.

Key Elements of the Immediate Component	
• meaningful engagement during unstructured time;	• untaught materials and minimal supervision;
• sensory preferences and special interest;	• formative assessment.

Meaningful Engagement During Unstructured Time

Meaningful engagement involves doing activities and using materials that the individual is drawn to use and keeps his attention. Meaningful activities and materials stimulate the pleasure or feel good center of the brain and can cause a sense of well being at any age.

The *Immediate Component* is concerned with brief periods of time when individuals need to entertain themselves. This includes a variety of unstructured times, such as:

- waiting periods while in the community (e.g., at bus stops, doctor's office, religious service, and when riding in a bus or car);
- brief periods between structured activities at school (e.g., after an individual has finished an activity and the next activity has not begun);
- brief periods during breaks at work;
- free time at home, especially when waiting for an anticipated event (e.g., dinner or favorite TV show) or when caregivers cannot give full attention to an individual (e.g., when caregiver is

doing dishes, brushing own teeth, paying bills, or making an important phone call).

In the *Immediate Component*, items may be needed for a short duration of 5–30 minutes or occasionally longer. Individuals may want to continue engaging with an item beyond the unstructured time or waiting time, which is a positive sign that it is a meaningful activity. However, do not allow individuals to engage with any one item to the point that they either get tired of it or that it becomes an obsession. Instead, provide a choice of several attractive items that are rotated.

Parents and others who support individuals with ASD cannot always anticipate when these individuals will need to entertain themselves, so it is sensible to have small portable items that can be used in a variety of situations and locations carried in a fanny pack or other container. Figure 4.1 provides examples of some easily carried leisure materials that are available in local stores and online.

Some materials are too big or awkward to easily carry from one setting to another. For instance, favorite items that involve moving one's body in space, such as a mini trampoline, a Sit-n-Spin, and a Ride-on Ball, may be unwieldy to move between settings. If an individual has a particularly strong attraction to a large item, duplicates should be kept in different locations where short periods of free time occur.

Access to Materials

Access to these materials should be given only during unstructured times, so that an individual will be motivated to use and sustain interest in them. The manner in which these materials are presented can vary depending on the individual and location. Some individuals with ASD have difficultly making a choice between items and should be given one item at a time. Individuals who are able to make a choice between several items can be given a container (e.g., fanny pack, daypack, basket, or tote) holding those favored items. The presence of the container signals that it is time to select an item for free time.

Sensory Preferences and Special Interests

In the *Immediate Component*, the selection of materials is based on individual sensory preferences and special interests, because they generate interest and sustained engagement. Carefully choosing materials reduces the need to try many materials or activities.

Knowing what an individual with ASD is attracted to or prefers, in general, will lead to the best match of activities and materials. If this information is not already know, it may be gleaned through observation or asking others who know the person well. Further methods of learning about preferences are discussed in Chapter 3.

Sensory Preferences

Materials in the *Immediate Component* are chosen with the sensory input that an individual with ASD prefers in mind. Many individuals with ASD have a strong preference for one or more types of sensory input, including taste, smell, hearing, vision, touch, and where one's body is in space (i.e., vestibular and proprioceptive).

Attraction to sensory input by individuals with ASD has been recognized for some time. As early as 1943, Kanner described sensory fascinations in persons with ASD (e.g., watching light reflecting from mirrors). Subsequent research has demonstrated that individuals on the spectrum tend to seek out and sustain interaction more with leisure materials that provide favored sensory input and avoid those that are related to sensory sensitivities (Gutierrez-Griep, 1984; Hochhauser et al., 2010; Little, 2012; Potvin et al., 2013; Rincover et al., 1977).

Many common toys, games, and other leisure materials provide sensory stimulation that may be sought after by an individual with ASD. The more that is known about an individual's preferences, the better for matching items to sensory preferences. An individual who likes tactile input may favor items they can squeeze (e.g., Koosh ball), stretch (e.g., Silly Putty), rub for certain textures, (e.g., knobby rubber ball), and/or make vibrate (e.g., Bumble ball). Good tactile items for individuals with ASD should be durable and interesting to touch. In contrast, an individual who is drawn to visual input may be drawn to flashing lights, or slow moving objects (e.g., motion or lava lamp) and/or objects that spin (e.g., top). An individual who is attracted to sounds may seek out crashing sounds, such as those found in some video games and/or soothing music.

Materials that provide the sensory input that Dan, Julie, and John seek are identified to use briefly during unstructured times. Dan already listens to music on his iPod Touch during short periods of unstructured time, but he could benefit from at least one other activity for waiting times. Since he likes crashing sounds and lights, he is also given an electronic handheld car racing game that provides sound and a moving visual display.

Julie continues to play video games mainly because of the visual properties and needs at least one other choice. Her desire for visual input is further provided for with a water ring toss game and Magna Doodle.

To provide the auditory input that John seeks, he is given Golden Seek 'n Sound books.

Special Interests

Another way to promote meaningful engagement during unstructured time is to use obsessions or special interests (Boyd, Conroy, Mancil, Nakao, & Alter, 2007). Many individuals on the spectrum have an intense, focused interest in a particular subject, objects, or action with objects.

Individuals who have a special interest in a subject or object are often attracted to catalogs, magazines, books, videos, maps, and objects (e.g., action figures) depicting an element of that subject. They may also seek to depict their special interest through drawing, clay modeling, or other creative mediums.

Some common actions that individuals with ASD tend to focus on are stacking, matching, sequencing, putting together (e.g., assembling and building), or actions that cause a reaction (i.e., cause and effect). Individuals who like assembling often like materials, such as puzzles, Qubits, Rubik's Cube, and puzzle lock toys; individuals who like building often like materials like blocks, Legos, and K'Nex. In addition, a number of apps for mobile devices (e.g., tablets, smart phones, and iPod Touch) involve putting something together.

Individuals who seek actions that cause a reaction are often attracted to arcade games available through a browser or app and video games. In addition, there are many other types of cause and effect materials, such as toy transportation vehicles that are activated by some action by the person.

Dan's, Julie's, and John's special interests are considered when choosing materials and activities. Dan continues to listen to his all-time favorite song, "Little Drum Boy" over and over again on his iPod. He enjoys his new Little Drummer Boy figurine and new wind-up toy of a marching drummer. His team is, also, looking for a simple drumming app that he will be able to use without training. Julie's special interest is snakes. She is pleased with her new rubber snake and book on snakes. John repeatedly bangs objects. He enthusiastically uses his new hammer and pegboard.

Untaught Materials and Activities with Minimal Supervision

Untaught materials are vital to the *Immediate Component*. Untaught materials and activities are those that can be used safely after they are either given to or simply demonstrated to an individual. The reason these materials and activities do not need to be taught is that the objects themselves dictate what to do with them. For instance, when a maraca is shaken or even casually moved, it makes a sound. When individuals notice movement causes the sound, they then shake or move it again.

Self-determined use of an object is a "focus" in this component. In the *Immediate Component*, self-determined use of an item means that an individual with ASD chooses and uses it in any way desired, as long as it is safe and not destructive. Sometimes an individual may focus on the sensory input or an area of special interest related to an object rather than the intended use. The item does not need to be used in a conventional manner. For instance, a maraca might be tapped against the individual's hand to make a sound rather than shaken to make a specific rhythm.

Materials and activities that require minimal supervision are a critical part of the *Immediate Component*, because caregivers and other support people need some times when their attention can safely be elsewhere. When the toys, games, and other objects reliably attract and sustain interest out of harm's way for brief periods of time, the need for continuous supervision is reduced.

Finding Materials for the *Immediate Component*

When looking for materials for meaningful engagement during short periods of unstructured time, consideration should also be given to:

- ease of use without being taught;
- age appropriateness of items.

Age appropriate means suitable for people of a particular age or age group. This means items are both appealing to and considered safe for an age group. Manufacturers of toys, games, books, movies, and video games have rating systems to determine age appropriateness and often design materials specific to a particular age group. These manufacturers often list the age materials or activities are intended for on their packaging. However, parents, caregiver, teachers, and service providers should use discretion related to the stated age level on packaging. An item considered safe for a particular age group may not be safe for an individual with ASD of that age who is severely affected by ASD.

A remarkable number of age appropriate toys, games, and other materials that provide the sensory input that an individual seeks or is related to his special interests can be found both in local stores and by using the internet. If you know exactly what material(s) will increase meaningful engagement during short periods of free time, you can phone stores or search online to find the item(s). If you do not know the precise material(s), but know the individual's sensory preferences and special interests, you will discover many suitable items locally and online. Figure 4.1 shows some examples of sensory input and special interests that may be attractive to individuals with ASD along with a sample of widely found toys, games, and other materials containing that feature.

Developing Leisure Time Skills for People with Autism Spectrum Disorders

Primary Attraction				Type	Examples	Age
Tactile	Visual	Auditory	Special Interest			
X				squeezing	Putty, Play Doh, Koosh Ball, stress ball	3+
X				stretching	Putty, Play Doh, Gak, Stretchy String, stretch bands	3+
X				vibrating	Jumping Joggle Bopper, Wiggle Writer, Fisher Price Cuddle Soother stuffed animal, Bumble ball	0+
X				textured: soft	Stuffed animals, blanket (silky, fleece),	1+
X				textured: rough	Knobby ball, textured sand roller toys	3+
X	X	X		textured	Oball Shaker, Tangle Creation Jr.	3+
	X		X	drawing	Etch-a-Sketch, Doodle Pads	3+
X	X		X	action figures	Transformers, super heroes	5+
	X			lights	Flashlights, themed lighted wands, glow sticks, lava lamps, water ring toss games	3+
	X			spinning	Tops, spin wands, magnetic spinning gears	3+
	X		X	pictures & graphics	Picture and graphic books, catalogues, magazines, maps	3+
	X	X		handheld games	Simon, arcade games	5+
	X	X		pictures with sound	Seek 'n Sound books	3+
		X		rhythm instruments	Bells, shakers, claves, triangles	3+
		X		listening	MP3 player, iPod, Micro Jammers, digital voice recorders	5+
			X	put together	Puzzles, Qubits, puzzle lock toys	3+
			X	building	Blocks, Legos, K'Nex	3+

Figure 4.1: Portable Leisure Materials

When you keep your eyes open and enlist help from the individual with ASD, family, and friends, you will come across an array of engaging materials in local stores. Various types of stores sell materials with sensory features or special interests that will capture and hold the interest of an individual with ASD. These include, but are not limited to department stores, toy stores, science stores, novelty shops, hobby shops, and sporting goods stores. Frequently, stores have a section with small items, such as Koosh balls and kaleidoscopes that may be perfect for a particular individual.

There are many ways of finding toys, games, and other materials that provide sensory input or relate to special interests on the internet. The first online approach is to google key words related to an individual's sensory preferences or special interests, such as spinning toys, toys with sounds, flashing light toys, squeeze toys, spinning toys, handheld games, rhythm instruments, building toys, and cause and effect toys. This will generate a selection of websites that carry the type of toy, game, or other leisure material desired.

The second online approach is to go directly to a company's website and type key words in the search box for that company. These sites may include Internet companies (e.g., Amazon.com), stores (e.g., Target or Toys 'R Us), and companies that specialize in supplies for individuals with ASD (e.g., AutismCommunityStore.com or National AutismResources.com) or special needs (e.g., SpecialNeedsToys.com or eSpecialNeeds.com).

The third online approach is to google "toys for autism spectrum." In addition to companies that specialize in individuals with ASD or special needs, more and more regular companies, such as Amazon.com and Toys 'R Us, list toys for individuals on the spectrum.

Finally, a wide variety of free and inexpensive apps can be found online that either provides the visual and auditory input that an individual seeks and/or incorporates his special interest. For instance, some apps created specifically to provide sensory input include Flashback, Sensory Electra, Miracle modus, Sensory Magma, and Art of Glow. Many game apps provide the types of actions that are preferred by individuals with ASD, such as cause and effect, stacking, matching, sequencing, and putting together. Periodically, new lists of apps for ASD, apps for specific subjects and more can be found online. Additional games that provide sensory input or are related to special interests can be found through browsers.

Formative Assessment

Observation is the main method of gathering information that will influence changes or additional materials for the *Immediate Component*. Observation of an individual engaged with the materials helps identify if the materials are being used safely and continue to be desirable, thus determining if they should continue to be used in the *Immediate Component*. Additional information on individual preferences and interests can result from observations. This informal assessment also informs decisions about activities and approaches to be used with an individual in both the *Exposure* and *Training Components*.

Summary

The *Immediate Component* reduces the need for constant supervision that occurs when individuals with ASD do not know how to entertain themselves during unstructured time. In this component, age appropriate toys, games, and other materials that provide preferred sensory input and/or incorporate special interests are utilized to help individuals with ASD to be meaningfully and safely engaged for short periods of time with little to no supervision. Because the materials used dictate what to do, use of these materials are untaught.

The Exposure Component of Leisure Development

Chapter 5

eaningful and satisfying leisure involves having a variety of activities in which an individual freely chooses to engage at home, school, work, and the community. Many examples exist of individuals with ASD participating in a wide range of leisure activities (Coyne & Fullerton 2014), attesting to the potential and capability of anyone with ASD to develop this important aspect of life. Despite these encouraging examples, recent studies suggest that individuals with ASD of all ages continue to engage in fewer leisure activities than both those with and without other disabilities (Badia, et al., 2013; Buttimer & Tierney, 2005, Hochhauser & Engel-Yeger, 2010; Orsmond, et al., 2004; Reynolds, et al., 2011).

The nature of ASD must be understood, if we are going to broaden leisure engagement. The restricted, repetitive patterns of behavior, interests, or activities that are inherent to ASD negatively impact and limit leisure participation. These patterns may include, 1) stereotyped or repetitive use of objects, 2) excessive adherence to routines or excessive resistance to change, 3) highly restricted, fixated interests, and 4) hyper-or hypo-reactivity to sensory input or unusual interest in sensory aspects of objects and the environment (APA, 2013). Furthermore, each of these characteristics can result in limited opportunities to even try a variety of activities. Please refer to Chapter 1 for more information about these characteristics and their impact on leisure engagement.

Since a person can only be interested in activities that they have seen or experienced, a narrow range of experiences with leisure activities perpetuates constricted leisure engagement. Not surprisingly, even when individuals with ASD do express an interest in new activities, they seldom engage in these new activities (Potvin et al, 2013). Not pursuing a novel activity may be due to a lack of opportunity, but frequently it relates more to challenges in coping with aspects of new activities (e.g., new materials, actions, environments, and people) and discomfort with certain sensory input (e.g., sounds, bright lights, textures, quick movements, physical proximity to people, and textures).

The *Exposure Component* is designed to alleviate the challenges related to the characteristics of ASD and lack of experiences with leisure activities by providing supported experiences with leisure activities with a high potential of being of interest. The primary purpose is to broaden leisure interests and pursuits in the home, school, work, and community. The key elements of the *Exposure Component* are listed below.

Key Elements of the Exposure Component	
• discovery of new leisure interests;	• supported, repeated exposure to new activities;
• guidelines for activity selection;	• formative assessment.

This approach reduces stress associated with a new activity, motivates participation, and promotes the discovery of new leisure interests.

Discovery of New Leisure Interests

In the *Exposure Component*, a systematic, structured approach is used that supports the challenges of ASD while providing an opportunity to experience activities for a period of time to see if one or more will generate interest. This systemically approach includes:

1. selecting activities;
2. planning for the activity;
3. preparing the individual prior to the activity;
4. supporting and guiding participation in the activity.

In this component, carefully chosen and planned leisure experiences are used to allow individuals with ASD to discover interests and to make more informed choices based on their experiences. The cycle of experiencing leisure activities and using experiences to refine interests and choices is self-determining for individuals with ASD. Through this component, individuals with ASD are given an opportunity to discover interests rather than rely on the opinions of family members and professionals when it concerns what type of activity is appropriate for them.

In addition to developing interests, this component helps individuals and the people who support them to better understand more about their strengths and challenges related to leisure activities. It is a process of discovery for both individuals with ASD and those that support them.

Guidelines for Activity Selection

Few individuals with ASD have a variety of activities in which they freely choose to engage. The vast majority has a restricted range of activities and do not understand their leisure options, so they will need assistance in broadening their interests.

There is no rule for how many leisure activities an individual should participate in. The range of possibilities, such as hobbies, sports, fitness activities, aquatics and water-related activities, arts and crafts, music, dance, drama, nature experiences, and games, are immense. However, individuals with ASD can only tolerate experiencing a limited number of new activities at any one time. Few activities and sometimes only one activity should be selected for exposure at a time. The process of developing new interests in activities occurs over time.

Chapter 5: The Exposure Component of Leisure Development

Individuals with ASD, parents, caregivers, teachers, and service providers may wonder how to select activities from the vast array of leisure possibilities. To guide people who support individuals with ASD to thoughtfully select activities for the *Exposure Component*, this section discusses two major topics, they are:

- guidelines for activity selection;
- prioritizing from activities that meet selection criteria.

The following section, starting with Figure 5.1, offers guidelines for selecting activities that are both personally meaningful to the individual and likely to be engaged in over time.

Figure 5.1: Guidelines for Selecting Leisure Activities

The activity is:

- a match with individual preferences and special interests;
- interest of family members and friends;
- age appropriate;
- readily available in person's home, school, work or community;
- done in a variety of environments;

- engaged in both alone or with others;
- economically feasible.

The activity has:

- potential for frequent and long term participation;
- social demands at person's skill level.

Match with preferences and special interests—Individuals with ASD must be afforded meaningful leisure experiences that will facilitate developing interests. What's meaningful is very individual. A diagnosis of ASD does not indicate what activities an individual should pursue.

Many individuals on the spectrum display skills, strengths, and talents associated with special interests, and often display extensive knowledge in a particular area of interest. These special interests may seem unusual because of the intensity with which they are pursued. Individuals with ASD, also, may have highly preferred objects, topics, or themes and sensory stimuli that they perseverate on across multiple settings. Incorporating these passions into activities can promote interest and sustained engagement in leisure activities (Baker, 2000; Boyd, Conroy, Mancil, Nakao, & Alter, 2007; Charlop-Christy & Haymes, 1998). The systematic matching of individual preferences and special interests with activities can also reduce the time spent trying new activities to broaden leisure interests and increase leisure satisfaction.

Because technology has become the entertainer for individuals with ASD, it must be discussed before delving into preferences further. Computers and mobile technology, such as tablets, smart phones, and iPod Touch, are very motivating, visually appealing, and enjoyable for most individuals with

ASD. As a result, individuals with ASD engage with computers and mobile technology more than other people and they may become fixated on them (Mazurek, Shattuck, Wagner, & Cooper, 2012; Orsmond, & Kuo, 2011; Potvin et al, 2013; Solish, & Minnes, 2010). The use of technology has both pluses and minuses that should be considered. If video games or other use of technology is selected as an activity for exposure, care must be taken to ensure that the use of technology does not become the only leisure pursuit.

Since a new activity has the greatest chance of becoming a desired activity if it contains features important to the individual, preferences in the following areas are taken into account in the *Exposure Component*:

- sensory input (e.g., touch, sound, visual, vestibular, and proprioceptive);
- special interests or passions (i.e., topics or objects of intense interest, in which they are very motivated to invest a lot of their time and energy);
- environmental conditions (e.g., indoor vs. outdoor);
- particular people.

Clearly, knowing what an individual with ASD is attracted to in activities or his or her preferences in general will lead to the best match of activities. Information about preferences and special interests can be gathered using techniques and tools described in Chapter 3, if this information is not already known.

Dan's team has brainstormed many possible activities that match his preferences and special interests. These matches are shown in Figure 5.2 for Dan. He has been fortunate that first his IEP team and now his Individual Support Team use this approach.

Chapter 5: The Exposure Component of Leisure Development

Figure 5.2: Match of Dan's Preferences to Potential Activities		
Preferences	**Possible Activities**	**Possible Settings**
Wind in face Being outdoors Motion Vibration	Bike riding (tandem for safety)	Paved bike paths Bike lanes
Motion Vibration Water	Swimming	Fitness center Community center Water park
Motion Vibration Jumping	Mini trampoline	Group home Work break area Fitness center
Water Blowing warm air Soft textures Creating sounds	Making felt covered balls with bells inside for cats	Group home Community center Crafts store
Being outdoors Motion Throwing objects Creating noise	Basketball (shooting baskets)	Group home driveway Neighborhood park School yard Work parking lot
Vibration Creating loud noise Hitting objects Favorite song: Little Drummer Boy	Drumming	Group home (using Wii or iPad) Drumming circle at store or with interest group Community Band
Listening to music	Using MP3 player or iPod	Group home Work Community, especially during waiting times
Being outdoors Listening to music	Going to summer outdoor concerts	Variety of community venues (e.g., parks, zoo)
Blowing warm air Vibration Odors Eating	Using air popcorn maker	Group home Work break area
Wind in face Being outdoors Motion Vibration Spinning	Going on amusement rides	Amusement or theme park Fairs and carnivals

From the leisure assessment discussed in Chapter 3, Dan's team knows that he is already enjoying a couple of these activities and that he had enjoyed several of these activities in the past, but has not had the opportunity to continue them.

Interest of family members and friends—Most of us do the majority of our activities with friends and family members. When family members and friends are interested in an activity, it usually means that an individual will have more opportunities to engage in the activity.

To expand leisure options for individuals who may always need some level of support for participation, it is especially important to identify common interests with friends and family members, who may become leisure partners and natural supports. This will also expand the number of opportunities that an individual has to share mutually meaningful experiences with people that an individual wants to spend time with. Families and friends can grow closer together through enjoying leisure activities together.

From the leisure interest surveys completed by Dan's friends and family (see Chapter 3), his support team knows that all of the activities in Figure 5.2, except making felted cat balls and drumming, are enjoyed by either a friend or family member. In addition, he has friends and family members who would like to do a number of these activities with him. For instance, his sister, Sarah, wants to ride the tandem bicycle with him; his friend, Bert, wants to swim with him; his co-worker, Ned, wants to play basketball with him; and his mother and Sarah want to go to outdoor concerts with him.

Age appropriate—Activities that are engaged in by people in the same age group are considered to be age appropriate. An advantage of age appropriate activities is that they provide a means to share interests and experiences with same age peers. These shared interests and experiences are a foundation to build friendships and natural supports.

Sometimes it is difficult to think of the wide-ranging possibilities for age appropriate leisure activities. To assist the reader, many of the extensive options in various categories (e.g., media, physical activity, games/crafts, events, and other) for individuals from five-years-old through adulthood are shown in the Age-Appropriate Activities List in Appendix A, page 119. It does not list all the extensive possibilities, but provides a solid start.

All of the activities listed for Dan in Figure 5.2 are engaged in by his peers in their early 20's. Hopefully, Dan will make some new friends in these activities.

Chapter 5: The Exposure Component of Leisure Development

Available in person's home, school, work, and/or community—An activity must be readily available in the individual's home, school, work, and/or community so that he will have ample opportunity to engage in it. Every community has different opportunities for leisure in the home, school, work, and community.

Dan's team determines that all of the potential activities in Figure 5.2 are possible for him to pursue in his home, work, and/or community, except amusement rides. There is no amusement or theme park near where he lives.

Determining activities available in your community—Clearly, to determine if an activity is readily available, one must be aware of what opportunities are available or could be pursued within an individual's home, school, work, and community. Information about the range of activities and settings where they can be pursued can be collected in a variety of ways, including:

- online search;
- asking people in your network or in various settings;
- observation of settings;
- reading brochures, community newspapers, bulletin boards, and directories.

Look beyond traditional sources when collecting information about resources. Both sources that serve everyone and those that serve individuals with special needs need to be considered.

Many organizations that serve a large number of individuals with ASD (e.g., school districts, local chapters of the Arc and local chapters of the Autism Society) could benefit from a local resource list of leisure activities for different age groups. The reproducible blank Settings & Resources Activities form in Appendix B, page 137 provides a means to develop a resource list for all types of activities and where or when each activity can be pursued in school, community, and home settings. Several staff members and/or volunteers can be assigned either different types of activities (e.g., physical activities, arts and crafts, and nature activities) or types of organizations (e.g., parks department, school, and youth organizations) to investigate, and then record the results on the form.

Figure 5.3 shows a sample completed page of the Settings & Resources Activities form that was completed specifically for 14 to 18 years olds in Portland, Oregon. This particular page focuses on physical activities, but additional pages list other types of activities (e.g., arts and crafts, nature activities and more). It is unique to Portland, which has a large Parks Bureau with many programs (e.g., parks/playgrounds, outdoor programs, community centers, and community schools), community colleges, clubs/organizations, and commercial recreation opportunities. Examples of specific clubs and various types of commercial facilities are listed; however, the possibilities are too extensive for this list.

Figure 5.3: Settings & Resources for Activities

Column groupings: *School* = Break/Between Classes, Recess, Extracurricular, Elective Classes/Specials; *Community* = Parks/Playgrounds, Outdoor Program, Community Schools, Community Center, Community Colleges, Clubs/Organizations, Commercial Recreation (the *Parks Bureau* bracket spans Parks/Playgrounds through Community Center); *Home* = Outside, Inside.

Leisure Activities	Break/Between Classes	Recess	Extracurricular	Elective Classes/Specials	Parks/Playgrounds	Outdoor Program	Community Schools	Community Center	Community Colleges	Clubs/Organizations	Commercial Recreation	Outside	Inside
Walking					✓					Volksmarche			
Jogging			✓	✓						y's, Fun Run		✓	
Riding a Bike					✓					Wheelmen	Rental	✓	
Playing Catch	✓	✓			✓	✓				✓	✓		
Skill Building Classes				✓									
Swimming			✓	✓	✓	✓	✓	✓	✓	y's	Fitness Center		✓
Aerobics/Slimnastics/Jazzercise				✓				✓	✓		Fitness Center		✓
Exercise Equipment				✓				✓	✓	y's	Fitness Center		✓
Weight Training				✓				✓	✓	y's	Fitness Center		✓
Racquet Sports								✓	✓	y's	Health Club	✓	✓
Skating					✓		✓	✓	✓		Rinks	✓	
Skateboarding	✓				✓							✓	
Dance Classes			✓	✓				✓	✓	Square Dance, Other Clubs	Dance Studio	✓	✓
Volleyball/Soccer				✓	✓			✓	✓	Leagues	Leagues	✓	
Being a Team Manager			✓					✓	✓	Leagues			✓
Golfing								✓			Golf Course	✓	
Horseback Riding										4-H	Stable	✓	
Hiking/Backpacking						✓				Sierra Club	Outfitters	✓	✓
Snow Shoeing						✓				Mazamas	Outfitters	✓	✓
Skiing						✓				Numerous	Areas	✓	✓
Boating										Numerous	Numerous	✓	
Ping Pong							✓	✓		Boy's Club			✓

Chapter 5: The Exposure Component of Leisure Development

Done in a variety of environments and situations—Many of us seek opportunities to engage in our favorite activities in a variety of settings, because it means that we can do the activities even more. For individuals with ASD, there are additional reasons to consider doing activities in different locations. First, being able to do an activity in more than one setting offers the opportunity to spend more time to enjoy the activity and improve skills in it. Second, those supporting individuals with ASD have a limited amount of time to prepare individuals for new activities, develop supports, and expose them to new activities. When an activity can be pursued in multiple locations (e.g., home, school, work, and the community), there is less need to develop new interests and skills. Therefore, more time can be spent involved in activities than in developing new interests.

Many activities can be pursued in multiple locations. For instance, Figure 5.3 exemplifies many environments where the listed physical activities can be pursued.

As can be seen in Figure 5.2, Dan's support team thought about both a variety of locations for activities and his preference for environments when they considered activities for him. All the activities listed in Figure 5.2 can be done in more than one setting.

Engaged in alone or with others—Activities that can be engaged in both with and without others are valuable. Individuals with ASD tend to engage in more solitary activities than their peers and become more isolated as they get older (Badia et al, 2012; Orsmond, & Kuo, 2011), but it is not always clear if solitary activities are a choice or a result of lack of opportunity and barriers encountered. When an activity can be done alone or with others, it provides an opportunity to choose to interact with others or not in an activity.

All the activities for Dan in Figure 5.2, except activities in the community, can potentially be done alone or with others. At this point, Dan needs someone with him in the community for safety reasons. It is advantageous for that person to act as his leisure companion.

Economically feasible—Cost is a factor in whether an activity is accessible to an individual. Most activities have some cost attached to them whether it is the initial purchase of equipment, maintenance of equipment, fees for participation, or other charges. If a person, his or her family, or an agency cannot pay the costs associated with an activity in some way (e.g., money, work exchange, or other creative means), the individual will not be able to continue to participate, which can result in grave disappointment. Therefore, it is important to consider if an activity is economically feasible.

Dan's support team still needs to assess how some of the activities listed in Figure 5.2 could be paid for and sustained.

Potential for frequent and long term participation—Activities that can be engaged in regularly and continued over time are critical and may become lifelong activities. When an activity is regularly scheduled or there is an opportunity to choose it on a regular basis, the need for predictability and routine is accommodated. Furthermore, there is ample opportunity to practice and maintain skills for the activity. In the Guidelines for Selecting Leisure Activities, regular or frequent participation is a minimum of 12 times a year for most activities and a minimum of 6 times per season for seasonal activities (e.g., skiing, snowshoeing, and sledding).

That is not to say that an activity that an individual wants to do can only be done now and then should be ignored. An individual should still be given opportunities to do a desired activity that does not meet this criteria whenever possible. However, the activity would not be a priority for the *Exposure Component*. For instance, Dan expressed an interest in amusement rides, but the only amusement park is far from where he lives. Consequently, he can only go to the amusement park once in awhile. He does not receive the same amount of preparation and support for this type of outing as he would for a regularly scheduled activity.

Dan could potentially do all of the activities in Figure 5.2 regularly, except going to the amusement park. Additionally, since he has enjoyed most of these activities in the past, they have a strong potential of becoming lifelong leisure pursuits.

Social demands at a person's skill level—The social demands of a leisure activity can significantly affect the enjoyment and success of individuals with ASD. Therefore, social demands should be matched to the person. If the social demands of an activity are not considered, an individual with ASD may become involved in an activity that is very uncomfortable and heightens anxiety. Too often individuals with ASD have difficulty with an activity or refuse to participate because the social skills required are too demanding given their current skills. Most individuals with ASD prefer activities that have few social demands (e.g., bicycling, photography, individual sports, gardening, arts and crafts) or predictable social demands (e.g., turn taking in a board game, clap at end of concert). Activities that are socially complex (e.g., team sports) and/or require much social interaction (e.g., parties) may not be suitable for some individuals with ASD.

Prioritizing from activities that meet selection criteria—As can be seen from the previous review of the activities for Dan in Figure 5.2, sometimes there are more activities that meet the guidelines than an individual can experience during a set period of time. The final consideration in selecting activities for the *Exposure Component* is to prioritize the few activities that will contribute the most to the individual's leisure satisfaction. Consider if the individual has a personally meaningful balance of:

- activities at home, school, work, and in the community;
- activities pursued alone and with others;
- active and passive activities.

In the *Exposure Component* the goal is to have at least one activity in each of the settings (e.g., home, school, work, and/or community) that is alone, with others, passive, and active. To prioritize activities for exposure, information about the individual's past and present leisure, and his or her feelings about leisure pursuits are vital. The valuable information collected about an individual on the spectrum, such as that described in Chapter 3, provides a solid base for decision making about where more activities would be beneficial. A summary form, such as the reproducible blank copy of the Leisure Lifestyle Profile in Appendix B, page 135 is useful to determine if there are activities in each of these areas for a person.

Start by looking at activities in the home. If the person has little or no satisfying leisure activity at home, this should be the first priority, since the majority of free time for all of us is spent at home. Ensuring that there is meaningful leisure at home is often forgotten, because the community is often the sole focus for leisure activities.

Both activities alone and with others at home should be considered, while bearing in mind that the bulk of our leisure pursuits at home are solitary for most of us. In addition, many individuals with ASD are more interested in an activity itself than in any social interaction associated with it. A common mistake is to err on the side of activities with others, so be sure to think about what the individual wants. In the end, it is all about what is personally meaningful and satisfying for the individual with ASD.

Continue this process for school, work, and in the community. Then, see if there are activities in each setting, alone and with others, and active and passive. Consider whether an activity can be pursued in more than one setting (e.g., home and community).

Dan's Leisure Lifestyle Profile (Figure 3.6) and past history, which were presented in Chapter 3, are reviewed to prioritize the new activities that he will experience. Dan's team discusses the following.

HOME: Meaningful leisure activities in his home are even more important for Dan, since his supported employment placement of only 15 hours a week leaves him with more leisure time than the average person. At first glance, his Leisure Lifestyle Profile (Figure 3.6) may appear to show a good balance of activities. A closer look reveals that he spends most of his leisure time in sedentary and solitary activities—listening to music and lying on a heat vent for hours on end or being near group home staff without interacting. However, he gets some exercise by shooting baskets outside for about 20 minutes a day when the weather allows and briefly jumping on a mini trampoline inside. To add another active activity that Dan could potentially do daily at home, Dan and his team decide that Dan will try playing the drums using Rock Band on Wii.

Drumming is prioritized for two additional reasons. First, it can potentially be done with his housemates in the future. Secondly, it can help him get back into drumming, an activity he did in high school, in preparation for joining a drumming circle or band in the community.

To partially accommodate the sensory input that Dan seeks when he lays on the heat register, two additional activities are prioritized for Dan to experience at home. These include making felt covered cat balls, which involves using a hair dryer, and making hot air popcorn. Both of these activities could also involve social interaction in the future, if Dan wanted to interact. For instance, he could give the cat balls to family, friends, animal shelters, etc., and he could share his popcorn with housemates and friends.

WORK: Most of us have activities that we do at work during breaks and lunch time. In addition to eating, it may include socializing face to face or via a mobile device, taking walks, listening to music, reading, playing video games, and more. Often individuals with ASD do not recognize the opportunity for leisure activities in the workplace.

Dan's work is sedentary and he engages in a sedentary, solitary activity, listening to music during breaks and lunch at work. He creates his own noise and excitement by occasionally setting off the fire alarm on the way to break or lunch. Everyone at work would prefer him to have an alternative stimulating activity than setting off the fire alarm. Dan and his team recently discovered that there is a covered basketball hoop mounted in the parking lot that employees can use. Dan expresses interest in shooting baskets there and a co-worker, Ned, who wants to know Dan better, says that he would like to shoot baskets with Dan.

Shooting baskets is a good leisure activity to prioritize for his workplace. In addition to providing natural supports, it expands a physical activity that Dan enjoys in one setting (i.e., home) to another setting, while offering an opportunity to build a friendship through a structured interaction at his current ability level.

COMMUNITY: Dan is not involved in community activities by himself at this point due to safety concerns, but he enjoys going to music concerts in small venues, family gatherings, or quiet restaurants with his mother or sister once or twice a month. He participates less than enthusiastically in walking with staff in his neighborhood. He is doing fewer activities in the community than when he was younger, because of lack of opportunity, but that is soon to change. During his Person Centered Planning meeting, his sister Sarah says, that she would like to get the cobwebs off the tandem bicycle that their mother and Dan used to ride together and bicycle with Dan twice a month. Dan's friend, Bert, wants to swim with Dan at the YMCA, where Dan can get a free membership. Dan is excited to once more have the opportunity to try two old favorites, tandem bicycling and swimming, and do activities in the community with two favorite people.

After considering all the information, Dan and his support team prioritized the activities shown in Figure 5.4.

Figure 5.4: Dan's Prioritized Activities for Exposure					
Setting	Activity	Active	Passive	Alone	W/others
HOME	Rock Band—Drums	X		X	In Future?
	Felted cat balls	X		X	In Future?
	Air Popcorn	X		X	In Future?
WORK	Shoot Baskets	X			X (Ned)
COMMUNITY	Bicycling	X			X (Sarah)
	Swimming	X			X (Bert)

Note that the number of activities prioritized for Dan to try out is unusually high, but it makes sense for him. First, he has an abnormally large amount of leisure time to fill as a result of his very short work week. Second, only two activities—drums with Rock Band and felted cat balls—are new to him. He has previously enjoyed the other four activities, but has not had the opportunity to do them for some time. The exposure to these last four activities is to see if he's still interested in these potentially lifelong activities and to determine what it will take for him to adjust to the new environments in which he does them. Finally, he also has natural supports who are eager to do three of these activities with him.

This process of selecting and prioritizing activities will be repeated a number of times over the years, as interests develop or change. Developing personally meaningful and satisfactory leisure interests is an ongoing process for most of us.

Repeated and Supported Exposure to New Activities

Due to the nature of ASD, repeated and supported exposure is crucial to broadening leisure interests and pursuits.

Repeated Exposure

Multiple opportunities to try out an activity are necessary to ensure that individuals have adequate exposure to an activity to discover if it is meaningful and enjoyable for them. Repeated exposure is also crucial for three other reasons. An individual: 1) may resist new activities, 2) take time to understand them, and/or 3) have diverse reactions to an activity on different days.

Just because a person with ASD does not respond positively the first time an activity is presented does not necessarily mean that an activity should be discontinued. Even when individuals have chosen and desire to participate in a new activity, they may initially react negatively to novel elements associated with the activity, such as using unknown materials, wearing unfamiliar clothes, new environments, people, or demands. As familiarity increases, tolerance also increases. Without repeated exposure to activities, they are unlikely to overcome any initial resistance and accept the new aspects of the activity.

Insight about the variables that make activities more or less positive for an individual may be gleaned from inconsistent reactions to an activity from day to day. If one day is difficult, plan better for the next one.

Gradually introducing an individual to an activity and using the type of supports discussed later in this chapter will help, but cannot guarantee acceptance of an activity. If an activity has been presented five or more times and a person consistently responds negatively to the activity, it may be time to try something else. The main objective is to give each person with ASD the chance to try a number of options to discover new leisure interests that he or she wants to pursue; not every activity will be meaningful and enjoyable.

Supported Exposure

The focus in the *Exposure Component* is on support for experiencing new leisure activities rather than skill development for an activity. Emphasis is on having enough support to try out an activity without undue stress. Most individuals with ASD, regardless of cognitive level and/or expressive language skills, need supports that specifically utilize their strengths and compensate for their challenges.

The steps for providing exposure to new activities include:

1. planning for the activity;
2. preparing the individual prior to the activity;
3. developing and providing supports;
4. supporting and guiding participation in the activity.

Planning for the Activity

The importance of planning in advance for exposure to new activities cannot be stressed enough. Careful planning makes the experience of a new activity more pleasurable and reduces stress for both the person leading the activity and the individual with ASD. The essentials for activity planning include:

- Know the individual.
- Identify activity.
- Identify and gather materials needed for activity.
- Determine how the activity will be set up and presented.
- Identify opportunities to make choices within the activity.
- Determine ways to encourage the maximum level of independence.
- Identify what could go wrong and develop an alternative plan.
- Develop visual supports and structure to show what the upcoming activity is, sequence of steps in the activity, environmental conditions (e.g., crowding, noise, lighting), suggestions on how to cope, and expectations.

The Activity Cards in Appendix D, page 163 illustrate these areas for planning a positive experience with specific leisure activities.

Preparing the Individual Prior to the Activity

New activities, environments, and expectations can cause immense distress for individuals with ASD. Unless they are adequately prepared for an activity in advance, they may refuse to participate in an activity. Therefore, individuals with ASD must be prepared sufficiently to reduce the stress associated with new situations and to motivate participation. The more individuals with ASD are prepared for an activity the better.

Such preparation supports their intense drive for predictability. Most individuals on the spectrum will benefit from the following strategies to prepare them for a new activity:

- Know the individual.
- Someone familiar with the individual scouts the situation and/or does the activity ahead of time to anticipate possible problems.
- On several occasions before the activity, tell the individual what to expect, exactly what will happen, what the activity entails from start to finish, and any possible sensory challenges (e.g., unexpected sounds, ambient noise level, lighting, etc.) in a visual manner (e.g., visual schedule, cartooning, written list, social narrative, and/or video modeling).
- If the activity will take place in a new setting, consider visiting it on a number of occasions, and include introducing new leaders, instructors, and companions to the individual.
- If using new materials in activity, allow the individual to look at or try them out ahead of time.
- Negotiate reinforcement or what they can earn.

Because of individual differences between persons with ASD, they may require various combinations of strategies to prepare them for new activities. Use the ones that will be most helpful to an individual.

For example, the night before a school trip to the science museum, Julie's parents prepare her by first describing the sequence with words and photographs. This sequence depicts bus ride from school, see exhibit hall 1, eat lunch, bathroom, see exhibit hall 2, and bus ride back to school. Next, they review behavioral expectations with a written list and what she can earn for following directions. Finally, they talk about the science exhibits and write down two important topics about it so that Julie will have meaningful comments to share when she goes to the science museum. The teacher uses the same approach to prepare the entire class just before going to the science museum. These steps help prepare Julie for this activity and the change in her school schedule.

More information about preparation for change can be found in the Transitioning Between Activities module at the free Autism Internet Modules website (www.autisminternetmodules.org/).

Developing and Providing Supports

Knowing what supports have been used effectively with the individual is crucial. The individual and the people who know him or her the best are a rich source of information on effective supports. Involving an individual in planning supports, as much as possible, usually results in the best fit and provision of supports the person will be more motivated to use.

The *Exposure Component* is not the time to add supports that will require training for the individual to utilize. It is time to use the types of supports that an individual is already familiar with or that make sense to the particular individual with ASD without being taught.

Because of the nature of ASD, most of these individuals, regardless of their cognitive level or severity of ASD, will need some type of the following:

- visual supports to convey instructions, meanings, routines, schedules, changes, expectations, and reminders;
- visual organization of the environment and materials to provide structure and predictability, while conveying boundaries, routines, and schedules;
- environmental modifications and/or accommodations for sensory regulation and to prevent interfering stimuli.

Visual supports—Visual supports are a key evidence-based support and the most universally used approach for individuals with ASD to assist in all areas of challenge. This approach helps minimize their difficulties in auditory processing, as well as attention and organization, while supporting the tendency to conceptualize ideas and experiences in a visual way. In contrast to fleeting auditory information, visual supports provide concrete information that remains available to help an individual to better understand the activity. These supports can convey instructions, meanings, routines, schedules, changes, and expectations. They might include, but are not limited to visual schedules, maps, labels, diagrams, templates, finished examples, checklists, pictorial or written reminders, graphic organizers, and computers or mobile electronic devices (e.g., smart phones, tablets, iPod Touch) that incorporate calendars. A glossary for these and other support terms can be found in Appendix C, page 148.

One particularly important type of visual support is visual schedules. Visual schedules allow individuals to view an upcoming activity, gain a better understanding of the sequence of activities that will occur, and increase overall predictability. The Activity Cards in Appendix D, page 163 provide pictorial mini-schedules for each activity like the one in Figure 5.5.

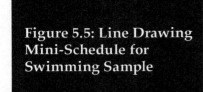

Figure 5.5: Line Drawing Mini-Schedule for Swimming Sample

The ability to understand different levels of abstraction varies between individuals with ASD. Visual supports need to be at the level that the individual understands even when stressed. This may be in the form of:

- objects and actions;
- photographs of objects and actions;
- black and white line drawings of objects and actions;
- written words which describe objects and actions.

Dan understands line drawings and uses a pictorial schedule, similar to those depicted in the Activity Cards in Appendix D. Julie understands print and generally follows written instructions. However, she does not always process print well when she is stressed, so she uses a pictorial schedule with words printed under each picture when she is introduced to new activities. John requires more concrete symbols, so he uses objects to represent activities.

Another evidence-based visual support is social narratives. Social narratives describe what will happen and what is expected. They may include photographs, illustrations, or videos to assist the individual understand the information. Social narratives are excellent for preparing individuals for novel activities through the use of written information. The Activity Stories for each activity in the Activity Cards in Appendix D are a type of social narrative.

The final evidence-based visual support discussed here is video modeling. Video modeling may be an effective support strategy to prepare for an activity, if watching videos is a meaningful activity for an individual. This strategy involves recording another individual (e.g., family member, peer, staff member) performing the new activity along with a simple narration about the process and requirements. An excellent example of using this strategy to prepare for a trip to the zoo can be found at the Autism Internet Modules website (www.autisminternetmodules.org/). (Browse alphabetically to Transitioning between Activities, then go to What are the specific transition strategies? and finally, go to Priming through Video).

Structuring a meaningful and predicable environment—Individuals with ASD thrive in predictable, well-organized, highly structured activities and environments. Structure and organization support the intense drive of individuals with ASD to find order and make sense of their world. Structure, organization, and modification of the environment assist individuals with ASD with difficulties in organizing, sequencing, and completing activities. By increasing predictability and understanding, highly structured activities and environments decrease the anxiety individuals with ASD may feel when they are confused. When individuals with ASD know exactly what is happening and what they are supposed to do, they are more apt to have a positive and enjoyable experience. When an activity lacks structure, it may set an individual with ASD up for failure and frustration.

Structured activities and environments promote a clear understanding of the schedules, activities, routines, expectations, and boundaries for both individuals with ASD and their support people. Mesibov and colleagues (2005) have identified the following key questions for structure that have been used extensively with leisure activities. These include:

- What am I expected to do?
- How much am I expected to do?
- Where do I do the activity?
- Where do objects belong?
- How will I know when I am finished?
- What will I do next?

An important, evidence-based strategy that uses this structure is called Structured Teaching. It is a visually based approach to creating highly structured activities and environments that support individuals with ASD across environments (Mesibov, Shea, & Schopler, 2005). This strategy involves a combination of approaches that rely heavily on the physical organization of a setting and predictable schedules. It involves a purposeful, systematic arrangement of the environment from physical layout of a room to routines/sequences used. Some components of structure and organization in this system include visual boundaries, visual organization of materials, and routines. Strategies that support structure includes, but are not limited to lines on floor, carpet squares on floor, color-coding, diagrams, jigs, finished box, first then sequence, labels, lists of materials, organizational checklists, positive routines, visual schedules, and work baskets. A glossary for these and other support terms can be found in Appendix C, page 148. Figure 5.6 provides an example of using a work basket and template for making a bead necklace.

A variety of tools, such as a countdown tool, can be used to indicate when an activity will be over.

Figure 5.6: Structured Work System and Template

Julie is experiencing roller skating for the first time. In addition to a schedule for the activity and a social narrative, the facilitator holds up a board with ten strips of paper on it. Then the strips are progressively removed during the activity to let Julie know how much "time" is left and when skating is over. This countdown tool was chosen because the removal of paper strips has no actual time increment. Each strip of paper can be removed after a different length of time, and, therefore, can be used flexibly if Julie does not appear to be able to continue skating for as long as was first anticipated.

Sensory supports—Many individuals with ASD have sensory sensitivities. Normal levels of auditory, visual, tactile, or other sensory input may be perceived as too much or too little. Sensory supports assist individuals with ASD to stay calm while maintaining the necessary level of arousal for an event or activity and/or reduces environmental stimuli that an individual wants to avoid. They also provide for the sensory needs and comfort requirements of individuals with ASD. Sensory supports might include, but are not limited to environmental modifications (e.g., changing lighting to reduce glare or brightness and putting up sound barriers to reduce noise), individual supports to lessen the impact of sensations (e.g., baseball cap or visor to reduce light and headphones to reduce noise), and supports for maintaining the necessary arousal for an activity (e.g., sensory diet).

Supports must be both individualized and flexible. Both the types and levels of support should be based on the needs and desires of the particular person.

Resources for support strategies—Some of the supports and concepts in the preceding section may be new to you, but there are a variety of resources that provide further information on these supports. Two resources in Appendix C, Support & Training Strategies (page 146) and Glossary of Terms for Support Strategies (page 148) will help you understand the supports better. In addition, practical information on how to develop and implement all of the supports strategies presented can be found at two excellent free online resources. These include the Autism Internet Modules (www.autisminternetmodules.org/) and the National Professional Development Center on ASD (http://autismpdc. fpg.unc.edu/content/briefs*) websites.

Developing supports—Developing supports does not need to be complicated or always look as professional as the figures in this chapter or Activity Cards in Appendix D, page 163. For instance, most people who support an individual on the spectrum can quickly draw the sequence of an activity using stick figures to create a mini-schedule. Many individuals already use supports that provide a template or can be use with minor adaptations.

More and more resources have become available to make the development of supports, particularly visual supports, more efficient and less time consuming. A growing number of websites provide useful tools for developing supports, such as downloadable supports that can be adapted for the

---

* Web addresses sometimes change. If this URL does not work, you may find what you are looking for if you: 1) Google the title or 2) use the domain name, such as http://autismpdc.fpg.unc.edu rather than http://autismpdc.fpg.unc.edu/content/briefs, and search that site.

needs of a particular individual. Two websites of particular note that provide free downloadable visual materials are pictureSET (www.setbc.org/pictureset) and do2Learn (www.do2learn.com). Pictures and symbols can also be downloaded from websites like Google Images. Meanwhile, smart phones and other mobile technology make capturing videos and digital images for visual supports straightforward while a growing number of apps make creating visual supports much easier. Three examples of useful apps are:

1. Visual Schedule Planner (https://itunes.apple.com/us/app/visual-schedule-planner/id488646282?mt=8) is designed to give an individual an audio/visual representation of the "events in their day" and can use video clips.
2. Stories2Learn (https://itunes.apple.com/us/app/stories2learn/id348576875?mt=8Description) is designed to create social narratives with photos text and audio messages.
3. Video Scheduler (https://itunes.apple.com/ca/app/video-scheduler/id482833959?mt=8) Originally designed to structure picture and video schedules, but video schedule function can be turned off to use as video modeling tool.

Supporting and Guiding Participation

In the *Exposure Component*, the focus is on the typical manner of doing an activity (i.e., adhering to rules of a game), whereas in the *Immediate Component* the focus is on using materials in the way an individual wants as long as it is safely. Family members, peers, caregivers, teachers, and service providers may be involved in supervising, guiding or directing individuals with ASD in activities. All the structure and supports discussed earlier in this chapter will help individuals to do an activity conventionally. However, guidance is also needed to prevent developing a pattern of doing an activity in an atypical or unconventional manner. Without such guidance, individuals with ASD may become preoccupied with a sensory aspect of an activity (e.g., Dan repeatedly rubbing a smooth surface), get stuck doing a part of the activity (e.g., Julie only jumping in a gymnastics class), or fixate on a special interest within the activity (e.g., John perseverates on the train at the zoo and, although he loves animals, he will not go look at them).

Individuals with ASD should be guided to do the activity in the conventional manner the first time, so they do not get stuck on doing it a different way. They tend to have a firm and sometimes unchangeable notion of all aspects of an activity (e.g., steps, materials, settings, environmental conditions, people present, and feelings about the activity) based on their first experience with it. Therefore, they may always do an activity in exactly the same way that it was performed originally or be very upset if some aspect is different. For the same reason, a negative or confusing experience is always remembered and should be avoided as much as possible. If you mistakenly misdirect an individual with ASD, fix it as quickly as possible, because it is extremely difficult to change later.

The person guiding the activity needs to assign meaning to events, actions, and show the way. Develop more independence by highlighting natural cues or provide visual sequences on when, where, and how to do activities. The picture sequences and written explanations in the Activity Cards (Appendix D, page 163) provide examples of how to provide the necessary information.

Depending upon the level of abstraction that an individual understands, meaning may be highlighted by a real object, photographs, line drawings, or written information. The written directions for making silk screen birthday cards in Figure 5.7 provides an example of the type of visual information that may be needed for an individual with ASD who reads, but has difficulty following verbal directions and demonstrations, such as Julie.

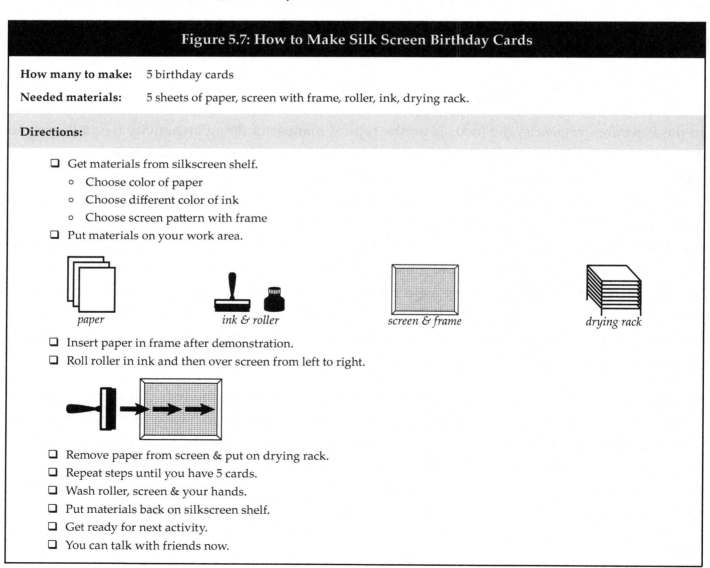

Figure 5.7: How to Make Silk Screen Birthday Cards

How many to make: 5 birthday cards

Needed materials: 5 sheets of paper, screen with frame, roller, ink, drying rack.

Directions:

- ❑ Get materials from silkscreen shelf.
  - ○ Choose color of paper
  - ○ Choose different color of ink
  - ○ Choose screen pattern with frame
- ❑ Put materials on your work area.

paper   *ink & roller*   *screen & frame*   *drying rack*

- ❑ Insert paper in frame after demonstration.
- ❑ Roll roller in ink and then over screen from left to right.

- ❑ Remove paper from screen & put on drying rack.
- ❑ Repeat steps until you have 5 cards.
- ❑ Wash roller, screen & your hands.
- ❑ Put materials back on silkscreen shelf.
- ❑ Get ready for next activity.
- ❑ You can talk with friends now.

The person guiding the activity should highlight critical information and direct effort. First, model or demonstrate the activity while providing a literal and clear description related to objects, actions, and people at the person's level of understanding. This commentary may sound similar to the types of information that a mother gives to a young child. Make reference to the mini-schedule or other supports verbally and with a point or other gesture. This process may be done through a live or video taped demonstration. This phase may not be necessary if the individual is already familiar with some parts of the activity.

Then, gradually introduce the individual to an activity with decreased expectations and/or partial participation, as needed. For instance, some individuals may only hold materials or be assisted to complete some of the steps at first. During this phase, highlighting relevant cues and providing assistance to prevent errors may still be appropriate. If an error occurs, model again using guided practice.

Finally, encourage full participation and as much independence as possible in an activity, while supervising and providing assistance, if needed, to prevent the individual from doing the activity wrong. Individuals with ASD often become prompt dependent and wait for directions when they only get verbal directions and prompts. Therefore, give directions and prompts through visual supports and avoid verbal directions and prompts, as much as possible. For instance, when an individual is having some difficulty, remind him or her how to ask for help with just prompts (i.e., point to his or her communication system).

Figure 5.8 (on the next page) provides additional tips to use when supervising, guiding or directing individuals on the spectrum in activities.

Figure 5.8: Tips for Guiding Exposure to an Activity

- Know the individual.
- Present activities at an appropriate level of difficulty.
- Reduce expectations the first time individuals are exposed to an activity.
- Pay attention to pacing issues and give ample time to respond.
- Let individuals finish what they are doing.
- Remain close to, but not always directly at a person's side
- Make sure individual has a means to ask for help, make a request, make a choice, and refuse.
- Speak calmly and softly.
- Speak literally and very specifically, e.g., "Put on your red swimsuit".
- Use "do" statements, e.g., "Hold my hand and walk," rather than "don't" statements, e.g., "Don't run."
- Use statements, e.g., "It's time to clean up" rather than questions, e.g., "Can you clean up now?"
- Allow time to process what is said and wait for a response.
- Help individual understand directions through visual supports.
- Provide choices and options.
- Identify key person(s) or a mentor the individual can go to if he or she is having trouble adjusting or understanding a certain situation.
- Be alert to body language and other behavior that signals anxiety or confusion.
- Read behavior as communication.
- Lower expectations when an individual is stressed.
- Reduce stressors.
- Provide access to comfort materials, such as a familiar object from home, and other sensory supports.
- Provide a location where the participant can go to relax and to regroup. Label the people, objects, and actions as they occur.
- Provide the participant with a visual menu of coping strategies.

Formative Assessment

Ongoing assessment is vital to determine which activities an individual enjoys and wants to develop more skills in through the *Training Component*. Feedback directly from an individual with ASD and observations by one or more people—who support the individual during an activity—provide valuable information about the degree of interest, effective strategies, additional supports needed, reactions to environmental factors (e.g., noise and crowding), and more.

If an activity does not work well, learn from what happened and plan better for the next time. Some beginning questions to ask, so that adjustments can be made are:

- What conditions may have contributed to the challenges?
- Was the environment too crowded or noisy?
- Was a good preview of what to expect provided?
- Did the individual expect something else?

Once an activity has been experienced a number of times, an individual with ASD should be given the opportunity to discuss or give some form of feedback (e.g., point to "Yes" or "No" cue cards, point to pictures, and accept or push away items representing the activity) about experiences with it and decide if he or she wishes to pursue the activity. Sometimes individuals with ASD indicate interest or a desire to continue to pursue and activity in unexpected ways that are difficult to interpret.

As much as possible, feedback should include:

- what an individual liked and disliked about an activity and why;
- what they think they did well and what was challenging;
- what things were different than expected;
- and more.

Knowing what an individual does not like provides valuable information, because we can learn as much from what an individual does not like as from what he likes. Individuals with ASD may willingly participate in activities that are scheduled and part of their routine even if they do not like an activity. A lack of protest may merely reflect resignation rather than interest in an activity.

Direct observation of an individual doing an activity provides much valuable information. Keeping a record of these observations is useful, so that the information will not be lost and can be reviewed when making decisions with the individual on the spectrum and his or her support people. Four tools are particularly useful in recording observations. These include the Activity Assessment Form (see description in Chapter 3), Environmental Assessment (refer to Figure 6.5 in Chapter 6),

Environmental Inventory (see Figure 6.6 in Chapter 6), and Leisure Lifestyle Profile (refer to Figure 3.6 in Chapter 3). Reproducible blank forms for each of these tools are provided in Appendix B for your use.

From assessment, such as those described above, we know that Dan showed significant interest in all the activities that he tried during the *Exposure Component*, except making the felted cat balls. He enjoyed the texture of the felt, hot air from the hair dryer, and tinkling of the bell in the balls, but did not demonstrate interest in the activity itself. He generalized use of the activity skills for shooting baskets, tandem bicycling, and swimming that he had learned and practiced over the years to the new settings.

Summary

To have meaningful and satisfying leisure, an individual with ASD must have a variety of activities that he or she freely chooses to engage in alone and with others at home and in the community. Many individuals with ASD have restricted interests and resist new activities. Additionally, they often have had very limited opportunities to try a variety of activities in a range of settings with different people. If an individual's leisure interests are narrow or unclear, then trying out new activities in the *Exposure Component* is crucial. In this component, individuals with ASD are exposed to activities with the greatest chance of becoming an interest in a systematic, structured manner that supports the challenges of ASD, so that interest in leisure activities can be broadened. Discovering interests takes time, because you have to try out different activities and settings. Careful preparation, support strategies, and guidance through an activity will increase the chance that each experience will be positive. Interests developed through the *Exposure Component* may be further developed through the *Training Component*. Ongoing assessment provides the information to adjust exposure to activities and, also, helps with decisions on what to focus on in the *Training Component*.

The
Training
Component
of Leisure
Development

Chapter 6

arents, caregivers, teachers, and service providers are concerned about the amount of ongoing support that individuals with ASD often require to participate in preferred leisure activities. When systematic training in the necessary skills for preferred leisure activities is provided, individuals with ASD can become as independent as possible in the activity. A few leisure activities that an individual can do independently or semi-independently with visual or other supports can outweigh having a dozen activities that will require intense support from others.

Having the opportunity to develop the necessary skills to participate in their preferred leisure activities gives the physical, emotional, and social benefits that are valuable to us all. For instance, increasing independence in leisure activities will enhance their sense of accomplishment and confidence. Furthermore, success in their chosen activities can increase the drive to continue to pursue those activities, as well as offer motivation to try and learn additional leisure activities.

The purpose of the *Training Component* is to develop the necessary skills and knowledge for the individual to participate, as independently and successfully as possible, in preferred activities in home, school, work, and community settings. After training, individuals with ASD should have sufficient activity and related skills to enable them to pursue desired activities without intense support from others. The key elements for the *Training Component* include:

Key Elements of the Training Component	
• development of leisure activity and related skills;	• systematic training;
• guidelines for prioritizing activities;	• formative assessment.

Leisure Activities and Related Skills Development

The *Training Component* emphasizes the simultaneous development and related skills of/for activities, because these combined skills are necessary for successful and independent functioning in a leisure activity.

Activity Skills

Activity skills are the motor skills (e.g., put face in water for swimming, throw ball for basketball) and/or the cognitive skills (e.g., knowing the rules, use of strategy to make decisions about moves, and concentration) that are necessary to be successful in an activity. Activity skills are vital to doing an activity, but they are sometimes narrowly conceived as the only type of skills necessary for autonomous pursuit of an activity. In addition to training in the activity skills for a particular activity, individuals with ASD require training in a variety of related skills that are necessary to be competent in the activity.

Related Skills

Vital related skills for competence in leisure activities in the *Training Component* include:

- awareness of free time;
- identification and use of resources;
- choice-making;
- initiation;
- social interaction;
- problem-solving.

Related skills are often not considered when teaching skills for leisure activities, because neurotypical individuals seldom need explicit instruction in these areas. However, due to the characteristics of ASD and challenges in incidental learning and generalization, individuals with ASD do not automatically learn or apply these essential skills in activities.

Related skills are often more difficult for individuals with ASD to learn than the steps for an activity and more confusing for them to know when to use. Therefore, these skills need to be an integral part of instruction of an activity (i.e., embedded instruction) rather than taught in isolation (Johnson & McDonnell, 2004; Johnson, McDonnell, Holzwarth, & Hunter, 2004; Reisen, McDonnell, Johnson, Polychronis, & Jameson, 2003).

In order to engage in even seemingly uncomplicated activities as independently as possible, an individual may need to learn and perform many related skills. For instance, although John, like many young children, enjoys and knows how to swing, he still needs to know when it is an appropriate time to swing and when to stop (awareness of free time), where he can swing (resources), how to make a choice to swing (choice-making), how to request a turn (social), and what to do if all the swings are occupied (problem solving).

Individuals with ASD cannot be allowed to fail or remain dependent in leisure activities, because they do not have the related skills. The following section describes the importance of the related skill areas in leisure training and provides examples of support strategies for each area.

Awareness of Leisure and Free Time

Individuals with ASD often do not differentiate between leisure and work. They may not:

- know that leisure or free time is time spent away from school, work, or domestic tasks and personal care activities;
- know that leisure or free time is an opportunity to have fun and engage in enjoyable activities of their own choosing;
- recognize when they have free time;
- know what activities they enjoy or prefer to do for fun.

These concepts frequently need to be taught using visual supports and concrete examples.

Dan may need to be taught to use a pictorial schedule with a symbol for leisure time and Julie may need to be taught to use a cue card of what indicates free time at home, school, and in the community.

Identification of Resources

To independently pursue an activity, it is necessary to know:

- where it can be done in the home, school, work, or community setting;
- what materials are needed for an activity (e.g., supplies, equipment, clothing, and money);
- what is needed for getting to and from an activity (e.g., transportation and registration).

Items needed for activity—Some individuals with ASD may need visual supports or organization systems to help them remember all the materials needed for a particular activity. Remembering, getting, and—in some cases—packing necessary equipment and supplies is important for independence. These steps may be accomplished with different types of supports.

Dan and Julie are taught to organize their materials for community leisure activities in different ways. For swimming, Dan is first taught to carry a pre-packed athletic bag with his swimsuit, towel, and grooming items (e.g., shampoo and comb) in separate compartments. Over time, he learns to pack the athletic bag by following a pictorial list. Julie has different needs and is taught to use the written checklist in Figure 6.1 to help her prepare items required for skating.

Figure 6.1: My Skating Checklist			
Time & Place:	4:00–6:00 PM, Tuesday Skate World (1220 NE Kelly Ave.)		
Money to bring:	Skating fee $ _____ For snack $ _____ Total $ _____		
Things to bring:	❑ skate bag ❑ skates	❑ socks ❑ knee pads	❑ elbow pads ❑ wrist guards	❑ helmet ❑ water bottle
Way to get there today:	❑ car ❑ bus	❑ walk ❑ cycle		
Friends skating today:	_____		

Purchasing leisure materials and equipment and paying for leisure activities are often needed to be independent in an activity and requires training.

Dan and Julie learn different ways to "pay" for leisure activities in the community. Dan is taught to use his membership card to the YMCA, which is attached to his athletic bag, for swimming in lieu of paying each time with money. Julie calculates how much money she needs for skating and snack with help from her mother (See Figure 6.1) and brings a dollar amount larger than the sum (i.e., $10.00 for a sum of $9.21). She gives an amount larger than the price of what she purchases and waits for change.

Transportation—Traveling within and to all environments in which activities occur is critical to independence. This may include the ability to travel safely by foot, bicycle, bus, train, and/or car. Individuals are most independent when they are also able to make their own arrangements for transportation whether it is via public transportation or a car driven by a family member, neighbor, caregiver, or friend.

Dan and Julie have different focuses related to transportation. Dan, who always needs someone with him in the community at this point, is taught to use a recorded message to ask his friend,

Bert, to drive him to the YMCA for swimming. Although Julie's mother will be driving her and her friends to skating, Julie needs to start learning about different ways of going places in order to prepare for making choices about modes of transportation in the future and to prepare for times when her mother may not be able to drive her. Initially, Julie's mother reviews ways people go places as in Figure 6.2. Julie is then taught to check off the option for the day. After her mother says, "Today I will drive you to skating," Julie checks car on her skating checklist (Figure 6.1)

Figure 6.2: Transportation Options

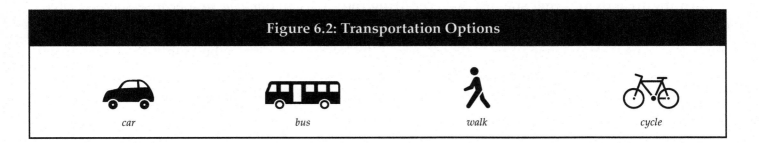

| car | bus | walk | cycle |

Choice-Making

Choice is central to leisure, contributes to independence, and is critical to the quality of life for all of us. Furthermore, when an individual makes choices, it increases motivation.

Because individuals with ASD may not understand the concept or have the skills for making choices, skills for making informed choices during leisure time often must be encouraged, and directly taught. Choice-making includes:

- knowing how to make a choice;
- expressing own preferences;
- selecting objects and actions;
- making own decisions.

Before training, it is important to determine what choices or decisions are essential to participate in an activity and what other choices are possible? For instance, can the individual chose when and/or where to do the activity and who to do the activity with? Examples of what choices are possible during an activity are presented in the Activity Cards in Appendix D, page 163.

Having a means of making a choice that is understood by the individual is important. Even individuals with ASD that have limited communication and/or cognitive skills can learn to make basic choices. They may make choices using real objects or a visual display of options, such as a choice board of pictures created with an app (e.g., My Choice Board).

Initially, the individual may only be able to choose between two preferred activities. Over time, the number of options for choice-making can increase. Further training of choice-making skills can enhance the ability to make choices, such as where and with whom they want to spend their leisure time.

Dan, Julie, and John all have difficulty making choices, and need to be taught different methods that reflect their current skills. For instance, Dan is initially taught to pair a picture from a choice book with an activity. Julie is taught to choose from a laminated written list of personally meaningful activities that she discovered during the *Exposure Component*. Because she is fixated on video games, video games are not on the list at first, but are used, instead, as a reinforcer after she has chosen and engaged in a different activity. John may initially be taught to choose from two objects, one that he likes very much and one that he does not like, so that he is naturally reinforced when he chooses the activity that he enjoys and is not reinforced when he chooses the other activity. Once he understands the choice-making process, he can learn to choose between two preferred objects or activities.

Initiation of Activities

Being able to initiate activities is critical to the independent pursuit of leisure activities. However, individuals with ASD often have difficulty initiating an activity, because they do not know when and how to begin an activity. Initiating an activity usually involves one or more of the following:

- gathering materials;
- moving to the appropriate location;
- engaging in the activity.

When an activity includes other people, it may also involve inviting others to do the activity or joining others in the activity.

Written or pictorial information on how to begin an activity may be needed to assist the individual with ASD to initiate the activity. For some individuals, the presence of the leisure materials may initially be the best cue to begin the activity. Visual schedules, Structured Teaching, and social narratives discussed in Chapter 5, can be employed effectively to teach initiation skills for an activity. Readers who would like more information about these approaches can learn more from the Glossary of Terms for Training Strategies in Appendix C, page 155 and the Autism Internet Modules at www.autisminternetmodules.org.

Social Skills

Social communication, cooperation, or other social skills are needed to respond appropriately and participate successfully in many leisure activities. Some activities could be engaged in without social interactions, but most would be more natural with casual conversation or other social interactions. Many activities also have unstated expectations, rules, or customs that are seldom taught because it is assumed that all people know them. Therefore, it is important to identify:

- social skills that may be required to do the activity (e.g., waiting in line, sharing materials, and taking turns);
- social interaction skills (e.g., conversational skills) that may be commonly used in an activity, but are not an essential part of the activity;
- social behaviors consistent with unwritten social rules (e.g., table manners, bathroom etiquette, and giving personal space).

Observing neurotypical people in the activity is an excellent method to determine what social skills the individual with ASD will need to be taught to be successful in an activity.

Essential social skills for an activity—Some activities are solitary and do not require interaction. For instance, numerous electronic games can be played alone. However, many leisure activities are of a cooperative or competitive nature and require social interaction of varying complexity with at least one other person. For example, most card games require turn taking, asking to join in the activity, requesting a card or cards, and other interactive behavior skills. It is often falsely assumed that the individual with ASD will automatically learn these skills by simply being included with typical peers. Yet, even basic social interaction skill, such as turn taking, may be difficult for the individual with ASD to learn without additional supports and training.

Dan, Julie, and John all have difficulty sharing and taking turns in board or video games. Because of their different abilities, they need to be taught different methods of taking turns. Dan and his friends are taught to use a turn taking board that has photos of the players in a circle and a rotating arrow that is moved to the next player at the end of a turn to help him recognize that there are other players and the sequence of turns. While playing video games, Julie is taught to hand her Nintendo DS controller to her friend when the screen reads "Player 2." Because of John's age and current skills, his support team decides to have him play Hungry Hippo, a game that involves being with others, but does not require taking turns. In the future, he can learn to receive a part of a game from the person before him, when it is his turn, and then pass the part on to the next person.

John, also, does not understand waiting his turn when others are using the swing, so he hits them. Although this may not be unusual developmentally, he needs a concrete way to understand what to do. The rule at this playground is to count to 100 and then say "My turn". Since John does not count, he is taught 1) to turn over a series of 20 cards on a ring, which takes approximately the same amount of time it would take a peer to count to 100, and 2) to hold out the last card, which has a picture of swinging with "My Turn" written on it, to request his turn.

The skills described above are all relatively basic. The social skills needed for an activity may be more complex. Consider, for example, the complexity in competitive team activities where participants must take turns, cooperate as a team, play against another group, and compete. These types of activities are likely to require significant training and/or supports.

Natural social interactions—Some activities can be engaged in an activity without social interactions, but the activity would be more natural if participants engaged in some interaction or conversation. For instance, one can participate in the game of Bingo without social interactions, but many people think of Bingo as an opportunity to socialize. Unless individuals with ASD have the skills for initiating, maintaining, and ending conversations, as well as interpreting social nuances, the "optional" socialization can negatively impact participation in leisure activities. Many lack these skills and consequently avoid many leisure activities.

One beginning step for individuals with verbal language and a desire to interact is to set a topic for a conversation of mutual interest.

For instance, Julie, who has excellent rote memory, is taught to use written sentences with pictures of what she can say about skating and Skate World in order to initiate talking with her sister, Bonnie, and friend, Tiffany, on their way to and from skating. The cue card includes some conversation starters, such as "How do you like Skate World?" In addition, she learns to use a combined written and pictorial conversational script to help continue the conversation.

Social behaviors—Individuals with ASD seldom figure out the unspoken social expectations, rules, or customs that everyone else seems to know without being taught. This lack of understanding and not following unspoken social rules or customs negatively impacts functioning in leisure activities and can make the world a confusing place (Myles, Trautman, & Schelvan, 2004). Parents, caregivers, teachers, and service providers must become social detectives to determine unspoken rules that the individual needs to understand and then find ways to directly teach them.

For instance, Dan needs to learn to look at objects rather than people in the shower room at the YMCA, and wait near the entrance to the shower room rather than near a person who is showering, if all the showers are occupied. He learns these behaviors with the aid of a pictorial list with a column for what to do and a column for what not to do (i.e., pictures with a slash mark through them).

Problem Solving Skills

Individuals with ASD often have difficulty identifying and solving a problem or asking for help. They may only have one solution (e.g., freeze, leave, or hit) to all their problems. They often persist with the same solution to a problem even when it does not help. Therefore, it is important to identify potential problems in an activity and teach how to deal with these problems.

Practicing solutions during natural opportunities or setting up situations in the location where an activity is done can prevent anxiety and frustration in the future. Social narratives and written or pictorial reminders of these responses to problems facilitate smoother participation.

Julie is taught to use the problem solving strategy in Figure 6.3 for her animation class.

Figure 6.3: Problem-Solving Strategies		
What I Can Do When I Have a Problem in Animation Class		
Problem	**What to Do**	**What to Say**
Difficulty doing activity	1. Keep trying 2. Approach helper	"I need help please."
No directions/materials	1. Approach helper 2. Do what others are doing	"I need help please." "Is this what I should do?"
Not enough materials	1. Borrow from friends or helpers	"Could I use that please?"
Seat taken	1. Find different area	"Can I share this area?"

Not all problems will be identified ahead of time, so some teaching will occur after unanticipated problems occur.

For instant, when Julie encountered a painter on a ladder blocking the front door to the roller skating rink, instead of walking around the building and going to another door, asking the painter to move, asking how long the painter would be there, or asking for help, she screamed and dropped to the ground. Her mother quickly drew a map of the route to a different entrance to the rink, which helped Julie to calm down and find her way to the side door. Later, a social narrative was developed to help Julie understand that there are different ways to enter buildings and what to do when the unexpected happens.

Guidelines for Prioritizing Activities

Before training can begin, careful consideration needs to be given to the activities for training. Individuals with ASD can learn only a limited number of activities at any one time. Therefore, few activities and sometimes only one activity should be prioritized for training at a time.

The first consideration in prioritizing is identifying activities that are likely to be done regularly and over time. It takes substantial time and effort on everyone's part for individuals to learn new activities. Individuals with ASD will likely require many training sessions with skilled instructors before acquiring the skills necessary to engage in an activity as independently as possible. Participation in the activities should continue far beyond when the training ends for the amount of effort to be worthwhile. The Guidelines for Activity Selection presented in Chapter 5 provides principles for identifying activities that result in long-term participation.

The second consideration is preferred activities. Individuals with ASD can learn to do almost any activity, but if the activity is not favored it is unlikely to be pursued in the future. Individuals must try out an activity, show signs of enjoying it (e.g., saying that it is pleasurable or showing positive effect, if they are unable to otherwise communicate pleasure), and demonstrate significant interest in it (e.g., saying that they want to continue to do the activity or choosing it from pictures) for an activity to be deemed a desired or preferred activity. Furthermore, instruction should focus on activities that are desired by the individual, so that it will be enjoyable and naturally reinforcing and, therefore, will be likely to motivate continued participation after training.

The third consideration is activities that require systematic training, given the individual's current skills and situation. Not all activities warrant training. An individual may already have adequate skills for an activity or the individual and his support people may be satisfied with the individual's current level of independence in the activity. The formative assessment described in Chapter 5, provides solid information for concluding if training is necessary.

The final consideration is activities that will contribute to a personally meaningful balance of activities for the individual. Consider if the individual has a satisfying balance of:

- activities at home, school, work, and in the community;
- activities pursued alone and with others;
- active and passive activities.

The rich information collected about an individual on the spectrum described in Chapter 3, provides a solid base for decision making about where more activities would be beneficial. For instance, Figure 3.6: Sample Completed Leisure Lifestyle Profile for Dan reveals a pattern that is examined to determine where more activities would be advantageous for Dan.

The following four questions need to be answered affirmatively for an activity to be prioritized for training.

- Is the activity likely to be engaged in regularly and over time?
- Is it a preferred activity?
- Does the activity require systematic training, given the individual's current skills and situation?
- Does the activity contribute to a meaningful balance of activities?

An example of responses to these questions for Dan after he tried out the activities in the *Exposure Component* is shown in Figure 6.4.

Figure 6.4: Prioritizing Dan's Activities for Training					
Setting	Activity	Can be done regularly	Preferred activity	Requires training	Contributes to balance
HOME	✓ Rock Band—Drums	X	X	X	X
	Felted cat balls	X		X	X
	Air Popcorn	X	X		X
WORK	Shoot Baskets	X	X		X
COMMUNITY	Bicycling	X	X		X
	✓ Swimming	X	X	X	X

Once activities have been identified that meet these four conditions, decisions can be made regarding the activity or activities that the individual will learn in the *Training Component*.

Dan's support team carefully considered each question as they completed this form. They had considered the Guidelines for Activity Selection before they initially selected these activities for the *Exposure Component*, so they already know that each activity can be regularly done and continued over time. From the formative assessment in the *Exposure Component*, the people who support Dan know that he showed significant interest in all the activities that he tried, during that component, except making the felted cat balls. In the latter activity, he enjoyed the texture of the felt, hot air from hair dryer and tinkling of the bell in the balls, but did not demonstrate interest in the activity itself.

The formative assessment indicates that he generalized the activity skills for making Air Popper popcorn, shooting baskets, tandem bicycling, and swimming that he had learned and practiced over the years to the new settings during the Exposure Component, although he had not done those activities for a number of years. (For information on how he initially learned some of these skills, refer to Chapter 3. In the new situations for shooting baskets and tandem bicycling that he will be doing at work and in the community, his natural supports (e.g., co-worker and sister) are able to easily support him, so training is not required. Although he has adequate swimming skills, swimming at the YMCA has new elements that require more support and training for him to be as independent as possible.

In Figure 6.4, it is clear that playing drums with Rock Band and swimming meet the four conditions. Teaching him to use Rock Band to play drums on Wii is an excellent choice because 1) he could do it daily; 2) he was enthusiastic about it when he tried it out in the *Exposure Component* and has, also, enjoyed playing the bass drum in his high school band in the past; 3) he does not have skills for this activity; and 4) he could benefit from an active activity at home. This has two more potential benefits. He could benefit from an interactive activity at home and may chose to do this activity with others at home in the future. In addition, he could benefit from more activities in the community and, after he increases his drumming skills, he could use them in a drumming group in the community.

Teaching him to go swimming at the YMCA is also an excellent activity because 1) he can do the activity at least once a week, has the opportunity for a free membership at the YMCA, and has a friend who wants to provide transportation and companionship for Dan in this activity; 2) he enjoys swimming and already has basic skills for it; 3) he has skills for swimming but not the related skills; and 4) he could benefit from an active activity with a friend in the community.

This process of prioritizing and determining the activities for training will be repeated a number of times over the years, as interests develop or shift, and circumstances in life change. It may be a long process for individuals to gain the activity and related skills to actively choose and engage in a variety of preferred activities at home, school, work, and the community.

Systematic Training

The focus in the *Training Component* is on the development of activity and related skills for the selected activity or activities. The major steps for providing training include:

- determine skills and supports to teach;
- prepare the individual prior to the activity;
- provide evidence-based training;
- provide ongoing practice;
- teach generalization of skills;
- teach purpose of instruction.

Determine Skills and Supports to Teach

The activity and related skills for activities, as well as how to use the supports and support structure for an activity, may all require instruction. The need for activity and related skills development is generally recognized. However, the need for teaching how to use supports and support structure is not equally understood. Supports will increase independence only when individuals with ASD are able to use them on their own, but they do not necessarily know how to use supports when they are first presented to them.

The specific skills or supports to be taught will depend on the abilities, skills, and needs of the individual with ASD. Once the activities are chosen, it is important to determine what instruction and supports are necessary for the individual to be competent and as independent as possible in an activity. One effective means to thoughtfully determine what needs to be taught and what supports are needed is an environmental assessment. In an environmental assessment, neurotypical individual(s) are observed doing the activity to identify the steps in an activity (i.e., task analyzed). Next, the individual with ASD is observed doing the activity to see how he presently does the activity compared to neurotypical individuals. Knowing what he does in an activity is important because it indicates his skills in that activity. He may be able to say what he should do or be able to use the skills or set of skills elsewhere, but showing strength in environmental assessment reveals what the individual does in the activity in a specific situation. Finally, activity and related skills, as well as supports or adaptations that will increase the individual's competence are identified.

Environmental assessment may take different forms depending on the activity and the focus of training. When the focus is on the activity skills alone, the form shown in Figure 6.5 is useful. In the environmental assessment form shown in Figure 6.5, the steps of an activity are broken down (i.e., task analyzed) to identify the activity skills, supports, and adaptations needed. When the focus is on activity and related skills, the form shown in Figure 6.6 may be more helpful. Reproducible blank copies of each of these forms can be found in Appendix B, pages 139 and 141.

As seen in Figures 6.5 and 6.6, Dan's support team decides to use two different environmental assessment forms to determine skills and supports for the two chosen activities, playing the drums with Wii Rock Band, and for swimming at the YMCA. This sample completed page contains just the first steps of over 20 steps for Dan to learn to drum with Rock Band using Wii. Dan needs to learn to do each step more independently and specific supports will be used to help him do so.

Figure 6.5: Completed Environmental Assessment Sample							
Name: *Dan*			**Activity:** *Rock Band (Drum) on Wii*				
Materials: Wii game system, Wiimote, Rock Band disc, sensor, TV, TV remote, drum kit, USB hub.							
What typical person does	**Person's performance**			**Needs**			**Instruction, Supports or Adaptation**
	Correct response	With prompts	Incorrect/not done	Teach	Adapt	Support	
1. Obtain materials			X	X		X	Digital photo Materials in box with photo on it
2. Insert yellow plug in hole			X	X		X	Digital photo Colors on TV input highlighted
3. Insert white plug in hole			X	X		X	"
4. Insert red plug in hole		X		X		X	"
5. Plug drums into USB hub & into Wii game system.			X	X		X	Digital photo
6. Set sensor securely in front of TV			X	X		X	"
7. Press power switch on Wii game system to turn on	X			X		X	"
8. Press eject button on Wii game system to open tray	X			X		X	"
9. Put Rock Band disc in game system	X			X		X	"
10. Press A button on Wiimote to turn it on			X	X		X	"
11. Turn on TV with TV remote	X			X		X	"

Figure 6.6 illustrates the use of a different environmental assessment form to help determine instruction and supports for activity and related skills for Dan for swimming at the YMCA. This form was chosen because Dan already has swimming skills, but the environment is new to him. Note that Dan already has adequate skills for swimming, but needs training and supports in the related skills.

Figure 6.6: Completed Environmental Assessment Sample			
Student: Dan	**Age:** 23		**Date:** February 18, 2015
Activity: Swimming	**Environment:** YMCA		
Area	**Skill**	**Competence**	**Training, Supports, or Adaptations**
ID TIME	Determine appropriate times to swim.	Does not read club's schedule for swim times.	Personal schedule of large, bold line drawings
RESOURCES	Arrange for transportation. Pay for membership.	Inconsistently asks for ride from buddy. Does not contribute.	Recorded request, reminder in schedule Free membership
CHOICE	Indicate desire to go swimming.	Does not indicate.	Choice board of large, bold line drawings
INITIATE	3:30 PM: Collect swimsuit, towel, athletic bag, membership card, snack, money.	Difficulty locating or collecting materials.	Prepacked athletic bag with material always in compartments
SKILLS	Enter front door and go to locker. Undress and put clothes in locker. Swim. Follow pool rules. Dress in locker room. Leave locker room when swimming over.	Difficulty locating door Completed Completed Completed Completed Difficulty exiting	Photo of door in mini-schedule/buddy Mini-schedule and buddy Mini-schedule Mini-schedule Mini-schedule and buddy Photo of door in mini-schedule/buddy
INTERACT	Greet and show card at counter to staff. Conversation with friends. Request friend to stop at snack bar.	Greets, trouble locating card. Repeats phrases. Goes by himself.	Card on cord attached to athletic bag Recorded conversation starters Recorded request
PROBLEM SOLVE	Ask for help if forget or lose something.	Does not ask for assistance.	"Help" reminder card in clear plastic outside pocket of athletic bag

Chapter 6: The Training Component of Leisure Development

Various aspects of an activity and setting can impact an individual on the spectrum's ability to learn skills for a leisure activity. Therefore, it is also important to identify the sensory stimulation (e.g., sights, sounds, lighting, temperature, personal space, and textures), organization of the space and materials, social demands, procedures, and expectations in the environment to determine if additional supports or adaptations are needed. The Environmental Conditions Form is included in Appendix B, page 142 to provide a means to record this information and begin thinking about supports.

Most individuals need supports that specifically utilize the strengths and compensate for the challenges of those with ASD regardless of cognitive level and/or expressive language skills. Refer to the section on Developing and Providing Supports in Chapter 5 for more information on supports. In addition, the Checklist of Support & Training Strategies and Glossary of Terms for Support Strategies in Appendix C, pages 146 and 148, are resources that can be used to help identify supports.

Prepare Individual Prior to the Activity

As discussed in Chapter 5, individuals with ASD prefer activities to be predictable and may resist new activities, environments, and expectations. Therefore, they must be prepared for an activity in advance to reduce the stress associated with new situations and to motivate participation. Before beginning instruction, supports and structure that will provide predictability should be in place. Effective techniques for preparing individuals on the spectrum for new activities, environments, and expectations are described in Chapter 5.

Provide Evidence-Based Training

Individuals with ASD require systematic instruction. Instruction in a typical recreation program with supports may be adequate for some individuals with ASD. However, many individuals on the spectrum require instruction that uses best practices for individuals with ASD. In accord with this need, more and more professionals who work with individuals with ASD are being required to use evidence-based practices (i.e., interventions whose efficacy with individuals with ASD has been validated through a stringent review of research published in peer reviewed journals).

The National Professional Development Center (NPDC) for Autism Spectrum Disorders (2014) has identified 27 EBPs for people between the ages of birth and 22 years that can be practically implemented in home, school, and community settings. Some of these evidenced-based practices are effective for teaching a variety of skills, while others have been shown to be effective for teaching specific skills. Of the 27 EBPs identified by the NPDC, 7 were shown to be effective for teaching leisure activity skills. These include:

- prompting;
- reinforcement;
- self-management;
- structured work systems;
- task analysis;
- visual supports;
- video modeling.

These strategies are often used in conjunction with each other. For instance, prompting, reinforcement, and visual supports are frequently used with other strategies.

The training strategies used will depend on several factors, including the needs of a particular individual with ASD, the activity, and the individual's past experience with the activity. Therefore, other EBPs can also be used effectively to teach leisure skills depending on the activity and especially when the related skills are embedded in instruction.

Dan's support team decides to use several strategies in conjunction with each other to teach Dan to play the drum part with Rock Band on Wii. The game is set at the beginner (easy) level and training utilizes a combination of prompting, mini-schedule, task analysis, time delay, video modeling, and reinforcement. Based on a task analysis of the activity, a pictorial mini-schedule of the steps for setting up and turning the game and system on and off is developed. Dan is taught to follow the mini-schedule using gestural prompts with graduated time delay, and as he learns to use the schedule to cue him to perform each step, prompting is faded. Video modeling showing what Dan sees is embedded in the game itself providing demonstration and practice in using the Wiimote game controller to manipulate the drum set. He simultaneously engages in the response while the video is shown. Selection of different rhythms is demonstrated and then practiced until Dan can select from the array of options.

Instruction is not necessarily as involved as in the above complex example for Dan. The same Tips for Guiding Exposure (Figure 5.8) apply when teaching skills.

You may not be familiar with all the evidence-based practices or how to implement them. The Glossary of Terms for Training Strategies in Appendix C, page 155 provides meanings for evidence-based and promising practices. In addition, there are two excellent online resources that provide enough information to get you started using evidence-based strategies. The Evidence-Based Practices Briefs in the National Professional Development Center on Autism Spectrum Disorder's website (http:// autismpdc.fpg.unc.edu/content/briefs*) includes step-by-step directions for implementation, and the

Autism Internet Modules' website (www.autisminternetmodules.org/user_mod.php) provides in-depth training modules for evidence-based instructional strategies.

Provide ongoing practice—Individuals with ASD need opportunities to learn, practice, and be reinforced for the skill or behavior frequently. Depending on the complexity of the skill being taught and the degree of challenge for the individual, the skills need to be taught very gradually and potentially over a long time until the individual with ASD uses the skill at the desired level of independence and/or with predetermined supports.

Teach generalization of skills—Effective teaching should lead to skills that are performed across the full range of trained and novel situations where the skill is appropriate. The goal is that learned skills and behaviors will be repeated or applied correctly in a new situation.

> Dan's team includes generalization. For instance, once Dan masters the steps involved in playing the drums with Rock Band, he selects new songs and rhythms that were not used during training to facilitate a generalized repertoire.

Since individuals with ASD have difficulty generalizing skills from one situation to another, they need the opportunity to practice skill(s) across materials, settings, people, and time of day. If an activity can be done in more than one way or can be done in more than one setting, the individual with ASD should be exposed to the different variations that can occur. In addition to incorporating multiple examples into the training situation, it is often useful to teach a variety of responses that may all achieve the same outcome (i.e., functionally equivalent responses).

> Julie is going to skate at different roller rinks in the future, so she needs to experience variations that occur in several roller rinks, such as paying in an area that looks different, paying a different amount, and getting a snack from a vending machine rather than the snack bar. Her support team uses this approach (i.e., general case programming), so that she can generalize skills to new roller rinks.

Teach Purpose of Instruction

Especially for individuals with near normal to above average intelligence, just teaching skills is not enough. Individuals with ASD may have difficulty understanding the relevance of instruction. The

---

* Web addresses sometimes change. If this URL does not work, you can may find what you are looking for if you: 1) Google the title or 2) use the domain name, such as http://autismpdc.fpg.unc.edu rather than the longer URL, and search that site.

purpose and importance of instruction in leisure skills needs to be explained explicitly so the individual is able to understand. It may be as simple as explaining what is being worked on and why.

Formative Assessment

Assessing the individual's progress needs to be an ongoing process. Formal data, informal notes, and anecdotal records all provide important information for showing the amount of progress towards targeted activity and related skills, the degree of generalization of skills, amount of dependence on assistance, and any behavior challenges that may indicate the need for changes in some element of the training strategies, sequence, or environment. When problems arise, those involved in implementation should come together to problem solve. Sometimes a very small change in training or the environment will make a major difference.

Training and support strategies are not always the issue. An individual with ASD and those who support him sometimes discover that he is not as interested in developing skills to pursue an activity as it first appeared. The effort to develop skills even with support strategies may simply exceed what the individual wants to do, yet he may still be able to do the activity without additional training through partial participation or more support. Some indications that an activity is not meaningful enough to the individual to warrant further training at that time are a lack of progress, despite systematic efforts to modify instruction, and/or a failure to select the trained activity when given a choice.

Summary

The development of leisure skills enhances our quality of life. The ultimate goal of the *Training Component* is that the individual has the activity and related skills to actively choose and engage in a variety of preferred activities at home, in school, and in the community. To accomplish this, individuals with ASD require systematic, carefully planned training. Although individuals with ASD have many common difficulties and characteristics related to leisure participation, it is important to individualize and design leisure training based on the unique learning needs of each individual with ASD. This involves the thoughtful selection of leisure activities, careful identification of targeted activity and related skills for these activities, and the selection and implementation of evidence-based training procedures. Blank forms that assist in individualizing are provided in Appendix B, while completed sample forms within this chapter illustrate the process.

Forms,
Charts &
Activity
Cards

Appendices

Appendix Contents

Leisure Behaviors & Activities List

Appendix A

Typical Leisure/Play Behaviors and Interest: Birth to Adolescence				
Development Age	Birth to 6 Months	7 to 12 months	13 to 18 months	19 to 24 months
Characteristics	Orienting: Mouths, licks, bites, body moves, babbles, vocal patterns	Repetitive manual manipulation	Observing behaviors of others	Repetitious: Pulling, pounding, throwing, jumping, climbing (locomotor exploration)
Social Interaction	Unoccupied behavior	Solitary Independent	Solitary Independent	Onlooker
# People	1	1 or 2	1 or 2	1 or 2
Examples of Activities & Materials	Senses and body: Other bodies, concrete objects, soft cuddly toys, mobile for crib, noisemakers, large plastic rings, etc.	Peek-a-boo, Where's Baby?, Patty cake, Treasure Hunt, This Little Piggy, Itsy Bitsy Spider, Horsey, etc. Squeaky play animals, unbreakable dolls, empty containers with removable lids, floating bath animals, rests of hollow blocks or boxes, etc.		Water play, sand play Crayons, 3-5 piece puzzle, large ball, tom tom, wagon, rocking horse, pull toys, pound toys, pans, wooden spoons large containers, sponges, etc.

Appendix A: Leisure Behaviors & Activities List

Typical Leisure/Play Behaviors and Interest: Birth to Adolescence				
Development Age	2 to 3 years	3 to 4 years	4 to 5 years	5 to 6 years
Characteristics	Investigatory: Climbing, running, jumping, digging; no give and take in play	Representative, imaginary, climbing, swinging, role playing	Taking turns, sharing toys	Systematic: Varied construction; conforms, some rivalry, increased doll play
Social Interaction	Parallel play	Association Play	Cooperative play One-to-others	Cooperative play Group
# People	2 or 3	2 or 3	2 or 3	2 to 5
Examples of Activities & Materials	Not yet ready for organized games Dress up, telephone play bean bags, housekeeping equipment, costume box, hollow blocks, large wooden beads, picture books, push-pull toys	Singing games (Here we Go Round the Mulberry Bus) Bubble set, clay, sand, farm and zoo animals' sets, costume box for dress up clothes, floor blocks with family figures, transportation play materials, steering wheel, large cartons, hammer and nails	Hide and seek, tag, red rover, sewing cards, King on the Mountain Finger paints, crayons, blunt scissors and paste, puppets, play luggage, housekeeping equipment, wood scraps, Play Doh	Simple circle games (Duck Duck Goose), jump rope, hopscotch, target toss, bat ball 8–20 piece puzzles, puppets, play circus, fix-it and try-it materials, tricycle and bicycle, stacking and nesting toys, plants

Typical Leisure/Play Behaviors and Interest: Birth to Adolescence			
Development Age	6 to 8 years	8 to 10 years	10 years and up
Characteristics	Construction, wrestling and tussling, curious about nature	Preoccupation with realism, like friends of same sex	Specialization of interest (hobbies, collections), yield to group, team spirit
Social Interaction	Group	Corporate Team	Competitive team
# People	2 or more	Variable	Variable
Examples of Activities & Materials	Low organized games (Steal the Bacon), not ready for team activities in which the group wins rather have the individual play Checkers, target games Plaster of Paris, papier-mâché, board & card games (Parcheesi, Go Fish), wagon, jump rope, marbles, pogo stick, kite, playhouse, puppets, boy & girl dolls, climbing apparatus, chalkboard, clay, nature crafts and games	Lead up games (Newcomb) and relays, writing to pen pals Steam engines, electro-magnets, old alarm clocks, sports, bicycle, skates, craft sets, hobby sets, live pets, board games, (Chinese Checkers), box hockey, table tennis	Regular sports with adult rules adapted to needs (tennis, basketball), news and poetry writing, band and orchestra, choral groups, social dances, creative dramatics Hobby sets, musical instruments, camera, sports equipment, electrical and scientific equipment, books of reference, tools, character dolls and materials for making doll clothes, table games (chess, dominoes, poker, etc.)

Appendix A: Leisure Behaviors & Activities List

Age-Appropriate Activities List Ages 5 to 8				
Media	Activity	Games/Crafts	Events	Other
Listening to music e.g., MP3, iPod, CD player, radio Watching TV or movies e.g., DVD, Blue Ray, On Demand, You Tube Reading or listening to books, audiobooks, and magazines Calling and texting on a cell phone	Playing at a playground Climbing trees or rocks Jumping rope Riding bike, scooter, or skate board Playing cards Playing ball games, e.g., T-ball, 4 square, keep-a-way, dodge ball, tether ball Playing team sports e.g., soccer, baseball, basketball, lacrosse Skating e.g., roller skating, ice skating, long boarding Swimming Going for walks or hiking Doing water sports e.g., fishing, boating, rafting Doing snow sports e.g., skiing, snowboarding, sledding, snowshoeing Riding horses Dancing or movement classes e.g., ballet, tap, yoga Doing gymnastics Doing martial arts	Playing video or computer games Playing board games Playing cards Playing with toys Doing puzzles Creating art projects e.g., coloring, painting, ceramics, Collecting, e.g., coins, stamps, sports cards, rocks Making and flying kites, paper planes, gliders Learning to sing Playing musical instruments Taking art or craft lessons	Going or giving parties, sleepovers Participating in special holidays Doing a religious activity Participating in school events Going to the movies Going to festivals, art fairs, music concerts Camping with family or groups Participating in clubs e.g., scouts, 4-H. cooking, gardening Attending sports events Attending or performing in plays, cultural performances, concerts, dances Attending trade shows e.g., trains, boats, cars	Hanging out with friends Visiting relatives Visiting community sites e.g., zoo, planetarium, museums, aquariums

Age-Appropriate Activities List Ages 9 to 12				
Media	Activity	Games/Crafts	Events	Other
Listening to music e.g., MP3, iPod, CD player, radio Watching TV or movies e.g., DVD, Blue Ray, On Demand, You Tube Reading or listening to books, audiobooks, and magazines Calling and texting on a cell phone	Using parks and playground Climbing trees or rocks Jumping rope Riding bike, scooter, or skate board Playing ball games, e.g., dodge ball, tether ball, keep away Playing team sports e.g., soccer, baseball, basketball, lacrosse, track and field Playing racquet ball, e.g., tennis, ping pong, Skating e.g., roller skating, ice skating, long boarding Swimming, diving Going for walks or hiking, climbing, hunting Doing water sports e.g., fishing, boating, rafting Doing snow sports e.g., skiing, snowboarding, sledding, snowshoeing Golfing, mini-golfing Riding horses Dancing or movement classes e.g., ballet, tap, yoga, aerobics Doing gymnastics Doing martial arts, karate	Playing video or computer games Playing board games Playing billiards or darts Playing cards or trading card games Playing with toys Doing puzzles Creating art projects e.g., coloring, painting, ceramics, jewelry Needle crafting e.g., knitting, sewing, weaving Woodworking, metal working, or stain glass Collecting, e.g., coins, stamps, sports cards, rocks Making and flying kites, paper planes, gliders Building e.g., Lego kits, robots, K'nex's Learning to sing Playing musical instruments Taking photographs, making videos Using a chemistry set for experiments Learning a foreign language	Going or giving parties, sleepovers Participating in special holidays Doing a religious activity Participating in school events Going to the movies Bowling Going to festivals, art fairs, music concerts, flea markets, or garage sales Camping with family or groups Participating in clubs e.g., scouts, 4-H, cooking, gardening Attending sports events Attending or performing in plays, cultural performances, concerts, dances Attending other events or trade shows e.g., trains, boats, cars, monster truck, air shows Participating in community gardening, volunteering	Hanging out with friends Visiting relatives Visiting community sites e.g., zoo, planetarium, museums, aquariums

Appendix A: Leisure Behaviors & Activities List

Age-Appropriate Activities List Ages 13 to 17				
Media	Activity	Games/Crafts	Events	Other
Listening to music e.g., MP3, iPod, CD player, radio	Using parks	Using parks	Going or giving parties, sleepovers	Hanging out with friends
Watching TV or movies e.g., DVD, Blue Ray, On Demand, You Tube	Climbing rocks,	Climbing rocks,	Participating in special holidays	Going on dates
Reading or listening to books, audiobooks, and magazines	running circuits, adventure courses	running circuits, adventure courses	Doing a religious activity	Visiting relatives
Calling and texting on a cell phone	Using exercise equipment, weight lifting	Using exercise equipment, weight lifting	Participating in school events	Visiting community sites e.g., zoo, planetarium, museums, aquariums
Making videos, You tubes	Riding bike, or skateboard	Riding bike, or skateboard	Going to the movies	
Using social media e.g., Facebook, chats, blogs	Playing ball games, e.g., dodge ball, hackey-sack,	Playing ball games, e.g., dodge ball, hackey-sack,	Bowling	
Participating in online groups e.g., science, math, history	Playing team sports e.g., soccer, baseball, basketball, lacrosse, track and field	Playing team sports e.g., soccer, baseball, basketball, lacrosse, track and field	Going to festivals, art fairs, music concerts, flea markets, or garage sales	
	Playing racquet ball, e.g., tennis, ping pong,	Playing racquet ball, e.g., tennis, ping pong,	Camping with family or groups	
	Skating e.g., roller skating, ice skating, long boarding	Skating e.g., roller skating, ice skating, long boarding	Participating in clubs e.g., scouts, 4-H, cooking, gardening, Lego Robotics, hiking, biking	
	Swimming, diving	Swimming, diving	Attending sports events	
	Going for walks or hiking, climbing, hunting	Going for walks or hiking, climbing, hunting	Attending or performing in plays, cultural performances, concerts, dances	
	Golfing, mini-golf, frisbee golf	Golfing, mini-golf, frisbee golf	Attending other events or trade shows e.g., trains, boats, cars, monster truck, air shows	
	Doing water sports e.g., fishing, boating, rafting	Doing water sports e.g., fishing, boating, rafting	Participate in community gardening, volunteering	
	Doing snow sports e.g., skiing, snowboarding, sledding, snowshoeing	Doing snow sports e.g., skiing, snowboarding, sledding, snowshoeing		
	Riding horses	Riding horses		
	Dancing or movement classes e.g., ballet, tap, yoga, aerobics	Dancing or movement classes e.g., ballet, tap, yoga, aerobics		
	Doing gymnastics	Doing gymnastics		
	Doing martial arts, karate	Doing martial arts, karate		

Developing Leisure Time Skills for People with Autism Spectrum Disorders

	Age-Appropriate Activities List Age 18+			
Media	**Activity**	**Games/Crafts**	**Events**	**Other**
Listening to music e.g., MP3, iPod, CD player, radio	Using parks	Playing video or computer games, role-playing or sports	Going or giving parties,	Hanging out with friends
Watching TV or movies e.g., DVD, Blue Ray, On Demand, You Tube	Climbing rocks,	Playing board games	Participating in special holidays	Going on dates
Reading or listening to books, audiobooks, and magazines	running circuits, adventure courses	Playing billiards, darts, shuffle board, or Bocci ball	Doing a religious activity	Visiting relatives
Calling and texting on a cell phone	Using exercise equipment, weight lifting	Playing cards or competitive trading card games	Participating in school events	Volunteering e.g., Meals on Wheels, Habitat for Humanity, tutoring
Making videos, You tubes	Biking, running, skate boarding	Doing puzzles, 3D	Going to the movies	Visiting community sites e.g., zoo, planetarium, museums, aquariums, library
Uses social media e.g., Facebook, chats, blogs	Playing ball games, e.g., dodge ball, hackey-sack,	Creating art projects e.g., coloring, painting, ceramics, jewelry	Bowling	
Participating in online groups e.g., science, math, history	Playing team sports e.g., soccer, baseball, basketball, lacrosse, track and field	Needle crafting e.g., knitting, sewing, weaving	Going to festivals, art fairs, music concerts, flea markets, or garage sales	
	Playing racquet ball, e.g., tennis, ping pong,	Woodworking, metal working, or stain glass	Camping with family or groups	
	Skating e.g., roller	Collecting, e.g., coins, stamps, sports cards, rocks	Participating in clubs e.g., cooking, gardening, hiking, biking	
	skating, ice skating, long boarding	Making and flying kites, paper planes, gliders, remote controls	Attending sports events	
	Swimming, diving	Building e.g., Lego kits, wood furniture	Attending or performing in plays, cultural performances, concerts, dances	
	Going for walks or hiking, climbing, hunting	Learning to sing	Attending other events or trade shows e.g., trains, boats, cars, monster truck, air shows	
	Golfing e.g., mini-golf, frisbee golf	Playing musical instruments		
	Doing water sports e.g., fishing, boating, rafting or going to water parks	Taking photographs, making videos		
	Doing snow sports e.g., skiing, snowboarding, sledding, snowshoeing	Using a chemistry set for experiments		
	Riding horses	Learning a foreign language		
	Dancing or movement classes e.g., ballet, tap, yoga, aerobics			
	Doing gymnastics			
	Doing martial arts, karate			

Assessment Forms

Appendix B

Leisure Observation Form Directions

Preparation

Set up an area with at least six items that provide an opportunity for different types of use and interaction. For example, a magazine would provide an opportunity for passive, solitary activity, whereas a ball would provide an opportunity for active social interaction. The area should be arranged so that different types of activities, such as table activities and physical activity can occur.

Explain to the individual with ASD that this is free time and that he can do whatever he wants in that area. Avoid direct participation in an activity unless the individual specifically requests your involvement.

Recording Information

After an adjustment period of at least five minutes, observations of behaviors are recorded on the Leisure Observation Form for four consecutive, five-minute periods. A timer can signal the end of five-minute intervals. Initially, four to six days of observations are often necessary to get adequate information. Behavior in three areas is recorded: social level, social interactions, and activity involvement.

Place a mark, such as the letter X under the appropriate column during each five-minute interval for social level and social interactions.

Social level includes:

- **Watches Others:** exhibits no behavior other than as an onlooker; is aware of others and is observing them.
- **No Activity:** unoccupied behavior, such as staring into space or self-stimulation, such as rocking; no contact with an external object or another person.
- **Engages Alone:** plays alone with a different object other than those used by peers within close proximity.

- **Engages Beside Peers:** approximates the action of one or more peers, but does not interact.
- **Interacts With Peers:** interests with peers doing same or similar activity; includes borrowing or loaning equipment.
- **Engages in Cooperative Activity:** mutually interacts with peers in doing an activity; activity cannot continue without cooperation, e.g., playing catch or checkers.

In the column on the right, describe materials selected, how they are used, who interactions occur with, where it occurs, and any other behaviors of note.

Appendix B: Assessment Forms

Leisure Observation Form														
Social Level							Social Interactions							Record Behaviors for Four Consecutive Five-Minute Periods During Unstructured Time
Watches Others	No Activity	Engages Alone	Engages Beside Peers	Interacts with Peers in Activity	Engages in Cooperative Activity	Interacts with Adult Only	No Response to Adult	No Response to Peers	Responds to Adult	Responds to Peers	Initiates to Adult	Initiates to Peer	Continues to Interact with Adult	Continues to Interact with Peers	Name: _____ Date: _____ Time: _____ Location: _____ Observer: _____ *Describe Activity (object involved, other people involved, place, behavior, etc.)*

Activity Assessment Form Directions

Purpose

The purpose of this Activity Assessment is to collect information on an individual's participation in an activity with as much input as possible from the individual and a support person who was present during the activity. The support person may be a family member, friend, respite care provider, child-care provider, babysitter, teacher, or other service provider. It's designed to be used with the Activity Cards in Appendix D, page 163, but can be used effectively to record responses to any leisure activity.

Directions

LEVEL OF INTEREST

Circle the graphic best depicting the overall feeling experienced by the participant. If the person enjoyed the activity, circle the happy face; if the activity was not enjoyed, circle the sad face; and if the experience was neutral, circle the Ho-Hum face.

PARTICIPATION

Record how independent the participant was during the experience. First circle one of the figures. The first figure indicates independent, the second means assistance was given, and the third reflects participation was resisted. After circling a figure, check the type of support that was needed. The types of assistance are:

- PA: physical assist;
- GA: gestural prompts;
- VA: verbal prompts.

CHOICES

Write brief comments regarding if you would recommend repeating the activity and any changes you would suggest for a successful experience for this participant.

Appendix B: Assessment Forms

Activity Assessment Form

| Name: | | Activity: | | Date: | |

1. Level of Interest:

Pleasurable   Negative   Ho-Hum

2. Participation:

All Myself   Needed Help   No

☐ Physical Assist

☐ Gestural Prompt

☐ Verbal Prompt

3. Choices:

Would you do it again? _____

What would you change next time? _____

Leisure Behavior Questionnaire

Name: Age: Respondent's Name   Date:

A. Please list up to five (5) activities that your child enjoys in each category and fill in the squares for each activity.

	Participation			Amount of Involvement		Level of Skill				
	Involved at least one time per week	Involved at least one time per month	Involved 2 to 3 times per year	Observes	Participates	None	Low	Average	High	Not Known
	☐	☐	☐	☐	☐	☐	☐	☐	☐	☐

1. Media (e.g., MP3 player, radio, magazines)

a.	☐	☐	☐	☐	☐	☐	☐	☐	☐	☐
b.	☐	☐	☐	☐	☐	☐	☐	☐	☐	☐
c.	☐	☐	☐	☐	☐	☐	☐	☐	☐	☐
d.	☐	☐	☐	☐	☐	☐	☐	☐	☐	☐
e.	☐	☐	☐	☐	☐	☐	☐	☐	☐	☐

2. Physical activities (e.g., swims, plays catch, hikes)

a.	☐	☐	☐	☐	☐	☐	☐	☐	☐	☐
b.	☐	☐	☐	☐	☐	☐	☐	☐	☐	☐
c.	☐	☐	☐	☐	☐	☐	☐	☐	☐	☐
d.	☐	☐	☐	☐	☐	☐	☐	☐	☐	☐
e.	☐	☐	☐	☐	☐	☐	☐	☐	☐	☐

Leisure Behavior Questionnaire (continued)

	Participation			Amount of Involvement		Level of Skill					
	Involved at least one time per week	Involved at least one time per month	Involved 2 to 3 times per year	Observes	Participates	None	Low	Average	High	Not Known
3. Games/crafts (e.g., computer games, puzzles, collections)	☐	☐	☐	☐	☐	☐	☐	☐	☐	☐
a. _____	☐	☐	☐	☐	☐	☐	☐	☐	☐	☐
b. _____	☐	☐	☐	☐	☐	☐	☐	☐	☐	☐
c. _____	☐	☐	☐	☐	☐	☐	☐	☐	☐	☐
d. _____	☐	☐	☐	☐	☐	☐	☐	☐	☐	☐
e. _____	☐	☐	☐	☐	☐	☐	☐	☐	☐	☐
4. Events (e.g., parties, fairs, movies, concerts)										
a. _____	☐	☐	☐	☐	☐	☐	☐	☐	☐	☐
b. _____	☐	☐	☐	☐	☐	☐	☐	☐	☐	☐
c. _____	☐	☐	☐	☐	☐	☐	☐	☐	☐	☐
d. _____	☐	☐	☐	☐	☐	☐	☐	☐	☐	☐
e. _____	☐	☐	☐	☐	☐	☐	☐	☐	☐	☐
5. Other (e.g., socializing, youth groups, museums)										
a. _____	☐	☐	☐	☐	☐	☐	☐	☐	☐	☐
b. _____	☐	☐	☐	☐	☐	☐	☐	☐	☐	☐
c. _____	☐	☐	☐	☐	☐	☐	☐	☐	☐	☐
d. _____	☐	☐	☐	☐	☐	☐	☐	☐	☐	☐
e. _____	☐	☐	☐	☐	☐	☐	☐	☐	☐	☐

Leisure Behavior Questionnaire (continued)

B. Please answer the following questions about this person. If you have a response which is not noted, please use the "other" category to respond.

1. This person spends the majority of his/her free time:

☐ alone

☐ watching others

☐ playing beside people without interaction

☐ interacting with others on a similar activity

☐ sharing and cooperating in play

☐ other (specify):_____

2. During free time, this person will usually:

☐ do nothing

☐ only participate when activities are initiated by others

☐ spontaneously initiate activity

☐ indicate need for assistance

☐ seek a playmate or friend

☐ plan an activity

☐ other (specify):_____

3. This person usually participates in activities located at:

☐ home

☐ park or playground

☐ school

☐ neighbor's home

☐ general community

☐ other (specify):_____

C. Please give your thoughts on the following:

1. List up to five activities that you personally enjoy doing:

a._____

b._____

c._____

d._____

e._____

2. How does your family usually spend its vacation?

_____

_____

3. List up to five leisure activities you would like to see this person pursue in the future:

a._____

b._____

c._____

d._____

e._____

4. List any difficulties you feel this person has in getting involved with leisure activities:

a._____

b._____

c._____

d._____

e._____

Appendix B: Assessment Forms

Leisure Interest Questionnaire for Family & Friends	
Name:	**Date:**

Directions: The purpose of this inventory is to determine the types of activities that you enjoy doing. It will, also, be used to identify possible leisure opportunities for your friend. Please take the time to think about your own leisure and complete this inventory.

1. List what you do for enjoyment or relaxation: _____

   - When you get home from school or work: _____
   - After dinner: _____
   - During break times at school or work: _____
   - During lunch time: _____

2. What do you like to do for exercise or fitness?
   _____

3. List clubs or groups in which you participate:
   _____   _____
   _____   _____
   _____   _____

4. List any classes you have taken for fun in the last two years:
   _____   _____
   _____   _____
   _____   _____

5. List some activities you enjoy doing.

   With your family:
   _____   _____
   _____   _____
   _____   _____

   With your friends:
   _____   _____
   _____   _____
   _____   _____

Leisure Interest Survey Directions

The Leisure Interest Survey can be used to determine leisure interests and patterns of individuals with ASD, family members, and friends.

1. List age appropriate activities available in your community in the first column. The Age-Appropriate Activity List in Appendix A is a resource for developing a list of activities, but it may not reflect all the activities done in your local area and may list some activities not done there. Add any other activities pursued by same age peers in your community to the list.

2. Ask individuals with ASD, family members, and friends to complete the form.

3. Individuals with ASD who are asked to complete this form should have the ability to answer the questions verbally, with a communication device or in writing. Assist them to complete the form as needed (e.g., read it to them and/or write the answers).

Resources in this book that may be helpful in completing this form:

- Completed example of this form in Figure 3.5 on page 43.
- The Age-Appropriate Activity List in Appendix A.

Appendix B: Assessment Forms

	Leisure Interest Survey								
Name:				**Date:**				**Age:**	
Activity	Do you enjoy it?	Did you do it in the last month?	How often?	Does anyone else in the family do it?	Where do you do it?	Who do you do it with?	Would you like to do it with your special friend?	**Comments**	

Leisure Lifestyle Profile Directions

The Leisure Lifestyle Profile offers an overview of the individual's present leisure pattern and skills in different settings and alone or with others. It is designed as a tool for planning for leisure engagement.

- Identify activities that the individual performs for a minimum of fifteen minutes, at least twelve times a year. List activities in the appropriate cell for where it is done and if it is done alone or with others (e.g., home alone, home with others).
- Indicate the individual's interest using the following code: likes = +; neutral = 0; and dislikes = -.
- Rate each of the following related skills in the appropriate columns using the key on the bottom of the Leisure Lifestyle Profile:
  - ID Time: Identification of free time for engaging in preferred activities.
  - Resources: Identification and utilization of necessary equipment, attire, money and resources for activity.
  - Choice: Selection of activity.
  - Initiate: Self-initiation of the activity.
  - Skills: Demonstration of skills necessary for participation in the activity.
  - Interact: Demonstration of social interaction skills required for the activity.
  - Problem Solve: Demonstration of problem-solving skills related to participation in the activity.
- Write notes, such as training and supports needed in the comment section.

Interpreting the Leisure Lifestyle Profile

The ultimate goal is that an individual has the activity and related leisure skills to actively choose and engage in a variety of activities in a variety of environments. Consider if the individual has a satisfying balance of:

- activities at home, school, work, and in the community;
- activities pursued alone and with others;
- active and passive activities.

An initial goal is a minimum of one activity in each grid. For an individual without activities in each grid, initial planning usually includes expanding leisure interests for a better balance through exposure to age appropriate activities of potential interest (i.e., Exposure Component). Both solitary and activities with others is important. The majority of free time is generally spent at home, so a higher number of activities at home is appropriate.

Once there are preferred activities in each grid, the development of activity and related skills necessary for independence becomes a major focus. The profile provides information for prioritizing necessary skills for instruction. Rather than adding more activities, many activities may also be expanded to other environments.

As the individual develops more activities and related skills, other variables may be added as well, such as variety in type of activities, actively levels, etc.

The completed sample page for this form in Figure 3.6 in Chapter 3, page 47 may be helpful in completing this form.

Appendix B: Assessment Forms

Leisure Lifestyle Profile									
Name:								**Date:**	
Activity	Id time	Resources	Choice	Initiate	Skills	Interact	Problem Solve	**Comments**	
HOME (Activity within property boundaries of home)									
Alone									
With Others									
COMMUNITY (Activity beyond property boundaries of home)									
Alone									
With Others									
SCHOOL OR WORK (Activity during recess, breaks, lunch, elective classes and extracurricular activities)									
Alone									
With Others									

- Record activities engaged in for at least 15 minutes, 12 times a year.
- Indicate interest with code: + = likes, 0 = neutral, - = not preferred
- Indicate level of independence or supports with code:
  - I = Independently completes without adaptations or supports.
  - IS = Independently completes predetermined adaptations or supports
  - V = Verbal cue or prompt require.
  - G = Gestural cue or prompt, such as point is required.
  - TA = Total assistance is needed.
  - NA = Not applicable; not required in activity or skill is not defined.

Settings and Resources for Activities Form Directions

Description

The Settings & Resources Activities form was designed as a means to develop a local resource list on leisure activities for different age groups. After it is completed, the form will include a list of activities available in a specific community and where the activities can be pursued in the home, school, and community. This resource can be used 1) to help identify potential leisure activities for the Exposure Component, 2) to identify activities for inclusion on individualized plans, 3) to determine settings to experience and learn activities, and 4) to identify settings for generalization of leisure skills. It is particularly useful for organizations that serve a large number of individuals with ASD (e.g., school districts, local chapters of the Arc, and local chapters of the Autism Society) to create a local resource with this form.

Procedure

1. Make a list of activities for your age group on the Settings & Resources for Activities form. The Age-Appropriate Activities List located in Appendix A, page 119, is a good resource for your list activities.
2. Survey where these activities are available in your community and check all categories that apply for each activity on the form. Write specific examples for clubs, organizations, and commercial facilities.

The Settings & Resources for Activities form is divided into three major settings: school, home, and community. These settings are further subdivided into settings or leisure time opportunities.

- The school section includes columns for naturally occurring opportunities to learn or participate in leisure activities. These include break/between classes, recess, extracurricular activities, and elective classes.
- The community section includes columns for parks department, community college, clubs/organizations, and commercial recreation.
- The home section includes whether the activity is done inside the house or outside. Check all that apply for the activity.

Resources in this book that may be helpful in completing this form:

- The Age-Appropriate Activities List in Appendix A.
- Completed sample page for this form in Figure 5.3 in Chapter 5, page 70.

												Leisure Activities		
												Break/Between Classes	School	Settings & Resources for Activities
												Recess		
												Extracurricular		
												Elective Classes/ Specials		
												Parks/ Playgrounds		
													Parks Bureau	
													Community	
												Community Colleges		
												Clubs/ Organizations		
												Commercial Recreation		
												Outside	Home	
												Inside		

Environmental Assessment Form Directions

The Environmental Assessment Form assists in determining what activity skills require training, supports, and/or adaptations to be independent in an activity.

To complete this form:

1. Select an environment and an activity for instruction.
2. Observe neurotypical individuals performing the activity and list the steps necessary to independently participate in the activity.
3. Observe and check off how the individual with ASD presently does each step.

   a. Correct response: indicates that the individual does the step independently.
   b. With prompts: indicates that the individual does the step with some level of prompts. It is an emerging skill.
   c. Incorrect/not done: indicates that the individual either does the step incorrectly or not at all.

4. Determine and check off whether a step will need to be taught, adapted and/or provided with supports.
5. Describe any instruction, supports, and/or adaptations needed.

Resources in this book that may be helpful in completing this form:

- A completed example of this form is shown in Figure 6.5 in Chapter 6, page 105.
- Information on training can be found in Chapter 6 and in the Glossary of Terms for Training Strategies in Appendix C.
- Ideas for supports can be found in the Checklist of Supports and the Glossary of Terms for Support Strategies in Appendix C.

Environmental Assessment							
Name:		Activity:					
Materials:							
What typical person does	Person's performance			Needs			Instruction, Supports or Adaptation
	Correct response	With prompts	Incorrect/not done	Teach	Adapt	Support	

Environmental Inventory Form Directions

The Environmental Inventory Form assists in determining what activity or related skills will require training, supports, and/or adaptations to be competent in an activity.

To complete this form:

1. Select an environment and an activity for instruction.
2. Observe neurotypical individuals performing the activity and list the activity and the related skills necessary to independently participate in the activity.

The following abbreviations are used for the skills:

- ID Time: Identification of free time for engaging in preferred activities.
- Resources: Identification and utilization of necessary equipment, attire, money, and resources for activity.
- Choice: Selection of activity.
- Initiate: Self-initiation of the activity.
- Skills: Demonstration of skills necessary for participation in the activity.
- Interact: Demonstration of social interaction skills required for the activity.
- Problem Solve: Demonstration of problem-solving skills related to participation in the activity.

3. Observe and record how the individual with ASD presently does the activity.
4. Determine and record what leisure activity and/or related skills will require instructions, supports, and/or adaptations.

Resources in this book that may be helpful in completing this form:

- A completed example of this form is shown in Figure 6.6 in Chapter 6, page 106.
- Information on training can be found in Chapter 6 and in the Glossary of Terms for Training Strategies in Appendix C.
- Ideas for supports can be found in the Checklist of Supports and the Glossary of Terms for Support Strategies in Appendix C.

Appendix B: Assessment Forms

Environmental Inventory			
Name:	Age:	Date:	
Activity:	Environment:		
Area	Skill	Competence	Instruction, Supports, or Adaptations
ID TIME			
RESOURCES			
CHOICE			
INITIATE			
SKILLS			
INTERACT			
PROBLEM SOLVE			

Environmental Conditions Form Directions

Place a check mark in each description that applies. Conditions of an environment that are not a good fit for the individual will require adaptations and/or supports at a minimum. (Refer to Support & Training Strategies and Glossary of Terms for Support Strategies for ideas and supports). Some conditions can significantly interfere with enjoyment and success. Environments in which adequate supports cannot be provided to overcome these effects should be avoided.

Adapted from Coyne, P. (2011). Used with permission.

Environmental Conditions				
Name:		**Location:**		
Conditions	**Frequently**	**Occasionally**	**Never**	**Support or Adaptation**
ENVIRONMENTAL FACTORS				
TEMPERATURE				
Cold				
Hot				
Indoor				
Outdoor				
NOISE LEVEL				
Quiet				
Some noise				
Loud				
LIGHTING				
Bright				
Average				
Dim				
Florescent				
Incandescent				
Other (specify):				

Appendix B: Assessment Forms

Conditions	Frequently	Occasionally	Never	Support or Adaptation
Environmental Conditions (continued)				
Name:				
SPACE				
Shared space				
Closer than 3' to others				
3' to 6' from others				
Farther than 6' from others				
Orderly				
Disorganized				
Other (specify):				
SOCIAL DEMANDS				
Alone				
In pairs				
Cooperative group				
Competitive group				
Other (specify):				
LENGTH OF ACTIVITY/TIME OF DAY				
1 hour or less				
2 – 3 hours				
4 – 5 hours				
More than 5 hours				
Morning				
Afternoon				
Evening				
Other (specify):				
PACE				
Relaxed - waiting				
Fast				
Alternate between relaxed and fast				
Breaks				
Constant				
Other (specify):				

Support & Training Strategies

Appendix C

Appendix C: Support & Training Strategies

Directions: The following are best practice supports for individuals with ASD. Check the types of support that will help the individual with ASD participate in the activity. Circle specific examples, such as templates when appropriate. Add information, such as who will make the support and by what date in the comments box.

Name:		Date:	
Activity:		Respondent:	

Visual supports to help minimize the individual's difficulties in auditory processing, attention and organization, as well as to maximize independence in participation.

	Comments:
☐ Object, pictorial or written schedule	
☐ Visual directions, e.g., templates, finished examples, mini-schedules, checklists	
☐ Work system to indicate start, sequence, and finish of activity	
☐ Checklists or reminder cards for rules and expectations	

Structuring for a predictable environment: Organization and modification of the environment to assist the individual's challenges in organization, so that he knows where to be, what to do, how much to do, with whom and for how long.

	Comments:
☐ Consistent routines and schedules with clear structure	
☐ Clear physical boundaries in the environment, e.g., lines on floor, carpet squares	
☐ Labeling or color-coding objects	
☐ Provision of clear beginning and ending to activities	
☐ Clear ending, e.g., timer, finished box or folder	

Sensory Support to support the intense sensory needs and comfort requirements of the individual.

	Comments:
☐ Reduce environmental distractions or add something to help e.g., visor, headphones	
☐ Sensory diet incorporating exercise, carrying heavy objects, swinging, climbing, rocking	
☐ Relaxation protocol	
☐ Breaks in and out of the activity area	
☐ Immediate materials, e.g., fidgets, for waiting times	
☐ Personal space for breaks	

Appendix C: Support & Training Strategies

Preparation for change to assist with the difficulty with new or different environments, activities, or expectations.	
☐ Prepare ahead with schedules, video ☐ Gradually introduce new situations ☐ Describe what to expect with visual supports, such as a mini-schedule or social narrative (e.g., Social Stories™)	Comments:
Communication supports to help the individual to communicate and understand communication.	
☐ Augmentative or backup communication systems ☐ Allowance for delayed processing time ☐ Use of gestures, models, visual supports and demonstration with verbal information by support person(s) ☐ Concrete, specific language used by support person(s)	Comments:
Social supports to help the individual relate well with others.	
☐ Provision of situation specific expectations of behavior with social narratives (e.g., Social Stories™) or other visual supports ☐ Trained leisure companion ☐ Circle of Friends or other supportive friendship approach	Comments:
Behavioral supports to increase appropriate behavior and prevent challenging behaviors.	
☐ Remove from stressful situations ☐ Functional Behavior Assessment ☐ Avoidance of disciplinary action for behaviors that are part of ASD	Comments:

Adapted from Coyne, P. (2011). Used with permission.

Glossary of Terms for Support Strategies[1]

Accommodation
Something needed or suited; adaptation.

Augmentative Communication
Any approach designed to support, enhance, or supplement the communication of individuals who are not independent verbal communicators in all situations.

Break card
A small card with pictorial and/or written information that can discretely be given to the individual when behavior is beginning to escalate.

Cartooning
A type of social narrative. The use of simple cartoon figures and other symbols, such as conversation and thought bubbles, in a comic strip-like format that is drawn to explain what people think, as well as what they say. An educator can draw a social situation to facilitate understanding or a student, assisted by an adult, can create his or her own illustrations of a social experience.

Choice-making
A strategy that can reduce problem behaviors, increase motivation, and develop personal freedom.

Color-Coding
Use of color to organize the environment or specific tasks. More under Visual Supports module; select "Visual Supports Across the Curriculum" at www.autisminternetmodules.org.

Comic Strip Conversation
A type of social narrative. A conversation between two or more people, which incorporates the use of simple drawings, and illustrates the quick exchange of information, which occurs in a conversation.

Countdown tool
A numbered or colored object used to count down the remaining items to be completed to finish an activity. A visual countdown allows an individual to "see" how much time remains in an activity, but no specific time increment is used. More at www.autisminternetmodules.org/ (Go to Autism in the Community then Transitioning Between Activities module; select "What are the Specific Transition Strategies and how do I implement them?" then select "Visual Strategies").

1. Adapted from Coyne, P. (2011). Preparing youth with autism spectrum disorder for adulthood. Used with permission.

Environmental factors

Aspects of the individual's experiences or surroundings, such as noise, temperature, sleep schedules, light, etc.

Environmental accommodations

Accommodations to the environment that will decrease the probability of a challenging behavior occurring. For example, the lights could be dimmed, if it is too bright for an individual with ASD.

Evidence-based practices (EBPs)

Practices supported through research presented in peer-reviewed journals. As of 2014, the National Professional Development Center on ASD has identified 27 EBPs. More at http://autismpdc.fpg.unc. edu/content/ebp-update.

Fidgets

Objects that can be squeezed or manipulated to assist with sensory regulation, such as a Koosh ball.

Finished box

A box, or specified place for the individual to place completed work jobs or tasks. More at www. autisminternetmodules.org (Go to Autism in the Community then Transitioning Between Activities module; select "What are the Specific Transition Strategies and how do I implement them?" Then select "Visual Strategies").

First then sequence

A visual sequence with an initial task, usually a less preferred, or non-preferred task is specified, and then, following completion of that task, usually a preferred task is presented for completion.

5-Point Scale

A visual representation of social behaviors, emotions, and abstract ideas on a scale that breaks social and emotional concepts into five parts. More at www.ocali.org/project/resource_gallery_of_ interventions/page/5_point_scale, or for further information, visit the Incredible 5-Point Scale Autism Internet Module at www.autisminternetmodules.org.

Functional behavior assessment (FBA)

A systematic set of strategies that are used to determine the underlying function or purpose of a behavior so an effective intervention plan can be developed. FBA consists of describing the interfering or problem behavior, identifying antecedent or consequent events that control the behavior, developing a hypothesis of the behavior, and testing the hypothesis. More at http://autismpdc.fpg.unc. edu/content/functional-behavior-assessment and www.autisminternetmodules.org (see Functional Behavior Assessment module).

Graphic organizer

An instructional tool used to illustrate content information. Some examples are outlines, timelines, tables, charts, webs, lists, and pictorial representations.

Jigs

A picture or line drawing which shows the layout of specific materials in their correct combination or sequence necessary for the completion of a task.

Labels

A visual tool that can help organize the environment for the child with ASD. More at www.autisminternetmodules.org (see Visual Supports module).

Mini-Schedule

A task list that communicates a series of activities or steps required to complete a specific activity. Mini-schedules can take several forms including written words, pictures, photographs, objects, or workstations.

Motivating factors

May include offering choices during activities and across the day, incorporating preferred materials into activities, allowing learners with ASD to engage in a preferred activity when completing an activity, tangible objects, breaks, or tokens.

Natural Supports

Refers to the use of person, practices, and things that naturally occur in the environment to meet the support needs of the individual.

People locators

A visual tool that provides individuals with ASD information about where the people in their life currently are in a format that is more easily processed by them. It can help reduce the anxiety and preoccupation some individuals on the spectrum feel when favorite people in their lives are not around. More at www.autisminternetmodules.org (see Visual Supports module).

Positive routines

Routines that support what should happen in an activity, transition, etc.

Power Cards

A visual aid and social narrative that uses an individual's special interest to help the individual understand social situations, routines, the meaning of language, and the hidden curriculum in social interactions. This intervention contains two components: a script and the Power Card. More at www.autisminternetmodules.org (see Social Narratives module).

Appendix C: Support & Training Strategies

Premack

A person will perform a less desirable activity to get to a more desirable activity.

Priming

A procedure that allows individuals to preview an activity or event before it occurs so that it becomes more predictable. During priming, an individual previews the materials that will be used in an activity, such as a schedule of events that will occur. More at www.autisminternetmodules.org (Go to Autism in the Community then Transitioning Between Activities module).

Reminder cards

Visual tools used to assist individuals with daily activities. They are simply a visual cue placed on paper, index cards, or other media, which are easily accessible for the student.

Sensory Activities

Planned and well thought out interventions that satisfy one's visual, auditory, tactile, gustatory, olfactory, vestibular, and/or proprioceptive needs.

Sensory diet

Planned and scheduled sensory-based activities selected to address specific needs of individual at various intervals throughout the day.

Social narratives

Describe social situations in some detail by highlighting relevant cues and offering examples of appropriate responding. Social narratives are individualized according to learner needs. They typically are quite short and may include pictures or other visual aides. More at www.autisminternetmodules.org/ (see Social Narratives module) and http://autismpdc.fpg.unc.edu/content/social-narratives.

Social Response Pyramid™

A visual representation of social understanding and social effectiveness to increase the effectiveness of responses. More at www.thegraycenter.org/social-response-pyramid/what-is-the-social-response-pyramid.

Social Stories™

A type of social narrative that describes a situation, skill, or concept in terms of relevant social cues, perspectives, and common responses in a specifically defined style and format. The description may include where and why the situation occurs, how others feel or react, or what prompts their feelings and reactions. Social Stories™ may exclusively be written documents, or they may be paired with pictures, audiotapes, or videotapes. More at www.autisminternetmodules.org (see Social Narratives module) and www.thegraycenter.org/social-stories

Structure

A purposeful, systematic arrangement of the environment from physical layout of a room to routines used.

Structured Teaching

A visually based approach to creating highly structured environments through a combination of procedures that rely heavily on the physical organization of a setting and predictable schedules. The five major components of structured teaching include physical organization/visual boundaries, schedules, routines, work systems, and task organization. More at www.autisminternetmodules.org (see Structured Teaching module).

Structured Work System

Designing the environment so that activities are visually displayed and expectations for completion are visually presented. These visually structured sequences clearly communicate four important pieces of information:

1. What activities to complete.
2. How many activities to complete.
3. How the individual will know when the activity or task is finished.
4. What will happen after the activity or task is complete (Mesibov et al., 2005).

More at http://autismpdc.fpg.unc.edu/content/structured-work-systems or www.autisminternetmodules.org (see Structured Work Systems and Activity Organization module).

Time timer

Displays a section of red indicating the allotted time. The red section disappears as the allotted time runs out. More at www.timetimer.com

Transition strategies

Techniques used to support individuals with ASD during changes in or disruptions to activities, settings, or routines. The techniques can be used before a transition occurs, during a transition, and/or after a transition, and can be presented in a verbal, auditory, or visual manner. These strategies attempt to increase predictability and may include, but are not limited to, visual supports, timers, bells, video priming, Social Stories™, and high probability requests. They are utilized across settings to support individuals with ASD. www.autisminternetmodules.org (Go to Autism in the Community then the Transitioning Between Activities module).

Verbal advanced warning

A warning provided to the individual as an auditory cue alerting them to an upcoming change or transition. This can be delivered at a certain time (e.g., five minutes prior to the completion of the activity or the time to transition). www.autisminternetmodules.org (see Transitioning Between Activities module).

Video priming

Videotaped instruction used to prepare individuals for upcoming transitions. www.autism internetmodules.org (see Transitioning Between Activities module).

Video Modeling

Recording another individual (e.g., adult, peer, sibling) performing the desired or targeted behavior(s). Subsequently, the individual watches the video before being asked to perform the target behavior. Video modeling can be used as a stand-alone method or be integrated within other methods, such as an activity schedule or a Social Story™.

Visual boundaries

Visually defines a section of the room, providing visual organization for the youth or young adult with ASD. A visual boundary can be created through a variety of means including furniture arrangement, labels, and color-coding. www.autisminternetmodules.org (see Visual Supports module and Structured Teaching module under What is Structured Teaching?) and http://autismpdc.fpg.unc. edu/content/visual-supports.

Visual cue

A visual cue is a picture, graphic representation, or written word used to prompt an individual regarding a rule, routine, task, or social response.

Visual representation

An image that shows a likeness of something.

Visual Schedule

A series of symbols, words, pictures, photographs, icons, and/or actual objects that show the individual what he needs to do and in what order it is to be done in a clear, structured sequence. The mode of the schedule is determined by the needs of the individual with ASD. More at www.autisminternetmodules.org (see Visual Supports module); and http://autismpdc.fpg.unc.edu/content/visual-supports.

Visual supports

Any tool presented visually that supports the individual as he moves through the day. Visual supports might include, but are not limited to visual boundaries, schedules, maps, labels, organization systems, timelines, people locators, Social Stories™, reminder cards, and scripts. More at http://autismpdc.fpg. unc.edu/content/visual-supports; www.autisminternetmodules.org/ (see *Visual Supports module*).

Visual Timer

Presents information related to time visually to "see" how much time remains in an activity before a transition to a new activity or location.

Workbaskets

A system for organizing materials into easily identifiable groups according to their use. The materials for each task are kept in one location, requiring the individual to follow one established process for collecting materials needed for an activity or task.

Glossary of Terms for Training Strategies [1,2]

Activity skills
Motor skills (e.g., put face in water for swimming) and/or the cognitive skills (e.g., knowing the rules) necessary for a leisure activity.

Antecedent based interventions*
Modifying the environment, antecedents, or setting events to prevent the need for challenging behavior. It is often used in conjunction with other evidence-based practices, such as functional communication training, extinction, and reinforcement.

Augmentative and alternative communication (AAC)
Devices to help individuals communicate and interact within their environment. This is accomplished through the use of switches, buttons, pictures, computers, and many other adaptive devices.

Backward chaining
Breaking down the steps of a task and teaching them in reverse order.

Chaining
Instructional procedure involving reinforcing a series of related behaviors, each of which provides the cue for the next (e.g., hand washing and showering).

Choice-making
A strategy that can reduce problem behaviors, increase motivation, and develop personal freedom.

Cartooning
A type of social narrative. The use of simple cartoon figures and other symbols, such as conversation and thought bubbles, in a comic strip-like format that is drawn to explain what people think, as well as what they say. An educator can draw a social situation to facilitate understanding or a student, assisted by an adult, can create his or her own illustrations of a social experience.

1. Definitions of terms were adopted or adapted from a number of sources, especially the National Professional Development Center on Autism Spectrum Disorders' Evidence-Based Practices Fact Sheets and the Autism Internet Modules.
2. Further information on how to implement most of these strategies can be found in the Autism Internet Modules at www.autisminternetmodules.org and/or in the Evidence-Based Practices Briefs at http://autismpdc.fpg.unc.edu/content/briefs.
* Strategies ending with * have been determined to be evidence-based by the National Professional Development Center on Autism Spectrum Disorders in 2014. Terms without * are either a subset of an evidence-based practice or have been determined to be best practices by other organizations.

Cognitive behavior intervention*

Learners are taught to examine their own thoughts and emotions, recognize when negative thoughts and emotions are escalating in intensity, and then use strategies to change their thinking and behavior. This intervention is often used in conjunction with other evidence-based practices including social narratives, reinforcement, and parent implemented intervention.

Comic Strip Conversation

A type of social narrative. A conversation between two or more people, incorporating the use of simple drawings, and illustrates the quick exchange of information, which occurs in a conversation.

Constant time delay

Fixed amount of time is always used between the instruction and the prompt.

Differential Reinforcement*

Providing positive reinforcement for desired behavior and the absence or lower rate of a problem behavior while ignoring inappropriate behavior.

Discrete trial teaching*

One-to-one instructional approach characterized by repeated or massed trials that have a definite beginning and end. Other practices that are used with DTT include positive reinforcement, task analysis, prompting, time delay, and reinforcement.

Embedded instruction

Skills taught in the context of naturally occurring activities and transitions.

Exercise*

A strategy that involves an increase in physical activity for a fixed period on a regular basis as a means of reducing problem behaviors or increasing appropriate behavior while increasing physical fitness and motor skills. It is often used in conjunction with prompting, reinforcement, and visual supports.

Extinction*

A strategy in which the consequence believed to reinforce the occurrence of the target challenging behavior is removed or withdrawn, resulting in a decrease of the target behavior. Other practices that are used in combination with extinction include differential reinforcement and functional behavior assessment.

Evidence-based practices (EBPs)
Practices supported through research presented in peer-reviewed journals. As of 2014, the National Professional Development Center on ASD has identified 27 EBPs. More at http://autismpdc.fpg.unc.edu/content/ebp-update.

Forward chaining
Chaining procedure that begins with the first element in the chain and progresses to the last element.

Functional behavior assessment (FBA)*
A systematic set of strategies that is used to determine the underlying function or purpose of a behavior, so that an effective intervention plan can be developed. FBA consists of describing the interfering or problem behavior, identifying antecedent or consequent events that control the behavior, developing a hypothesis of the behavior, and testing the hypothesis.

Functional communication training*
A systematic practice that replaces inappropriate behavior of subtle communicative acts with more appropriate and effective communicative behaviors or skills. The alternative response is a recognizable form of communication, such as vocalization, manual sign, or Picture Exchange Communication System.

General case programming
An instructional process, in which the variations of essential behaviors necessary for successful performance and the full range of stimuli that may be encountered in relevant situations and all variations of those behaviors and that are of that skill in relevant situations are identified. The goal is to generalize a skill set learned during structured teaching situations to relevant real-world settings and situations.

General case programming
An instructional process that uses multiple examples that sample the variations of essential behaviors necessary for successful performance and the range of stimuli that may be encountered in relevant situations.

Generalization
Response in other settings and with persons other than those that were present during the initial learning. That is, the learned behaviors are demonstrated in untrained settings.

Hidden curriculum
The rules that we all know but were never taught.

Modeling*

Demonstration of the desired target behavior that results in imitation of the behavior by the learner and leads to the acquisition of that imitative behavior. It is often combined with other strategies, such as prompting and reinforcement.

Natural cue

Naturally occurring cue that individuals rely on to let them know what they need to do.

Naturalistic intervention

Providing cues, prompts, and instruction in natural environments to elicit and reinforce communication and social behaviors.

Parent-implemented intervention*

Programs in which parents are trained by professionals in home or community settings to carry out some or all of the interventions with their own child.

Peer mediated instruction*

Teaching peers without disabilities to engage individuals with ASD in social interactions in both teacher-directed and learner-initiated activities.

Picture Exchange Communication System*

Six phase instructional program beginning with teaching individuals to give a picture of a desired item to a communicator partner in exchange for the item.

Pivotal response training*

Applying the principles of applied behavior analysis to natural environments to teach pivotal behaviors including motivation, responding to multiple cues, social interaction, social communication, self-management, and self-initiation.

Positive reinforcement

The presentation of a reinforcer that maintains or increases a desirable behavior; it should result in the behavior getting stronger and the person getting reward for his behavior.

Power Card Strategy

A visual aid and social narrative that uses an individual's special interest to help that individual understand social situations, routines, the meaning of language, and the hidden curriculum in social interactions. This intervention contains two components: a script and the Power Card.

Appendix C: Support & Training Strategies

Priming
A procedure that allows individuals to preview an activity or event before it occurs so that it becomes more predictable. During priming, an individual previews the materials that will be used in an activity, such as a schedule of events that will occur. More at www.autisminternetmodules.org (Go to Autism in the Community then Transitioning Between Activities module).

Progressive time delay
Time between giving the instruction and giving a prompt is gradually increased.

Prompting*
Verbal, gestural, physical, model, and visual prompts given by an adult or peer before an individual attempts to use the skill. These procedures are often used in conjunction with other evidence-based practices including time delay and reinforcement or are part of protocols for other practices, such as pivotal response training, discrete trial teaching, and video modeling. Prompting procedures are considered foundational for the use of many other evidence-based practices

Reinforcement*
An item, activity, or event that immediately follows a particular behavior, resulting in an increased likelihood that a behavior will recur in the future. Includes positive reinforcement, tokens, point systems, graduated reinforcement systems. Reinforcement is a foundational evidence-based practice that is almost always used in conjunction with other evidence-based practices, such as prompting, pivotal response training, discrete trial teaching, and functional communication training.

Reinforcer
Anything that follows a behavior and increases the likelihood that the behavior will occur.

Related skills for leisure
Skills beyond the motor and cognitive skills that are necessary to be successful in an activity. These include awareness of free time, identification and use of resources, choice-making, initiation, social interaction, and problem solving.

Response Interruption/Redirection*
Providing another activity that appears to serve the same function as a problem behavior, e.g., offering popcorn in place of eating a pencil.

Scripting*
Written sentences or paragraphs and/or videotaped of phrases and sentences, which individuals with ASD can say in a given circumstance and can memorize or carry with him. Scripts are used for indi-

viduals who have difficulty generating novel language, particularly when under stressed, but have excellent rote memories. It is often used in conjunction with modeling, prompting, and reinforcement.

Self-Management*

Teaching individuals to discriminate between appropriate and inappropriate behaviors, accurately monitor and record their own behaviors, and reinforce themselves for behaving appropriately. It is often used in conjunction with other evidence-based practices including modeling, video modeling, and visual supports.

Sensory regulation

The ability to attain, maintain, and change arousal levels appropriately for an activity or situation.

Social Narratives*

A written intervention where social situations, relevant cues, the thoughts and feelings of other people, and responses are described in detail.

Social skills training*

Group or individual instruction designed to teach individuals to appropriately interact with typically developing peers.

Stimulus Control

Using reinforcement to teach a person to perform a certain behavior under very specific stimuli.

Structured play groups*

Use of small groups with typically developing peers and clear delineation of theme and roles by adult leading the group to teach a broad range of outcomes. Other strategies that are part of structured play groups include prompting and scaffolding.

Structured Teaching

A visually based approach to creating highly structured environments through a combination of procedures that rely heavily on the physical organization of a setting and predictable schedules. The five major components of structured teaching include physical organization/visual boundaries, schedules, routines, work systems, and task organization.

Structured Work System

Designing the environment so that activities are visually displayed and expectations for completion are visually presented. These visually structured sequences clearly communicate four important pieces of information:

1. What activities to complete.
2. How many activities to complete.
3. How the individual will know when the activity or task is finished.
4. What will happen after the activity or task is complete (Mesibov et al., 2005).

Task analysis*

Process of breaking a skill down into smaller, more manageable steps in order to teach a targeted skill that requires several steps to be performed in a certain order. Task analysis can also be used to take a much larger group of skills, such as those used in a complex vocational task like cleaning a cafeteria, and break them down into phases. A number of evidence-based practices can be used in the instruction of a skill that has been broken down with task analysis including, but not limited to: visual schedules, video modeling, social narratives, discrete trial training, pivotal response training, and time delay.

Technology-aided instruction and intervention*

Use of a broad range of devices, such as speech-generating devices, smart phones, tablets, computer-assisted instructional programs, and virtual networks, to increase or maintain and/or improve recreation/leisure, daily living, and work capabilities.

Time delay*

Prompt fading strategy, in which a delay is inserted between giving an instruction and prompting. It is always used in conjunction with a prompting procedure, such as least-to-most prompting, simultaneous prompting, are graduated guidance.

Video Modeling*

Recording another individual (e.g., adult, peer, sibling) performing the desired or targeted behavior(s). Subsequently, the individual watches the video before being asked to perform the target behavior. Video modeling can be used as a stand-alone method or be integrated within other methods, such as an activity schedule, a Social Story™, prompting and reinforcement.

Visual Supports*

Concrete cues that provide information about an activity, routine, or expectation and/or support skill demonstration. They can take on a number of forms and functions, such as photographs, icons, drawings, written words, are objects, environmental arrangement, schedules, graphic organizers, organizational systems, and scripts.

Activity
Cards

Appendix D

Directions for Activity Cards

The purpose of the Activity Cards is to provide a structure for exposing individuals with ASD to new activities while minimizing anxiety and stress. The cards are designed to be easily used by family members, friends, respite care providers, child care workers, babysitters, teachers, and service providers. It contains 48 activities that are grouped into arts and crafts, board and card games, community activities, hobbies, physical activities, and sensory crafts.

Activities in most categories consist of one Activity Card that provides the information necessary to do that activity. Because of the complex nature of community activities, there are three cards for each activity in this category. These include:

- "Get Ready" cards to help prepare the individual for the activity;
- "The Real Thing" cards to show the real experience of the activity;
- "Review" cards to help the individual review the activity.

The Activity Cards are divided into sections that assist the facilitator of the activity to both effectively structure the activity and help an individual with ASD understand the sequence and variables in an activity. The front of each card provides information for the facilitator. The back of each card provides written information on the activity that is designed to be read to an individual and a visual sequence for the individual with ASD to follow. The cards are divided into the following sections:

1. **Activity symbol** on the top, left side of each card represents the activity. This picture of the activity can be copied and used on a visual schedule and/or posted to indicate where an activity is happening.
2. **Title** of the activity is provided at the top of each card.
3. **Materials** list the items that are used in the activity and must be gathered in preparation for the activity.
4. **General Guidelines** provides the basic steps in an activity and tips on presenting the activity. Facilitators should use their knowledge of an individual with ASD to decide if steps need to be broken down or simplified.
5. **Furthermore** provides variations in the activity to encourage expansion. (In some cases, this may mean breaking down or expanding the activity.) This section does not appear on every card.

6. **Activity Stories** are provided on the back of each card. These written stories introduce an activity. They may provide a variety of information, including what the upcoming activity is, sequence, environmental conditions (e.g., crowding, noise), suggestions on how to cope, and expectations. Depending on an individual's language and learning level, the wording may need to be simplified or visual images added to enhance understanding of the content. Activity Stories should be reviewed with an individual on a number of days before the activity and just before the activity.

7. **Visual Sequences** are provided on the back of each card. They consist of a series of line drawings that depicts the sequence of steps in an activity from beginning to end and sometimes, also, includes choices within the activity. When an activity is done in a different order than what is shown, pictures can be cut and pasted. The mini-schedules are important both to prepare an individual for an activity and to follow during an activity.

SWIMMING (THE REAL THING)

Materials:
- Bag with swimming suit, towel and money

General Guidelines:
1. The activity story and/or visual sequence provided can offer the keep elements of the experience.
2. Review the rules of safety in transition, arrival, and around the pool when ready to swim.
3. Greet the staff and pay the swimming fee in a manner as previously described. Note any needs for training, such as greeting.
4. Assist the individual as necessary to change into their swimsuit and again, note what skills may need to be worked on in training.
5. Provide concrete information as to how long the individual may stay and how they will know it is time to go.
6. Assist as necessary in the drying off, and redressing into street clothes. Note what skills may need to reviewed in training.

Furthermore:
There is a wide variety of sensory experiences to anticipate at a swimming pool. Some are obvious, such as moisture and fluid movement. However, be sensitive to other experiences as well. The ceilings above pools are many times echo chambers increasing sound. Crowds play a big role and can cause sudden splashes or movements. Water temperatures can feel different to different people making it uncomfortable. Transitioning between the warm showers to the cool feeling pool takes time to adjust. There are also many social requirements to know in the locker, no staring or commenting when others dress. Remembering all your clothes before you leave. Many pools have extra equipment for individuals with special needs. Be sure to check.

Activity Story
I walk into the swim area. I will greet and give the cashier my swim card or money.
I walk into the locker room. I will take off all my clothes and put on my swim suit. I will put my clothes into my bag. I will put my bag into a locker. I will ask for help if I need help.
I will take a shower before I walk to the pool.
I will walk to the pool. I will only jump in the pool where the life guard tells me I can.
I will swim and/or play in the water.
I will get out of the pool when I am asked and walk to the locker room.
I will take off my swim suit, dry, and put my clothes on in the locker room.

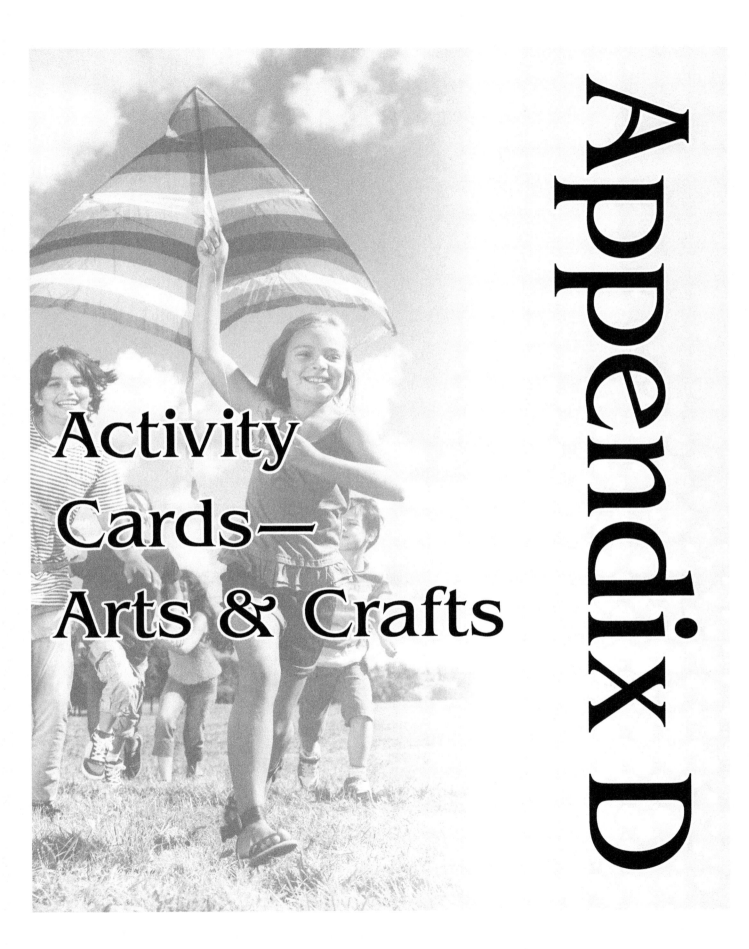

Activity
Cards—
Arts & Crafts

Appendix D

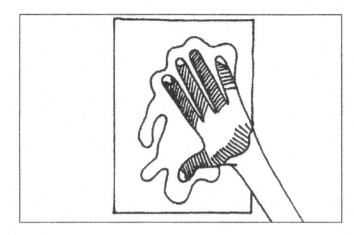

FINGER PAINTING

Materials:

- Finger paints
- Finger paint paper
- Several of the following:
    - Cornmeal
    - Sand
    - Beans
    - Cotton Balls
    - Rice
    - Sponges
    - Noodles
    - Potatoes
- Protective clothing
- Protection for the surface to paint on

General Guidelines:

1. The activity story and/or visual sequence provided can offer the key elements of the sensory experience.
2. Assist as necessary to retrieve a sheet of the finger painting paper. The individual could keep a plain sheet or maybe choose to cut the paper into a particular shape.
3. Assist as necessary to select colors of paint and scoop some on the paper. Some individuals will only use finger paint as their sensory preference.
4. Assist as necessary for individuals to select and retrieve small portions of the variety of textures to add. If it is difficult or too messy to retrieve the items by hand, consider putting the items in small paper cups as individual portions.
5. Assist as necessary to experience a variety of the textures. Some individuals will not vary their choices without encouragement, maybe from a buddy.
6. Finger painting is open-ended with no clear ending. Some strategies for ending this activity may be; when the paint is gone, when the paper is covered, a timer, or bringing a bucket of water for clean up.

Furthermore:

Many individuals with ASD have difficulty with textures. This is a great opportunity if they don't mind the sticky paint. For those individuals that are hesitant, modifying how they finger paint is helpful. Having lines on the paper, maybe a small circle, and encouraging the individual to touch the paint a little, and then touching the circle. It's a start, and using a buddy system to have the individual touch the circle, then the buddy adds to a picture leaving simple touches to be added. Some individuals are sensitive to cold and prefer warm sticky substances. Warming the paint may make the paint more tolerable for some. Some of the individuals who are more eager for exploring textures, there are some other options than the ones listed above. Consider adding textures under the paper. Bubble wrap is fun, or different fabrics. Increasing objects in the paint may include using toy cars to make tracks on the paper or through the paint. Shaving cream is also fun especially if the finger paint is powder and can be mixed in while working the shaving cream like paint.

Activity Story

Today I will finger paint. I will put my hands in a soft paint and spread it around on paper.

I will choose how I want to use the paint. Sometimes I will make swirls. Sometimes I will draw shapes.

I will choose something to put in my paint. I can choose hard or soft things to paint with. I can choose both. I can choose many things to paint with.

I might feel funny with paint on my hands. I might feel my hands are sticky.

When I am done painting, I will wash my hands. I will get all the paint off my hands.

I will not touch my picture until the paint is dry.

GROWING SPROUTS

Materials:

- Egg cup or other small bowl
- Paper
- Permanent pens
- Cotton balls
- Spray bottle including water
- Beans or alfalfa sprouts

General Guidelines:

1. The activity story and/or visual sequence provided can offer the key elements of the experience.
2. Egg cups are usually used to hold soft boiled eggs. They come in different shapes and sizes. Craft stores have glass paint to offer different looks by individual or row of cups.
3. Assist as necessary for the individual to plan the face or preferred decorations on paper first. Then assist as necessary to transfer the design. If the cup is easily held, maybe use tracing paper. If not, you may need to brace it by snuggling it into a cut-out bottom of a cardboard box, or other stabilizer.
4. Assist as necessary to sprinkle the seeds on top of the cup. An item like candy sprinkler holder or sugar sprinkler may work also.
5. Mist the cotton balls with water from the spray bottle. Dipping can work also, but many times it becomes too drenched for the cup.
6. The seeds will need consistent spraying of water for the seeds to grow. Create a reminder chart or note on a calendar when the cups should be misted again.
7. Assist the individual to use the sprouts in creative ways; on a salad, or on a sandwich maybe. Using the sprouts makes the growing of them more functional or important.

Furthermore:

Growing grass is fun in the cups as well. Grass can be trimmed as hair if you have made the cup a face. It could also be fun to grow a row of them with a variety of faces and haircuts. The beans or alfalfa sprouts do grow faster but grass makes the project intriguing.

Activity Story

Today I am planting some seeds in an egg cup. When the grass grows it will look like hair. Seeds take time to grow and need water every day.

I will first decide on what king of face to draw. I could be happy, surprised, or maybe sad. I will choose a color and paint my cup.

After I have drawn the face on paper, I will draw it on the egg cup. Sometimes holding the cup is difficult. I can ask for help if I need it.

I put cotton balls in the cup. I take a few seeds and put or shake them on top of the cotton balls.

I will take the spray bottle and spray the cotton balls until they are wet. I will be careful to not spray a lot of water. I will not get anything but the cotton balls wet.

I will mark on my calendar to water my seeds every day. Soon I will see the seeds sprout.

When the sprouts are tall I can eat them. I will decide to eat them on a salad or sandwich. I will not eat the cotton balls.

*When they grow it will look like hair growing out of the top of a head. I can cut the grass like hair.

PAINTING SHIRTS

Materials:
- T-shirt
- Fabric paint brush, pens
- Stencils of shapes (optional)

General Guidelines:
1. The activity story and/or visual sequence provided can offer the key elements of the experience.
2. A sample of a shirt or additional sequences, such as presenting the tools of the project left to right or visually presenting a step-by-step visual of the project.
3. Assist as necessary for the individual to select a t-shirt to paint. It could be an old one or new from a fabric store.
4. Assist as necessary to put a piece of cardboard or poster board inside the t-shirt. The size does not need to be exact but support the fabric where the individual will be painting. Some individuals may need another piece of cardboard underneath to pin and hold down the t-shirt.
5. Assist as necessary to determine if a stencil will be used. If so, assist the individual to determine what shape they prefer. Make available a picture or sample of both stencil and free design.
6. Assist as necessary to select color choices. Presenting the tubes/pens in an array allows the individual to make a clear choice rather than another linear, first this than that, interpretation.
7. Assist as necessary to squeeze paint in the appropriate area and brush paint on. Some individuals may have difficulty squeezing and need the paint presented in small cups. There should be a brush per paint color to ensure the paint color is clear. The individual can then go back and blend with another brush specifically for that purpose.
8. Assist the individual to color in the shape or the free design with appropriate amount of paint. Some individuals will need smaller amounts in the cups or the understanding of maybe "1 squeeze". If using pens, the individual can color as if coloring on paper, just softer.
9. Some individuals may want to paint both sides of the shirt. Allow the first side painted to dry then repeat the steps.
10. Allow the shirt to dry.

Furthermore:
Consider using different techniques to vary the project. Using rubber bands to bunch up the fabric will allow you to make circles in the design. Using rocks or ping pong balls inside the rubber band shapes can make bigger circles or they can be painted a different color, also giving the circles distinctive colors. Spray bottles mixed with some paint can also make interesting patterns.

Activity Story
Today I will paint on a shirt. The shirt may be white or maybe an old shirt. I will paint a shirt to wear.

The shirt will have a piece of hard paper inside. I do not want the paint to go through. I will paint the front and back of my shirt.

I will squeeze, scoop, or color the paint on my shirt. I will use a small amount of paint. I will not use a lot of paint.

I will paint the shirt with the designs I want. I can paint with many colors. I can paint with one color. I can paint in shapes. I can brush or color with a pen the paint on my t-shirt. I will only paint my shirt.

I will not touch the paint on the shirt until it is dry. When the paint is dry, I can turn it over to paint again.
When the paint is dry, I can wear my shirt.

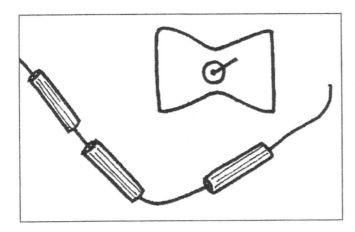

PASTA CREATIONS

Materials:
- Different shaped macaroni (large and small)
- String for necklaces or bracelets
- Pin or earring backs
- Metal barrettes
- Magnets
- Food coloring
- Acrylic varnish
- Clear acrylic
- Craft glue
- Scissors

General Guidelines:

1. The activity story and/or visual sequence provided can offer the key elements of the fun.
2. Provide choices in pictures for the individual to see and choose from. Then have the individual select what kind of macaroni to use. Some individuals will only see the pictures as what they must use. Assist as necessary to show the individual different choices rather than the sample.
3. Assist the individual to participate in any of the steps for making the jewelry.
    - If painting, dip the macaroni in water that has food coloring. Allow to soak for at least 30 minutes. Place the pieces on wax paper to dry. Turn the pieces over every 15 to 20 minutes. To dry faster, put the pieces on the lowest setting and microwave for 2 to 3 minutes. Turning the pieces over every 30 seconds.
    - Assist gluing the now dry pieces on to the jewelry shape the individual has chosen. Use a strong glue to keep the pieces attached.
    - Assist the individual to spray the jewelry with acrylic varnish. This will preserve the pieces from breaking easily. The varnish will need to dry.
    - Some individuals may prefer to paint the macaroni after gluing the plain pasta on the jewelry pieces. Glue the pieces on. Use the acrylic paint gently with a soft brush to paint the macaroni. When dry, assist the individual to spray with acrylic varnish to preserve.
    - Some shapes, such as a pin, could be stronger by cutting the shape from poster board. Necklaces or bracelets, typically, use hollow macaroni, such as elbow or penne. Making a hole in other kinds of pasta for a necklace of bracelet is trickier. The hole must be made when the pasta is soft from dying/painting. When the pasta is wet from the paint the pasta can rip. Some individuals could become frustrated.
4. Assist as necessary for the individual to understand when the project is finished. Making the jewelry does have a clear ending. When the paint/dye is dry and the varnish has also dried, the project is finished.
5. Some individuals will wear their jewelry. Encourage individuals to share their art.

Activity Story

Today I will make jewelry from macaroni. I can wear jewelry. I can make a necklace, a bracelet, earrings, or a pin.

I will paint my macaroni. I might use water to color my macaroni. The water will be different colors. I will put my macaroni in the water to color my macaroni. Sometimes I will paint my macaroni with a paint brush. I will decide what color I want.

I will wait for my macaroni to dry. Sometimes it is hard to wait for paint to dry. I will wait for the paint to dry.

I will spray my jewelry. The spray will make my macaroni shiny and hard. Sometimes it is hard to spray. I will ask for help. Sometimes macaroni breaks. Sometimes the macaroni will not break. That is okay, I can make more macaroni.

I will wait for the spray to dry. Sometimes it is hard to wait. I will wait for the spray to dry.

When the spray is dry I can wear my jewelry. Sometimes I can give my jewelry to friends and family.

POTTERY: CANDLE HOLDER

Materials:

- Clay measured as 1 lb. & 1/4 lb.
- Wire to cut the clay (optional)
- Dull knife
- Ruler
- Rolling pin (optional)
- Cookie sheet and oven

General Guidelines:

1. The activity story and/or visual sequence provided can offer the key elements of the project.
2. Cut one pound of clay in half with a wire or break off.
3. Assist as necessary for the individual to take part of the clay and make a pinch bowl. Instructions how to make a pinch pot is provided in the Activity Car - "Pottery – Pinch Pot."
4. Assist as necessary to guide the individual to make the base of the cup. Take another lump of clay and using the individual's hand or a rolling pin to flatten the clay. The shape should be approximately 1". Use a template or cookie cutter large enough for the cup to sit on for creating a base.
5. Assist as necessary to place the cup on the base. The cup and base will need to be secure. The individual will need to gently push down on the inside of the cup. The cup will also need to be smoothed on the outside of the cup and gently smooth the two together.
6. Assist as necessary to roll out another lump of clay. This will be the handle. Roll the clay out until it is snakelike in shape. For the handle to hold its shape, the snake must be about ¾ to an inch thick. Using a ruler and dull knife, cut the snake to 6". Smooth one end and place onto the cup, making sure it is adhered. Using a little water while smoothing will help it stick as well. Shape the other end of the clay into a hook and put the other piece of clay near the bottom of the cup. Smooth the end to adhere to the cup.
7. Assist to check the size by putting a votive candle in, or use a fake candle.
8. Assist as necessary to place the cup without the candle in it on the cookie sheet. The cup needs to bake at 350 degrees for one hour. After one hour, check if the cup is dry and hard completely through. If not, add more time.
9. When the cup is cool, add the candle.

Furthermore:

Rolling the handle of the cup may be the hardest part. Some individuals may need a model to follow whereas others will need a paper template. Drawing on the parchment paper from underneath offers one way to draw a pattern. A paper template to lay on the flatten piece of clay requires the skill to cut around. A dull or plastic knife can cut through the clay with minimal safety issues. Battery operated candles would also minimize the safety issues of flames.

Activity Story

Today I will make a candle holder. A candle holder holds a candle so it won't fall over.

I will roll the clay out into a ball, place my thumb in the middle, and push down. Sometimes the clay is hard to push. I will ask for help. I can ask for help to push a hole in my clay.

I will squeeze the sides of the hole. I will squeeze all the way around the clay. I will make my hole bigger. I will not make my hole too big. Sometimes the hole gets too big and breaks. If my hole is to big I can ask for help. I will ask for help to make my hole bigger.

I will make my hole so big I can make a fist and put it in the hole. My hole is now a bowl.

I will not know if my bowl will be a candle holder. I will put a candle into the bowl. Sometimes the bowl is too small. I can squeeze the sides of the bowl more.

I will take some more clay. I will flatten the clay with my hand or rolling pin. My bowl will sit on this clay.

I will use a cookie cutter as a template to cut around my clay. My clay will look like a circle.

I will put my bowl on the circle. I will softly push on the bottom of the bowl. I will gently smooth the outside where my bowl sits on the circle. Sometimes the bowl will not stick. I can ask for help. I can ask for help to make my bowl stick to the circle.

I will take more clay. I will roll my clay. My clay will look like a snake. I do not want my clay to be small. I do not want my clay to big. I will take my ruler and measure my clay. My clay cannot be too long. My clay cannot be too short. I will use my ruler and measure my clay.

I will take my clay and put it on my bowl. I will make one end stick to the bowl. I will make a loop with my other end of clay and place it on the bowl to make a handle. Sometimes I gently rub the end so it is smooth on my bowl. Sometimes I dip my finger into water and smooth the end of my clay on my bowl.

My bowl and clay look like a cup. My cup will hold a candle. My candle holder is a cup.

I will put my cup on a cookie sheet. My cup will go in the oven. Ovens are very hot. I will not touch hot things. I will not touch the hot oven. I will not touch the hot cookie sheet. The cup will be in the oven for a long time. I can set a timer to tell me when it is done. I will wait. Sometimes it is hard to wait. I will wait for my cup.

I will wait to touch my cup until it is cool. I will put my candle in my cool cup.

I will place a candle or fake candle (switch operated) in my candle holder I made.

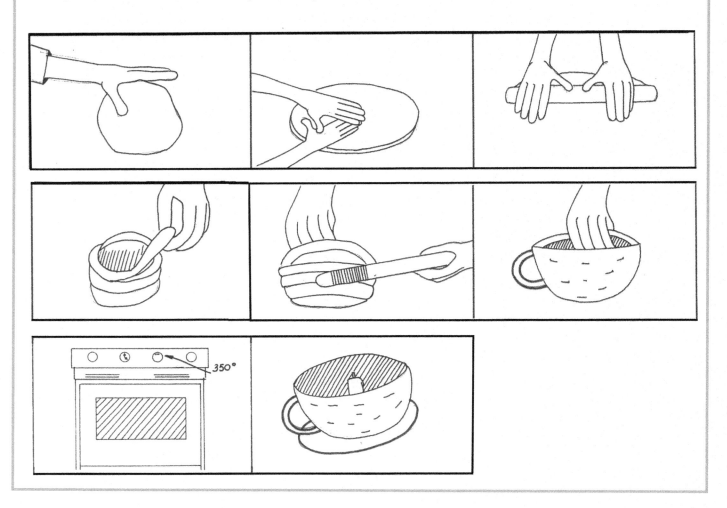

POTTERY: COIL POT

Materials:

- Clay 1lb. broken into two pieces
- Lazy Susan or something that turns
- Wax paper or parchment paper for surface
- Craft stick with string wrapped around it
- Rolling pin (optional)
- Ruler (optional)
- Cookie sheet and oven

General Guidelines:

1. The activity story and/or visual sequence provided can offer the key elements of the project.
2. Assist the individual to take a ½ lb. of clay and flatten it into a circle with their hand or rolling pin. Offer a template to show how big and thick.
3. Assist the individual to take the other piece and break it into smaller pieces to roll. Have the individual roll clay into shapes like snakes or ropes. Again, it may be easier to have a sample of what is expected to help determine the size. A ruler showing the length or coiling it around the base is an alternative.
4. Assist the individual to make five or six of the rolls. When they are finished rolling, assist them to begin putting the coiled rolls around the base. The coils must be smoothed to the base and each layered. Assist and model for the individual how to gently smooth and push the coils to stick. Dipping a finger in water before smoothing is effective. Some individuals may not be able to gently connect the coils without damaging the pot. An alternative may be putting the pot into a bowl roughly the same size. The individual could then moisten their finger and just smooth the inside running their finger around the softened, moist clay.
5. When all the coils have been layered and smoothed together, assist the individual to place the coiled pot on a cookie sheet. Bake the coiled pot at 350 degrees for one hour. Check the pot after one hour and if the pot is still moist, add more time.
6. Assist the individual to remove the coil pot from the oven. Some individuals are not safe around hot items, such as ovens or hot cookie sheets. Assist them to stay back, maybe with a concrete prop, such as behind a table, chair, or counter.
7. When the pot is cool, remove the coil pot from the cookie sheet. Assist and encourage the individual to use their coil pot to demonstrate the project had a purpose.

Furthermore:

There are some difficult issues in this project as the pieces of coil and the base must be accurate for success. Consider easy ways to offer assistance. The wax paper or parchment paper on the table could be drawn on for the base size. Hand or rolling pin flattening can then be used to match the shape. The same strategy could work for the length and width of the coils. Another idea for the coils is to put a piece of string taped to the table for a template or even use a piece of the tape.

Activity Story

Today I will make a coil pot of clay. A coil pot is a bowl you make out of clay by rolling pieces of clay to layer into the shape of a bowl. I will take a piece of clay and make it flat. Sometimes I use my hand to flatten the clay. Sometimes I use a rolling pin. I will flatten my clay to look like a circle. I will make my circle as big as the paper circle.

I will take more pieces of clay and roll them on the table. My rolls of clay might look like a snake or a piece of rope. I will roll the clay to be long and thin. These are the coils for my coil pot. I will make my coils as long as the _____ (*ruler, tape, string, paper template) tells me to. I will make four to five coils as long as the* _____ tells me.

I will take one of my coils and lay it around my circle. I will smooth the clay so my coil and circle will stay together. I will dip my finger into water and smooth the inside of the bowl. I will dip my finger in water and smooth the coil to the circle on the outside. I will stick my coil and circle together. Sometimes it is frustrating to make the coil and circle stick. Sometimes I may push too hard. I can ask for help when my coil is not right. I will ask for help to make my coil pot.

I will place the next coil on top. I will smooth the coils together. I will make the coil stick to the other coil. I will do this until I do not have any more coils. I will have coils stacked and stuck on each other. The coils are stuck on a base. I have a coil pot.

I will put my coil pot on a cookie sheet. I will put the coil pot into the oven. Ovens are very hot and can be dangerous. I will ask for help to put my coil pot into the oven. The coil pot is in the oven for a long time. I will set a timer so I know when my coil pot is done in the oven.

After my coil pot comes out of the oven it will be hot. I will not touch my hot pot. I will wait for my coil pot to cool.

I will have a coil pot. I will find things to put in my coil pot and hold them for me.

POTTERY: PINCH POT

Materials:

- 1 lb. of clay

General Guidelines:

1. The activity story and/or visual sequence provided can offer the key elements of the project.
2. Assist as necessary to retrieve a lump of clay as big as the pot the individual would like to make. Roll the lump into a ball.
3. Assist as necessary to put a thumb into the clay making a hole in the middle of the ball. Try to make the hole straight down into the ball for easier pinching.
4. Assist as necessary to squeeze around the edges of the bowl. Sometimes the individual may have difficulty understanding the different pressure needed to shape the bowl. Modeling or doing hand over hand will create the pressure and prevent the sides from becoming misshapen. Work around the sides of the bowl until they are evenly thinned.
5. Assist as necessary for the individual to use a small amount of water to smooth the inside and out. Modeling that using only one or two fingers into water will keep the clay from softening too much.
6. Assist as necessary to place the pinch pot on a cookie sheet and bake at 350 degrees for one hour. Check the pinch pot after one hour to ensure the pot is completely dry. Add more time if it is needed.
7. Making a pinch pot has a natural finish. Assist and encourage the individual to show the purpose of their project by finding items to put in it.

Activity Story

Today I will make a pinch pot of clay. A pinch pot is a bowl you make out of clay by pinching the clay into the shape of a bowl.

I will roll a lump of clay into a ball. The ball will be the size of my bowl. Sometimes I can add clay and make my bowl bigger. Sometimes I can make my ball smaller. My bowl will be smaller.

I will press my thumb into the center of the clay ball to make a hole. I will try to make a big hole. Sometimes it is hard to make a hole. Sometimes the clay is very hard. If my clay is hard to push I can ask for help. I will ask for help to make the hole in my clay.

I will squeeze the clay around my hole. The clay will squeeze thin. I will squeeze all around the hole. I will make the sides of my bowl the same all the way around. My hole is big. My hole is now a bowl. Sometimes it is hard to squeeze the bowl so it is the same all around the hole. Sometimes it is frustrating to see bowl sides are not the same. I can ask for help when my bowl is not right. I will ask for help to make my bowl. I can make another one if the sides are not the same.

I will put my bowl on a cookie sheet. I will put the bowl into the oven. Ovens are very hot and can be scary. I will ask for help to put my bowl in the oven. The bowl is in the oven for a long time. I will set a timer so I know when my bowl is done in the oven.

After my bowl comes out of the oven it will be hot. I will not touch my hot bowl. I will wait for my bowl to cool. When my bowl is cool, I can find things to put in it.

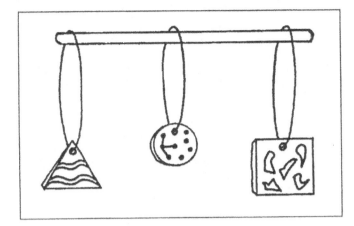

POTTERY: WIND CHIMES

Materials:

- Clay
- Cookie cutters or templates of shapes from poster board
- Rolling pin
- Dull knife
- String or yarn
- Dowel or coat hanger
- Decorations, such as beans, beads, shells (optional)
- Cookie sheet and oven

General Guidelines:

1. The activity story and/or visual sequence provided can offer the key elements of the project.
2. Assist as necessary for the individual to select a piece. Some individuals may need to be given a set amount so the task is not frustrating. With a rolling pin, roll out the clay or use a can to press the clay out flat. The flattened clay should be an inch or more. This will help prevent breakage.
3. Assist as necessary for the individual to select a shape. A variety of cookie cutters or poster board templates can be appropriate choices. Cookie cutters or templates should be presented in an array and not in a line. This will prevent the individual from using one at a time in sequence.
4. Assist the individual to make a hole at the top of their shape. Tools for making the hole could be a small dowel, top of a pen or pencil.
5. Assist as necessary to place the shapes on a cookie sheet and bake at 350 degrees for one hour. Sometimes individuals are uncomfortable with heat as it radiates out the oven and may not want to stay close as they bake.
6. After cooling, encourage the individual to paint or decorate the shape. Paint or glued on glitter makes it bright and fun.
7. Assist as necessary to put string through the holes or their chimes. Tie to a dowel or coat hanger and hang.

Furthermore:

There are other ways to decorate if the individual is interested in a more intricate process. Adding beads or other objects and putting them into the clay before baking creates a different look. Beads may melt and add a whole different look. This technique is a little more challenging as pushing the items into the shapes can damage the shaped clay. Baking as well needs to be monitored carefully in case the items burn. Using air drying clay can be used in either activity, cutting and baking, or cutting and adding items. It will take longer to dry. Some individuals can be patient and use a calendar to tell them when the cut-outs will have dried.

Activity Story

Today I will make a wind chime. A wind chime is made of clay. Shapes are cut out of the clay. Chimes hang in the wind. Sometimes the chimes make noise in the wind. I will make a chime to hang in the wind.

I will get some clay. I will roll the clay out so it is flat. I can use my hand to make the clay flat.

I will cut shapes out of the clay. I can use cookie cutters. I can use paper shapes. I will cut my shapes out of cookie cutters. I can make my shapes out by cutting around a paper shape. Cutting out paper shapes is hard. If I need help because cutting is hard, I will ask for help.

I will need to make _____ shapes. I can cut out _____ shapes with cookie cutters or my paper shapes.

I will put a hole in the top of my shapes. I will make a small hole. I will not tear the clay.

I will put my shapes on a cookie sheet. My shapes must cook so they are hard.

I will wait while my shapes are in the oven. The oven is very hot. I will not touch the oven. I will not touch the cookie sheet when it comes out of the oven. I will not touch the hot things.

I will wait until the shapes are cool. I will not touch the shapes until they are not hot. Sometimes waiting is hard. I will wait for my shapes.

I will paint or glue items on my shapes. I will make them look different with special items. I will wait for the glue to dry.

I will hang my shapes. I will put the string through the hole on top of my shapes. I will tie my shapes to a _____.

I will hang up my wind chime. I will watch my chime blow in the wind.

Activity Cards—
Board &
Card Games

Appendix D

CANDY LAND BINGO

Materials:
- Candy Land Bingo by Hasbro
- White paper

General Guidelines:
1. The activity story and/or visual sequence provided can offer the key elements of the game.
2. Assist the individual to deal colored bingo boards to each player. Distribute the markers according to the variation chosen to play. See "Furthermore" below for suggested variations.
3. If necessary, assist as necessary to match a marker to the correct color circle to understand the purpose of the markers.
4. Assist as necessary to flip spinner or roll dice.
5. Assist as necessary to retrieve the correct color marker and place on the correct circle.
6. Assist as necessary in understanding the games ends when all circles are filled or if one of each color marker is placed..

Furthermore:
The whole card of colors and markers can be confusing for some individuals. Try covering some of the board with white paper, determining how many rows should be shown. Also, each turn has many steps when broken down and this, too, can be overwhelming. Consider options, such as modifying the number of colors on the spinner orhaving the matching colored markers sitting next to the spinner colors with only one matching skill in place, attaching the spinner to a heavier material to make spinning easier, or putting the markers in a container and drawing out a man to match. This also facilitates turn taking as you pass the container. The markers provided can be tipsy for some and another option would be to make your own markers more easily controlled.

Activity Story
Candy Land Bingo is a game I play with friends. I can play with one, two, or three friends.

There are four different colors of markers. There is one board with many different colored circles on it. There is a spinner with an arrow that points to one color.

When it is my turn, I will flick the spinner to make it go around. When the spinner stops, I will see what color it is pointing at. I find a marker that matches that color. On the board, I place it on a circle that matches the marker.

I will wait for my friends to use the spinner, pick a marker, and match it on the board. When it is my turn, they hand me the spinner. When my turn is over, I hand them the spinner.

We play the game until someone wins. Someone wins when they have markers on matching colors that go straight up, down, or across like one side or an "X".

Sometimes I might win, sometimes my friend will win.

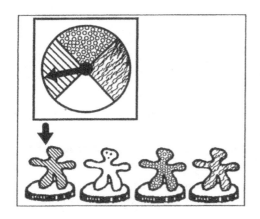

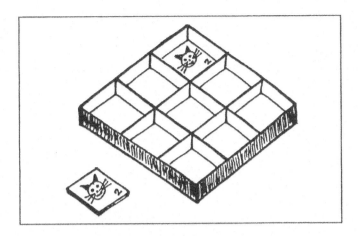

LOTTO

Materials:

- Lotto Grid (optional)
- Set of produced and/or personalized cards

General Guidelines:

1. The activity story and/or visual sequence provided can offer the key elements of the game.
2. There are a variety of ways to play this game. Here are a few suggestions:
   a. Place a number of cards out face up. Four is a good starting number and add more or less to minimize frustration. Mix up the matching cards and present to the individual either face up or down depending on the understanding of the individual.
   b. Place ½ the cards face down on the table and ½ in a stack face up. Take turns turning cards over till one is matched. Then go to the second card in the stack, turn until a match is found, and continue.
   c. Put all the cards face down. Take turns turning two cards over until a match is found, remembering to return the cards back over if they don't match.
   d. Placing the cards in the grid assists the movement difficulty when working on a flat surface. For some individuals it can limit accessing the card from the grid.

Furthermore:

Games are easier with clear rules. The back and forth of turns is easier than introducing the idea of an extra turn with each match. It can become confusing for some individuals. If using the grid, passing it to the next person is a clear indicator of turns. Consider having a dealer that gives a card to match if you are using step "b" above. There are many produced lotto cards but personal varieties are fun too. Pictures or sketches of family, pets, favorite animals, items, or maybe classmates are fun.

Activity Story

Lotto is a game to play with friends.

First, I place all the cards face down, so you can't see the picture on them. The cards fit into a grid which holds them.

Each person gets a turn.

When it is my turn, I turn two cards over and look at the pictures. If the pictures are the same, they match.

If two cards match, I will take them and keep them. I can then turn two more over.

If two cards do not match, the pictures are different. If the pictures are different, I will turn them back over so the pictures can't be seen.

When the cards don't match, my turn is over. I will need to wait and watch until everyone has a turn then it is my turn again.

I can watch and try to remember where the cards are when it is not my turn.

The game is over when all the cards are matched.

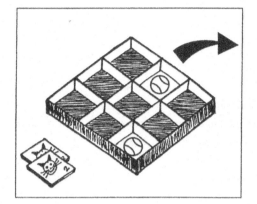

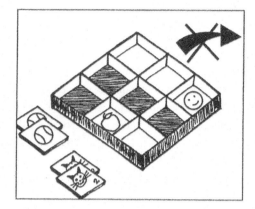

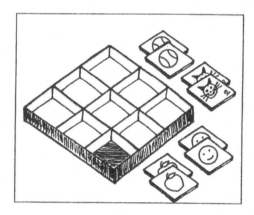

MR. MOUTH

Materials:

- Mr. Mouth or Tomy Frog Mouth by Hasbro

General Guidelines:

1. The activity story and/or visual sequence provided can offer the key elements of the game.
2. Assist as necessary to assemble the arms and head in the game board according to the game instructions.
3. Assist as necessary to distribute the chips. Another option is deal a different color to each participant, take turns, and deal the same color chip to each again or pick one chip after everyone has had a turn. See "Furthermore" for more expansion suggestions.
4. Decide who will turn the mouth on and off. Assist as necessary.
5. Assist as necessary to place chip and flip.

Furthermore:

This game has a great deal of variations making it good for a wide range of individuals. The head of the mouth can be removed, the colored chips varied, or simply using the flipping hand are some of the variations. The actual flipping motion is difficult at first to manage for some individuals. One hand can be set up as a practice. The rotating head has the advantage of giving a visual turn taking opportunity. You can't get the chip in when the head isn't facing you. However, there are other means to build turn taking when the head is off. Consider having one chip where each has a turn flipping, retrieving, passing off to the next person. To curb continuous flipping, have one person deal chips after the participant has had a turn. Mr. Mouth has a natural finish, when the chips are gone the game is over whether you count the successes or not.

Activity Story

Mr. Mouth is a game you can play by yourself or with others.

There are round chips that are different colors. Each player gets to pick a color. Sometimes someone chooses a color I want. That's ok, I can choose another color.

Someone turns the "head "on to move. The head goes around and the mouth opens and shuts.

I try to get the chips in the mouth by placing the same color chip on the same color hand. When the mouth is open, I pull the hand down and let it go off of the hand. The chip flips toward the mouth.

The game is finished when all the chips are flipped, one person gets all their chips in the mouth, or when all the chips are in the mouth.

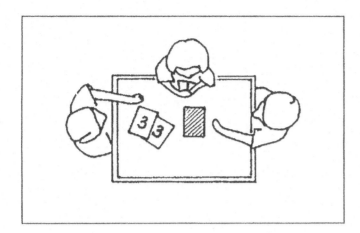

UNO CARD GAME

Materials:
- Deck of Uno cards sorted as necessary (see "Furthermore")
- Cardholder (optional)

General Guidelines:
1. The activity story and/or visual sequence provided can offer the key elements of the game.
2. Assist the student to pass seven cards to all the players.
3. Assist as necessary to hold cards in hand or in card holder away from other players.
4. Assist as necessary to draw a card and either match or follow the card's directions.
5. Assist as necessary to identify that the game is over when either player is out of cards.
6. This card game can be very confusing for individuals. See Furthermore for suggestions of the variety of playing strategies.

Furthermore:
Rules for card games need to be concrete, clear, and static. Uno is a game that can change with every turn. There are many ways to modify how to use the cards to play. Some suggestions are limit the number of cards by color, cover up the numbers with taping white paper and match just the color, or play with the cards face up in front of the player so all participants can help match. Cards could be dealt in groups of three or five rather than seven. When dealing, the cards cold be placed face up or face down on a template showing how many to disperse.

Activity Story
Uno is a card game you play with friends.

I will get seven cards. The cards will have numbers and colors on them.

One card is placed in the middle of the table. When it is my turn, I take one card that matches the color or the number.

If none of my cards match, I pick one off the stack of cards in the middle of the table.

I may see other cards too. A card that says draw four tells me to take four cards from the stack in the middle of the table. Draw two tells me to draw two from the stack.

I can play my cards with draw four or draw two. I can put an "S"or "R" down if the color matches.

I may also see color cards with no number but "R" or "S." If I get an "R", it means the person who just had a turn gets another turn. If I get an "S", it means the next person must skip a turn. If the person before me gets an "S", I have to skip my turn or if he/she gets an "R", I get another turn.

When I have only one card left, I must yell "Uno" so everyone knows.

The game is over when someone has no cards left. I can have no cards left and win.

Sometimes, I will have cards left when the game is over.That's okay, I may win next time.

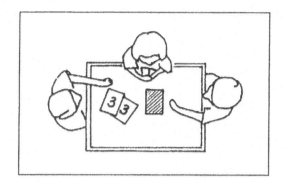

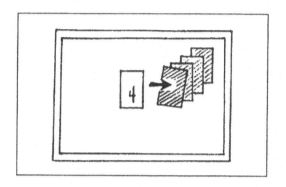

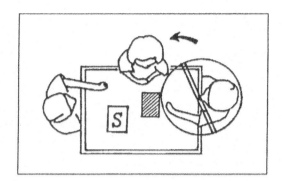

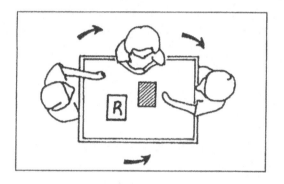

WAR CARD GAME

Materials:

- Standard deck of cards with or without kings, queens, jacks, jokers, and aces removed depending on the game.

General Guidelines:

1. The activity story and/or visual sequence provided can offer the key elements of the game.
2. Separate the deck evenly by the number of individuals playing (two players is definitely easiest, but three could play).
3. Assist as necessary for the individual to turn over the top card of their deck.
4. If turning the card over is difficult, start with the deck face up and the cards will be uncovered as the top one is removed.
5. Assist as necessary to determine who has the highest number. That person takes all the cards and puts them in a specific place close to them.
6. This game has a natural concrete "finish"; it's when the stack in front of the player is gone. Check who has the most cards if the individuals want to compete.

Furthermore:

It may be overwhelming at first to use the whole deck. Try using a limited number of cards that will successfully hold their attention. Gradually increase the cards as the individual is interested. This game has a natural ending, when the cards are gone from the stack. If this is confusing, consider having only one deck that individuals take turns reaching for. The cards remain in the center to determine the largest number and collection.

Activity Story

War is a card game that you play with another person.

Each person gets the same number of cards.

When each person has their cards, they are stacked and placed face down.

In unison, each person turns over one card. The person with the highest number card gets the two cards and places them in their stack. Now, turn over the next card. Who has the highest number? You do this until the game is finished. The game ends when your stack of cards is gone, or when one person gets all the cards.

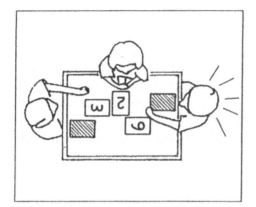

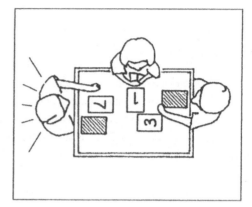

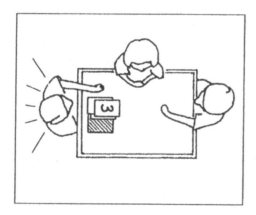

Activity Cards— Community Activities

Appendix D

BOWLING (GET READY)

Materials:

- Picture schedule

General Guidelines:

1. The activity story and/or visual sequence provided can offer the key elements of the experience.
2. Some individuals may need a more detailed sequence, such as getting on a bus, paying to play, getting shoes, picking a ball and going to a lane.
3. The individual may need the exact amount of money in a coin purse or a match money card. They may also need a visual sequence if you plan on buying snacks or drinks.
4. It is always good to develop and review concrete information, such as how you will be going to the alley, with whom, how many games you will play, and how to tell when it's time to go home.

Furthermore:

For some individuals, you could have a plastic set of bowling pins to practice on. Although, be clear, maybe through pictures, that this will look different at the actual alley. Try your best to prepare the individuals for all the sensory experiences that may happen at the bowling alley. Maybe borrow some bowling shoes so they can see the difference. Download the sounds and let them listen.

Activity Story

I will go bowling on _____.

I will ride on the bus or in the car to get to the bowling alley.

I will go bowling with my friends or family. There will be other people at the bowling alley.

I need money for bowling. I will put the money in my wallet.

I can think about what it will be like when I go bowling. I will need special shoes. I will wait my turn. I will roll my ball when it is my turn.

It may be loud at the bowling place.

I will think about all the things I will do while bowling.

BOWLING
(THE REAL THING)

Materials:

- Money for admission and food or drink

General Guidelines:

1. The activity story and/or visual sequence provided can offer the key elements of the experience. Review the rules of safety, possibly even practice. Note what skills or awareness may need to be addressed in Training.
2. Some individuals may need further break down of the steps than provided visual sequence. Assist the individuals necessary in paying and requesting the right shoes. Your "Get Ready" card should have prepared you for the method to pay.
3. Using the visual sequence, assist the individual as necessary with all the routines, such as putting on the shoes, selecting a ball, bowling skills, and returning the shoes. The success or frustrations may be important information for determining what needs to be trained or not. Other individuals may need more concrete steps, such as objects or actual photos.

Furthermore:

There are many different opportunities during bowling besides the act of rolling the ball. Social conversations that stop or start with playing turns, complimenting good scores or offering a comforting word for bad rolls, etc. Again, make note of behavior that might need further teaching. Teams could be encouraged for a social opportunity or make note of the teams and fellow participants at the alley. Some bowling alleys have bumper guards for ensured success. Be aware of sensory issues and accommodate when possible. Head phones can block out the loud sound of crashing, or maybe sitting a short distance away but still available for their turn.

Activity Story

Today I am going bowling. I remember, and think about our planning to go.

I will go in the car or bus to get to the bowling place.

When I get to the bowling place, I will need to get special shoes. Sometimes I have to wait until people in front of me get their shoes. Sometimes I can get my shoes first. I will get in line.

I will change my shoes. Then I will get my bowling ball.

(*change if using the ball rolling adaptor). I sit and wait for my turn. When it is my turn I hold my ball up. I walk to the line and roll my ball down the lane.

I try to hit the pins. Sometimes I knock many down. Sometimes my ball goes in the gutter and I miss them all.

When the balls hit the pins it makes a loud noise. That's okay, if I don't like it I can cover my ears.

When the bowling is over I put my ball away. I change my shoes. I give the special ones back.

My friends and family think it is fun to go bowling.

BOWLING (REVIEW)

Materials:

- Schedule
- Photos or video of their bowling trip

General Guidelines:

1. The activity story and/or visual sequence provided can offer key elements of the experience.
2. If other visuals were used to break down sequences, have the individual put them back in order with descriptions or gestures.
3. Using a score sheet or visuals, talk about how they and others played the game. How many pins were hit? This is enhanced if photos are taken on cell phones and can trigger a memory.
4. As much as possible, allow the individual to reflect on their experience independently. Resist the typical ask and answer retelling. This might be easier if done closer to the experience as possible. Review what happened at the bowling alley when you get back or the next morning.

Activity Story

I will think about my bowling trip. I will tell my family or friends about what I did.

I went to the bowling place with _____. I went in a _____.

When I got to the bowling place, I got some special shoes. I put the shoes on.

I went and got a bowling ball.

I rolled the ball _____ times. I hit _____ pins. My score was _____.

It was loud when people hit the pins.

I think I might go bowling again.

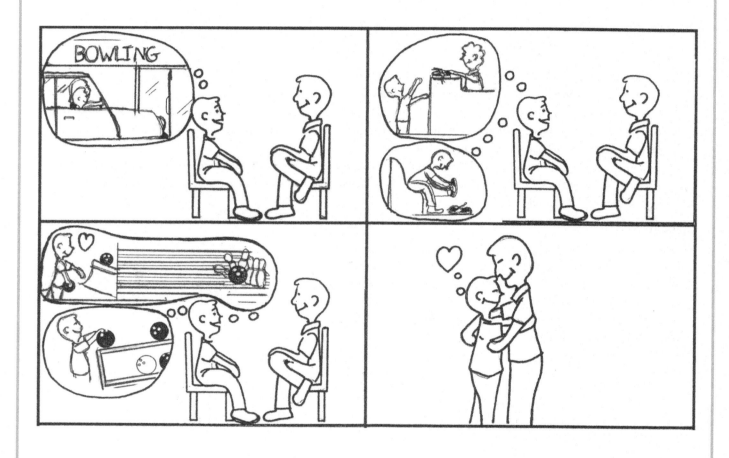

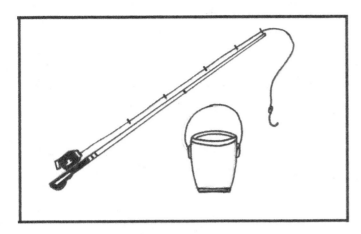

FISHING (GET READY)

Materials:

- Stories about fishing
- Pictures and video of fishing
- Map of fishing place

General Guidelines:

1. The activity story and/or visual sequence provided in "Fishing (The Real Thing)" can offer the key elements of the experience.
2. Assist as necessary, using objects, pictures, sketches, or written lists to review the whole process involved with fishing. Provide the steps in the individual's preferred manner of step-by-step tasks.
3. Provide a sequence from finding a pole, deciding on bait, picking a spot, baiting a hook, casting, catching, or catching and releasing, getting the fish off the hook, and cleaning up.

Furthermore:

There are many concrete steps involved in fishing. As listed above many items must be gathered, organized and used in a routine way. Having the information presented in a step-by-step manner makes preparing and starting to fish much easier. As does knowing if the individual plans on cooking up the fish or letting it go back in the water. Maybe there are family members or friends that love fishing and can share stories and pictures. YouTube or other apps available on line can be effective also.

Activity Story

Today I will get ready to go fishing. I will go fishing with my friend or family.

I will look at a map with my friend and decide where we will go to fish.

My friend will show me what to pack for fishing. I am ready to go fishing with my friend.

My friend will get me a fishing pole. My friend will show me how to put a hook on it.

I will be very careful with my hook. Hooks are very sharp and can stick me. I need a hook on my fishing pole to catch a fish.

I will practice throwing my hook into the water by swinging my pole. My friend will show me how to swing my fishing pole.

I will let my friend pull on my pole so I can know what a fish bite feels like. I will feel the tug like a fish on my pole.

I will practice waiting for a fish to bite. Sometimes the fish bites when I put my hook into the water. Sometimes the fish will not bite for a long time. I will know I must wait for the fish to bite.

FISHING
(THE REAL THING)

Materials:
- License, if necessary
- Fishing pole with hook
- Bait
- Container for fish that are caught
- (Needle nose pliers)

General Guidelines:
1. The activity story and/or visual sequence provided can offer the key elements of the experience.
2. Provide the individual the physical boundaries to stay within. At a fish farm, give them a specific area to stand in, i.e., by a river or stream and be sure to set how close to the water is okay to stand, and how far to walk up and down.
3. Assist the individual by providing their preferred method of step-by-step tasks. Using sketches, pictures, or objects show them how to bait the hook, cast, hold the pole, and then reel in. Tug on the line to show them how it feels if a fish bites. Note what skills may need to be addressed in training.
4. Provide a system to indicate waiting time and when to recast if they don't feel a bite. Use a timer, watch, or other mechanism so they don't continually recast but don't wait too long.
5. Provide assistance as necessary when the individual does catch a fish. How to get the hook out, save or return the fish, and how to clean up. Make sure the individual understands we keep fish for eating and if they don't choose to eat it then it should got back in the water. There are many reasons we fish.

Activity Story
Today I am going fishing. I will go with a friend to a fish farm or river. I will stand by the water. I will not get in the water. My friend will show me where to stand to be safe.

I will get bait on my hook. I will use my pole to swing the bait into the water.

Now I wait for a fish to swim by and eat the bait. Sometimes a fish comes by fast. Sometimes it takes a long time for a fish to come and eat the bait. Sometimes no fish come.

Waiting is difficult but I can look around me and see all kinds of pretty things.

If a fish eats the bait on my hook, I will tug on the line. I will pull the fish in to the edge of the water. My friend will help me get the fish off the hook.

I can let the fish go back in the water or I can keep it to eat. The fish will flop and wiggle. Fish don't like to be out of water.

If I catch a fish or if I don't, it will be time to go home eventually. I can take my fish home or I can go home without a fish. It doesn't matter because I went fishing. It was fun.

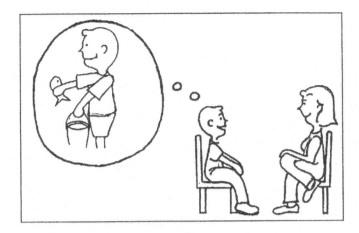

FISHING (REVIEW)

Materials:

- Pictures, sketches, video
- The fish when appropriate

General Guidelines:

1. The activity story and/or visual sequence provided can offer the key elements of the experience for recalling the event.
2. Sequence your pictures, sketches, or words to talk about the day. What was most fun? Not fun? Note if training could enhance the activity.
3. Fishing is a shared experience. In recalling the events, have each share how it went for them. You can ask questions like, "Who got the most bites?" "Which fish was bigger or biggest?" "How will you cook the fish?"Or "How did you get it back in the water?" Having a picture or video from a cell phone can provide natural prompts to asking and gaining information.

Activity Story

I went fishing. I caught _____ fish. I went to a fish farm or river to fish. It was fun.

I went to the fish farm or river and stood carefully by the water. I did not get wet. I helped put bait on the hook. I threw the bait in the water by swinging the pole. I had to wait for a fish to come by. It was hard to wait but I did it!

A fish came by and took a bite of my bait. It made my line wiggle. I pulled my hook in. There was a fish.

My friend helped me take the fish off. It wiggled and flopped. That is okay. Fish wiggle and flop out of water.

We put it back in the water. It swam away.

OR

We put the fish in our basket.

We put more bait on and fished again. When we were done, we went home.

IN THE PARK
(GET READY)

Materials:

- A map or picture of the park
- A marker for drawing on the map/photo
- A photo of the individual's friend on the equipment (optional)

General Guidelines:

1. The activity story and/or visual sequence provided can offer the key elements of the experience.
2. Present the individual with a map or actual photo of the park.
3. Assist the individual to understand the boundaries by drawing on the map or photo. Use a drawing of the actual barriers.
4. Present the individual equipment or structures and assist the individual in anticipating how to use them. If there is a specific number of turns or defined use for each, assist the individual to understand the timing.
5. Assist the individual to understand how to use the equipment. A photo may be helpful.
6. Assist the individual to transition from one piece of equipment to another. Using a marker and arrows can indicate the movement.
7. Assist the individual to understand when it is time to go. Provide concrete indicators, such as a timer or number of turns left.

Furthermore:

There are additional opportunities in going to such an active place. Examples may include; interacting with others that are on the equipment, asking a friend to come slide, or basic social greetings. Other opportunities could be asking a friend to play catch or tag. It's difficult to know how many other individuals may be in the park but practicing appropriate social behavior would be helpful no matter what.

Activity Story

I will be going to the park. I will look at my calendar and it will tell me when I will go to the park.

IN THE PARK
(THE REAL THING)

Materials:

- Water and/or snacks
- Boundary markers
- Drawings or photos of park equipment

General Guidelines:

1. The activity story and/or visual sequence provided can offer the elements of the experience. Ideally having photos of the actual park can help orientate the individual.
2. Safety is always first anytime the individual is moving around and throughout open space. Especially when crossing streets or around traffic. Know exactly how much assistance or supervision the individual needs.
3. Provide concrete information on the boundaries in the park. These may include verbal understandings, concrete flags, cones, rope, etc.
4. Take time to assist the individual on each piece of equipment to encourage varied experiences and note areas needing training. This also encourages the individual to utilize all the different equipment rather than routines.
5. Provide concrete information about when it is time to leave. Whether by counting down turns on the slide or setting a timer.

Activity Story

I will go to the park.

There are swings, slide, climbers, tether balls, etc. at the park.

I will stay on the grass, behind the rope, in front of the trees when I am at the park.

First, I will play on the _____.

Then I will play on the _____.

I can ask for help from my family or friend if I need help.

I will try one new thing while at the park.

The bell, alarm, and/or counting will tell me when it is time to leave.

I will come to the park again. My calendar will tell me when I go to the park.

IN THE PARK (REVIEW)

Materials:

- Visuals
- Pictures or video of the individual at the park

General Guidelines:

1. Using the activity story and/or visual sequence card can be a starting point in recalling the activities the individual participated in.
2. Assist the individual to organize, whether by verbal or visuals, the schedule of the park through usage of the equipment.
3. Assist as necessary to discuss verbally, or match pictures of themselves, indicating what they did that day. Maybe if they shared the equipment, who was there and playing.
4. If appropriate, schedule another trip to the park.

Furthermore:

It's easy to fall into question/answer when finding out about an activity of an individual. As much as possible encourage discussion with the recall. Utilizing video the individual made about someone, or someone made about them, that needs describing. Telling as much about the surroundings as the equipment. Was there a dog? Did someone fall down and cry? Who was there? Was someone else on the swing? Attempt to match the physical activity to a social comment.

Activity Story

Today I went to the park. I went with friends.

I will show my family pictures of the things I did. I will show my family the map.

I will tell my family about the park. I will tell them the things I did.

If I need help to remember I can ask my friend. I will ask my friend to help me tell my family what I did at the park.

I will tell my family I will go to the park again.

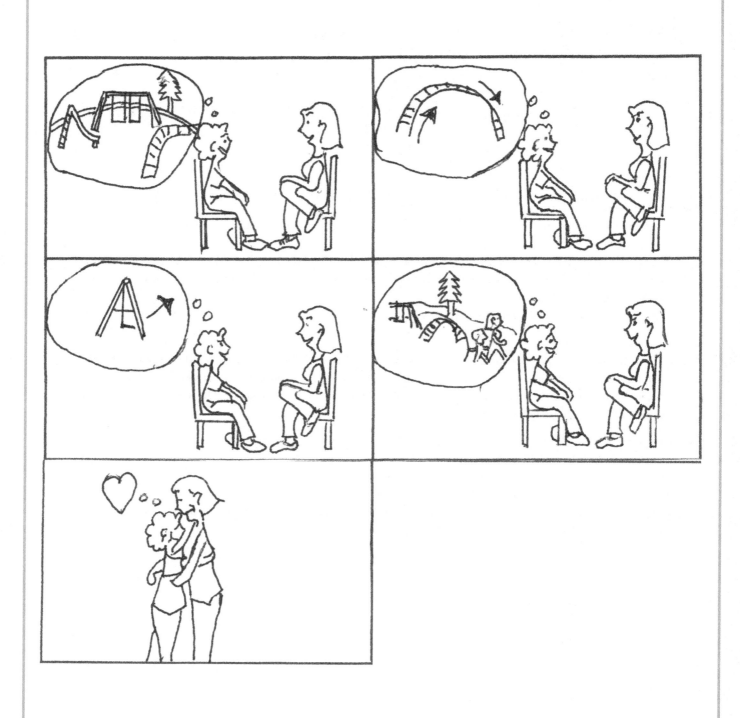

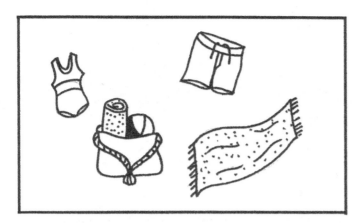

SWIMMING (GET READY)

Materials:
- Bag for supplies
- Bathing suit
- Towel

General Guidelines:

1. The activity story and/or visual sequence provided can offer the key elements of the experience.

2. Assist the individual to understand the coming events by using step-by-step task break down in the preferred system verbal/written/picture. Assist as necessary to collect and pack the items. For swimming you will need your suit, a towel, sometimes a swim cap or other hygiene items.

3. Assist the individual as necessary to anticipate the appropriate system to pay at the swimming center. It could be a set amount, or coins to be counted out when the individual enters or coins taped to the card for easy handling. Note what skills may need to be addressed in training. In addition, discuss/practice what social comments may be needed in the activity, such as a greeting at paying.

4. Assist the individual to anticipate through discussions/visuals pictures, how they will go and return by car or bus. How long they will stay and who might be going also? Is this a private swim or public?

Activity Story

I will look at my calendar to see when I will go swimming.

I will go swimming on or after _____.

I will look at my calendar to see what I need to take to the swimming pool. When it is time to, I will get my bag. I will put my swimsuit and towel in my bag.

I will take my swim card or money with me to get into the pool.

SWIMMING (THE REAL THING)

Materials:

- Bag with swimming suit, towel and money

General Guidelines:

1. The activity story and/or visual sequence provided can offer the keep elements of the experience.
2. Review the rules of safety in transition, arrival, and around the pool when ready to swim.
3. Greet the staff and pay the swimming fee in a manner as previously described. Note any needs for training, such as greeting.
4. Assist the individual as necessary to change into their swimsuit and again, note what skills may need to be worked on in training.
5. Provide concrete information as to how long the individual may stay and how they will know it is time to go.
6. Assist as necessary in the drying off, and redressing into street clothes. Note what skills may need to reviewed in training.

Furthermore:

There is a wide variety of sensory experiences to anticipate at a swimming pool. Some are obvious, such as moisture and fluid movement. However, be sensitive to other experiences as well. The ceilings above pools are many times echo chambers increasing sound. Crowds play a big role and can cause sudden splashes or movements. Water temperatures can feel different to different people making it uncomfortable. Transitioning between the warm showers to the cool feeling pool takes time to adjust. There are also many social requirements to know in the locker, no staring or commenting when others dress. Remembering all your clothes before you leave. Many pools have extra equipment for individuals with special needs. Be sure to check.

Activity Story

I will walk into the swim area. I will greet and give the cashier my swim card or money.

I will walk into the locker room. I will take off all my clothes and put on my swim suit. I will put my clothes into my bag. I will put my bag into a locker. I will ask for help if I need help.

I will take a shower before I walk to the pool.

I will walk to the pool. I will only jump in the pool where the life guard tells me I can.

I will swim and/or play in the water.

I will get out of the pool when I am asked and walk to the locker room.

I will take off my swim suit, dry, and put my clothes on in the locker room.

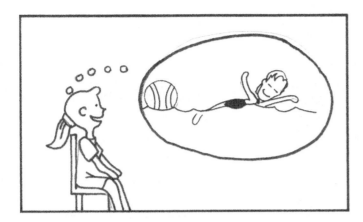

SWIMMING (REVIEW)

Materials:

None

General Guidelines:

1. The activity story and/or visual sequence provided can offer the key elements of the experience for recalling this event.
2. Using the preferred visuals, recall the sequence of events with the individual. Photos or video from a cell phone or camera can enhance recall and commenting.

Furthermore:

Recalling and retelling events to share with others is difficult for most individuals. Asking questions help share facts but it may be difficult to comment in a broader story telling. Having the individual take photos or video of a peer, then having them share it after, can help both the story teller and listener build communication skills..

Activity Story

I went swimming on _____.

I swam and played in the pool.

I will look at the pictures _____ took while I was at the pool.

I will look at the calendar to see when I will swim again.

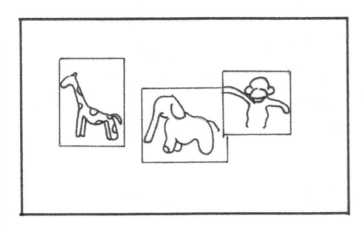

THE ZOO
(GET READY)

Materials:

- Pictures of zoo animals
- Plastic zoo animals
- Large sheets of paper
- Pen

General Guidelines:

1. The activity story and/or visual sequence provided can offer the key elements of the experience.
2. Review with objects and/or pictures for what the zoo looks like, and the different animals that live there. Remember individuals learn from a natural context or the real thing, but benefit from pre-teaching expectations.
3. Place objects and/or pictures on the map in the appropriate area for your zoo.
4. Move around the map; first go see the elephants, then the tigers, etc. Show where the restrooms will be.
5. Using the activity story and/or visual sequence, preview the activity discussing smells and sounds.

Furthermore:

This activity could be presented as one goal a day for preparation. The first day, categorize the animals, and take time to find the pictures and/or objects. If possible learn about their natural habitat, what they eat, etc. Another day, develop the map and discuss it.

Activity Story

I will be going to the zoo on _____. Today I will plan our trip.

I will find pictures of animals that live in the zoo. I will draw a map of where the animals live in the zoo.

I may go to the zoo with my family or buddy. I will stay by whoever I go with. This is one rule.

There is a train at the zoo. If I want to ride the train, I will tell my family or buddy.

I will think about the animals I will see. I will think about what I will see or hear at the zoo.

In _____ days, I will go to the zoo.

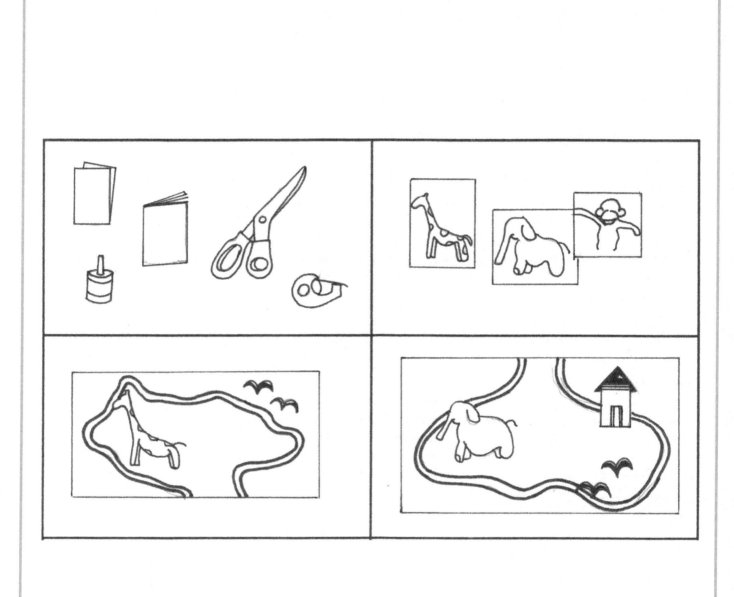

THE ZOO
(THE REAL THING)

Materials:

- Money for admission and/or snack

General Guidelines:

1. First, complete the preparation exercise. The activity story and/or visual sequence provided can offer the key elements of the experience.

2. Review any rules to get there safely. Practice other rules, such as staying with a buddy, looking carefully where you walk, or not talking to strangers.

3. Determine how much time is expected to view each animal and have a system for the individual as needed. For example, use a stop watch alarm set for minutes, reading a card, or walking across the front of the cage three times.

4. Your preparation exercise should have decided if there is time for a lunch or snack break. A visual card can help determine when, what to choose from, and how to get the food. Each zoo has different types of places to get food.

5. Provide the individual concrete information for when it will be time to go. For example, "We will see the penguins and then we will leave." or having animal cards to take away as the animals are viewed. When they are all gone it's time to leave.

Activity Story

Today I am going to the zoo.

I will see many animals. There may be many people there too.

When I walk around the zoo, I will walk with my family or buddy.

Sometimes the animals smell different. I may think they smell different. I may think they smell bad. I can walk away with my family or buddy.

Sometimes the animals make loud sounds. I may think the sounds are too loud and I can walk away with my family or buddy.

If I am hungry or need to go to the bathroom, I will tell my family or buddy. I know where to go because I can use my map. My map tells me where places are located at the zoo.

If I get tired, I can tell my family or buddy. We can sit and rest.

After we have seen the animals, we will go back to the car or bus. It will be time to go home or back to school.

THE ZOO
(REVIEW)

Materials:

- Map made during preparation
- Any pictures taken at the zoo
- Any items bought as souvenirs

General Guidelines:

1. Besides the map created at the preparation stage, the story and/or visual sequence provided can offer key elements to review.
2. Pull out the previously made map. Have the individual move around it as you did on the day of the visit. Place pictures in the correct places on the map.
3. Encourage the activity in any way possible for the individual to remember it and retell their experience. A nonverbal individual could point or manipulate visuals. For more verbal individuals you could discuss smells and sounds and what they thought.

Furthermore:

Depending on how tired the individual is, review when you get back or first thing the next day. You can also use the map as an extra leisure activity, pretending to go to the zoo. Recall is an important part of building positive experiences for leisure. How was it? Did they enjoy it? Now is the time to use the Activity Assessment Form.

Activity Story

I went to the zoo and saw the animals.

I can tell my family or friends about what I saw and did.

I will say, "First, I went to the _____ and saw the _____. Next we saw the _____.

I will tell them my favorite animal was _____.

I ate _____ for lunch or snack.

I can show them my map and or pictures taken and show them where I walked.

My family and friends will like to know about my trip to the zoo. It will make them feel happy to hear me tell them about the zoo.

Activity Cards— Hobbies

Appendix D

CALL A FRIEND

Materials:

- Pictures of friends
- Friends phone numbers
- Words/sketches or pictures of interest (topic starters)

General Guidelines:

1. The activity story and/or visual sequence provided can offer the key elements of making the phone calls.

2. Assist the individual as necessary to write friends name or get pictures. Most phones have the capacity to program phone numbers and add pictures as well. Some individuals may be frustrated by the steps and prefer punching the numbers from a written list.

3. Assist as necessary for the individual to use a step-by-step system to make the phone call. On a cell phone the individual has multiple steps, on a land line there are fewer steps. Create the sequence according to the communication check list the individual is familiar with. Note skills for further training.

4. Assist the individual to create a notebook or other medium to have topic starters. Listing their interests and listing their friend's interest to prompt questions.

5. Some individuals may need script outlines, including prompts like a greeting, questions from the interest list, and a farewell. Other individuals may need prompts to say goodbye by listening for phrases like "I have to go now."

Furthermore:

Sometimes individuals get repetitive and persist in repeatedly calling. Have a tally chart or mark a calendar to indicate how many times they may make phone calls. Other individuals may need a reminder system that they are not to call 911 unless there is a definite need for it.

Activity Story

Today I will talk with a friend on the phone.

I will decide what I want to ask my friend. I will decide what I want to tell my friend.

I will use the phone and call my friend. Sometimes the buttons are confusing. I may get confused calling my friend on the phone. I can ask for help if I need it.

When my friend answers the phone, I will tell my friend what I want to say.

When my friend answers the phone, I will ask them what I want to ask.

I will listen carefully to what my friend says. I will answer my friend's questions.

I will listen carefully for when to say goodbye. Sometimes I can decide when to say goodbye. Sometimes my friend will say goodbye.

When my friend says goodbye, I will say goodbye and hang up.

GROWING PLANTS

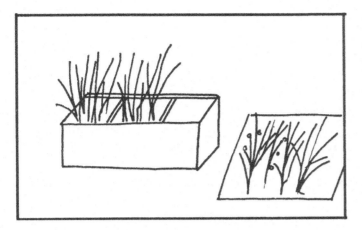

Materials:
- Container of prepackaged windowsill herbs or flower pots
- Potting soil
- Seeds
- Trowel
- Spray bottle or watering can

General Guidelines:

1. The activity story and/or visual sequence provided can offer the key elements of the experience.
2. Herb gardens are available in prepackaged containers. Open the package and follow the directions, or add a visual sequence as the individual is use to following. The following steps are an expansion on using the prepackaged growing herbs.
   a. Arrange in a sequence on a flat surface these items; package, seeds, and spray bottle. Assist as necessary to sprinkle the seeds. Using a sprinkle container, such as a clean candy shaker for cookies, or a sugar container can make distributing the seeds more even.
   b. Assist as necessary to spray water inside the container to moisten but do not wash the seeds away.
   c. Assist as necessary to create a calendar of when to water. The directions from the package should tell how often is necessary.
   d. Discuss how long the herbs will take to grow and what the individual can do with mature plants; use them for food or transplant to continue growing.
3. Assist as necessary to gather the containers. Line up the pots, soil, seeds, plants, and trowel. This provides a clear visual of the items to be used and in what order. Some individuals benefit from visual instructions on how to use the tools and complete the process.
4. Assist as necessary to add soil to the top of the pot or create a little mound on top as the water will condense it.
5. Assist as necessary to dig the appropriate size hole for the seeds or plants. The package or tag on the seeds or plant will indicate how deep. Cover the seeds with soil or put soil around the roots of the plants then gently pack it.
6. Assist as necessary to fill watering can and water the new seeds or plants. Have the individual touch the soil to feel the dampness in the pot.
7. Assist as necessary to develop a system for keeping track of when to water again. Have the individual once again feel for dampness in the soil. The individual will need to make sure the plants have enough water but not too much.
8. Watch the plants grow. One suggestion is to take measurements as the days go on to track how they mature. Or take pictures on set days to determine how they are growing.
9. If planting herbs or other edibles, discuss with the individual how they will be harvested and used.

Furthermore:

Growing your own food has become very popular. Growing flowers is also exciting, especially watching the plants grow from seed to bloom. However, some individuals have difficulty waiting for the seeds to mature until bloom or harvest. Planting seedlings may assist in earlier satisfaction. Having a picture of a mature plant and tracking how fast it is growing (see step 8 above) can also assist in the patience needed to grow plants. Many areas now have community gardens readily available. Whether the individual grows plants in the garden or simply visits and helps a gardener, it's fun to get in the soil and watch things grow. If the individual is sensitive to soil or weeding, a variety of garden gloves are available of different textures.

Activity Story

Today I will start growing an herb garden. I will plant the seeds to grow.

I will unwrap the package of paper. I will find the packet of seeds.

I will sprinkle the seeds on the soil as the directions tell me to.

I will use the spray bottle to water the seeds. I will stop when the dirt is a dark color.

I will mark on my calendar when I am to water them. I will keep them watered to grow.

I will look at the picture of the grown herbs. I will wait for my herbs to grow. When they look like the picture they will be grown.

I will cut or pick the grown herbs. Many herbs need to dry. I will put my cut herbs on a paper towel to dry. I will mark my calendar for two days. In two days, my herbs will be dry.

I will put my dried herbs in plastic bags. I will write the name of the herb on a piece of paper and put that in the bag too. If I need help, I will ask for help.

I will decide if I give my herbs to family or friends. I will save some of my herbs to cook in my food.

LISTENING TO AUDIOBOOKS

Materials:

- Computer or tablet with audiobook(s) downloaded
- Headphones (optional)
- Finished box (optional)
- Hard copy of the book (optional)

General Guidelines:

1. The activity story and/or visual sequence provided can offer the key elements of listening to the audiobooks.
2. Assist the individual to retrieve the source of the audiobook. Turn the system on, click on the icon for the audiobook. The individual will need to determine how they will listen to the audiobook. Using headphones might be an option. Other individuals will need a quiet corner for listening.
3. Assist the individual to start the audiobook, or if started, find where they left off. If they finish an audiobook, assist as necessary to request another by typing the genre in the search engine.
4. Assist the individual to determine a "finished" time, such as after the end of ____ chapters or having a set amount of time for reading by setting an alarm on a clock or stop watch. Assist the individual to return the system/audiobook to a designated area and this is another indicator of when reading time is considered finished.
5. There are many ways to engage individuals in reading. See "Furthermore" below for some suggestions.

Furthermore:

Early readers have some unique needs. Some look at a book and think the one page is the "whole" piece. The main character or subject can be lost. Others have difficulty just listening and/or keeping the body still. Suggestions would include listening with the book present. For early types of books, it may be helpful for a familiar person to record on the tablet. This allows the reader to indicate page turns as well as catch the attention as the voice is familiar. Another technique is to copy the main character in the story, laminate it, and use it. The reader can modify the story reading by adding prompts if necessary. Richard Fowler has a series of books that come with a laminated main character in the story (mouse, chicken). He then put slits in the pages for the character to move through the book. Some individuals may be able to use a book that has Velcro on the characters and need to match then turn the page, match again or pull the same one off the Velcro and move the same piece. Again, depending on the individual, familiar voices work best.

More experienced readers may enjoy listening to the audiobook without the book. However, sometimes they can become stuck on the same story or even on a particular section. Assist the individual as needed to overcome the temptation. Make a chart to show how many times they may repeat and then move on. Most audiobook sites offer a sample of a book. Broadening the scope of what the individual reads can be assisted by teaching them to use this addition to ordering audiobooks. Libraries now have a selection of audiobooks available for download and some show a picture before downloading, which can give information on what the book is about.

Activity Story

Today I will listen to an audiobook. Sometimes audiobooks are read from a tablet and I listen to it. Sometimes the voice is someone I recognize. Sometimes it is not.

I will use headphones so I can hear my audiobook. It is quiet and I can hear the story better.

I will get my tablet and turn it on. I will tap the picture of an audiobook or other icon. When it is open, I will tap on the picture of my audiobook.

I will check how loud the story sounds. Sometimes it is too loud and hurts my ears. Sometimes it is so quiet I cannot hear it. I will turn the tablet down if it is too loud. I will turn the tablet up if it is too quiet. Sometimes it's hard to sound just right. If the sound is not right, I can ask for help. I will ask for help to make the sound just right.

If my story is over, I will choose another story. I will go to the tablet's library and choose another story to listen to. Sometimes it is hard to find another story. I will ask for help if I am confused. I will ask for help finding another story to listen to.

When listening time is over, I will turn off the tablet. I will put it into the basket. I will listen to my audiobook another day.

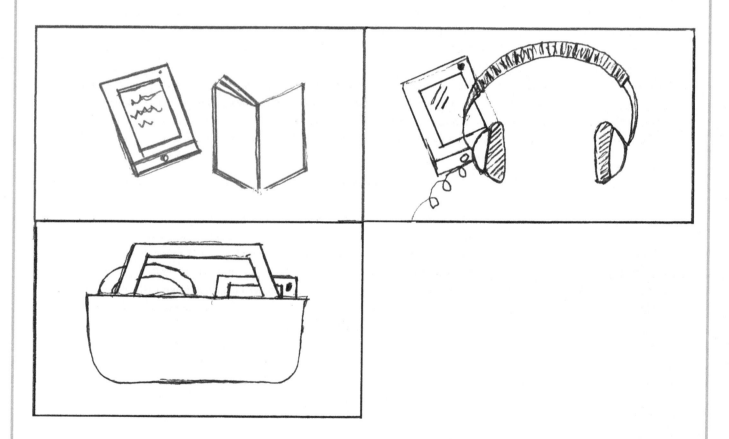

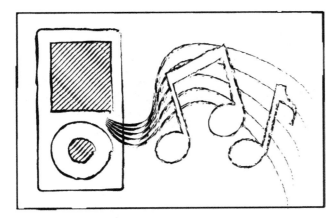

LISTENING TO MUSIC

Materials:

- Music source, such as cell phone, MP3, iPod, etc.
- Headphones (optional)
- Choice card to select genre or songs

General Guidelines:

1. The activity story and/or visual sequence provided can offer the key elements of the experience.
2. Assist as necessary in using the technology to listen to music. Typically there are seven steps the individual may need assistance with; to turn the system on, select a music icon, select the song or album, start the music, and know how to pause and stop the music. Then continue by turning the system off. These steps need to be presented in the style the individual is accustomed to using for step-by-step instruction. Some individuals utilize a system, such as a written form, a list of sketches depicting the buttons to push, or actual pictures of the system, and the button or icons to push.
3. Assist as necessary for the individual to find or choose music to play.

Furthermore:

Some individuals are too sensitive to ear buds or other headphones. There are strategies offered by Occupational therapists to desensitize wearing the headphones. But some individuals simply cannot tolerate them. Those individuals may need a stop and go system, indicating if this is a time they can listen to music, such as riding on a bus, or if they need to stop since others around them do not want to hear the music. Another issue with headphones is getting tangled up in the cords of headphones. Most are wireless but if the individual is using the wired headphones, they may need instructions or help to put the wires behind clothes, in a hat to keep them from being tugged on. To make informed choices or try new ones, the individual may need a system indicating how they feel about genres or artists. One opportunity may be to make a chart indicating positive or negative responses. Different types of music and artists could be played and the individuals would indicate on it their preferences. Doing it with friends or family can demonstrate that everyone has their own tastes. For some, having a picture or sketch of a few choices on a menu means the music may vary by a certain group.

Activity Story

Today I will listen to music.

I will find my music player. I will find my check list to play my music.

I will turn on my player. I will tap on the music symbol. I will look at what songs are on my player. Sometimes I will play music that sounds fast. Sometimes I will play music that is slow. Sometimes I will play music that is loud. Sometimes it might be quiet. I will choose the music I will listen to.

I will push on the song I want. I push the arrow. My music will start playing. Sometimes my music does not play. When my music does not play I might get frustrated. When I am frustrated, I will ask for help. I will ask for help if my music does not play.

When I am done listening to my music, I will press the stop music button. I will turn off the player. Sometimes someone tells me to stop my music. Sometimes it is frustrating when I am told to stop listening to music. I will stop and think about another time to listen. I know I will listen to my music again.

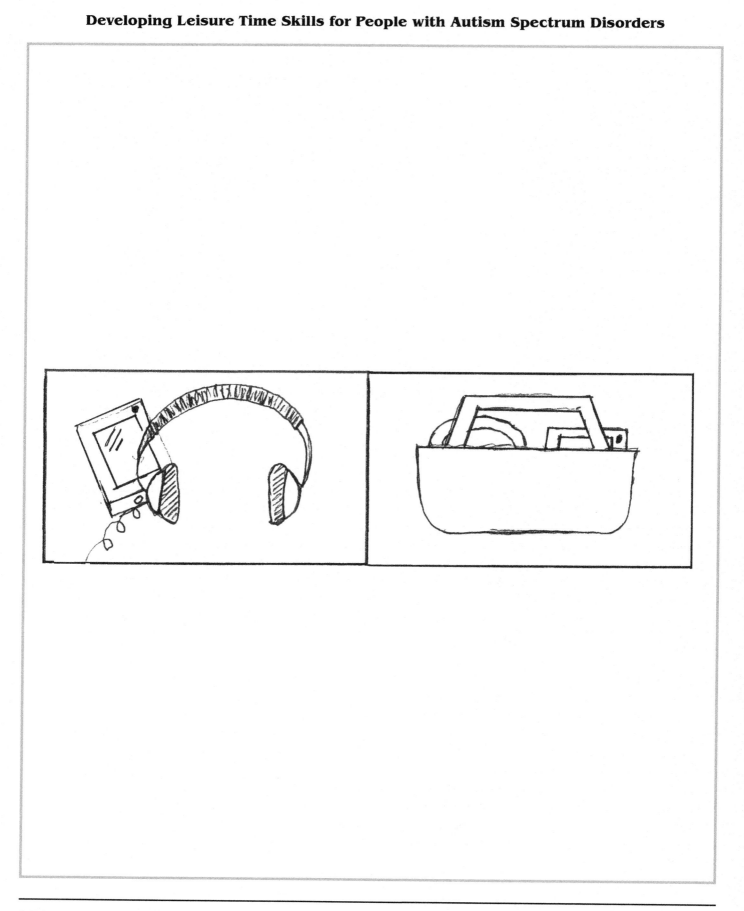

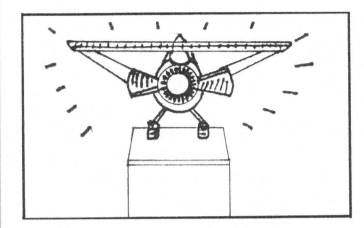

MODELING

Materials:
- Model kits: (cars, boats, planes, droids)
- Model glue as needed

General Guidelines:
1. The activity story and/or visual sequence provided can offer the key elements of the project.
2. Assist the individual to select their model kit. Sometimes there is a group project, such as a group at a hardware store doing bird houses, an organized Girl or Boy Scout troop or art classes. These opportunities may have limited visual instructions. Some individuals may need developed instructional list. Some individuals may be able to discern the steps as modeled by an instructor. They may only need minimal help to clarify for success.
3. Assist the individual with pre-made kits since they have different requirements. The following lists are issues to consider and suggestions for successful participation.
    a. Most kits come with step-by-step instructions. Some come in thorough breakdown of steps. Others are broader instructions assuming the reader can fill in information. Some provide the step-by-step but not clearly arranged on the directions. Cutting the paper into steps that move from left to right is an easy correction. Broad directions, when cut-up, can be enhanced with missing steps. Some individuals would benefit from the cut-up directions being presented one at a time.
    b. Most kits ask that you remove the items and ensure you have all the parts. Most individuals benefit from the picture on the front. Some individuals would benefit from kit pieces being presented in smaller containers, holding only the pieces necessary for that step.
    c. There is a varied complexity to the kits that create a unique frustration for individuals that need clear starts and finishes. When the project takes longer than the time available, make sure you have a plan to show how much time the individual has to work on it. Some ideas might be to show visuals of how many steps to do this session or set a timer to show how much time. Make sure you include information when the next opportunity will be to work on it.

Furthermore:
Many times, social opportunities are tied to model building. Some hobby or craft stores have group times set aside to work on individual's model just to offer help to each other. Droid builders have competitions as ways to contact others and learn from and socialize with others that have similar interests.

Activity Story
Today I will work on building a model. A model looks like a real thing but smaller. A model can be of a car, boat, and ship. I will pick a model I want to build.

I will make a model that looks like _____.

I will have many pieces to make my model. Each piece goes with the other. Sometimes there are pictures that tell me how to put the pieces to make my model. Sometimes I will listen or watch to see how to put my pieces together.

Sometimes I will use glue to put my pieces together. Sometimes I will snap my pieces together. I will put pieces together to make a model.

My model will look like _____ when I put pieces together.

Sometimes I will finish my model and I will look at it. Sometimes I will have more pieces to make my model. That's okay, I will finish my model another time.

SCRAPBOOKING

Materials:

- Pictures, coins, other collectable items
- Paper if using hard copy
- Downloaded program for computer use

General Guidelines:

1. The activity story and/or visual sequence provided can offer the key elements of the project.
2. Individuals will need to decide how they will do their collecting of important things. Obviously, a coin collection must be in a notebook. However, there are many programs on the computer that are structured to collect pictures on their own boards. Many photo programs allow you to organize photos that are downloaded or scanned in. Sometimes these programs offer pages with frames like paper albums.
3. Assist as necessary for whichever is selected by providing a written or visual check list. The computer program will need to be set up but then can simply be visited to add the pictures or sketches using the steps.

For computer scrapbooking:

    a. Turn on the computer.

    b. Assist as necessary to find the correct icon and click on it for the site the individual is using.

    c. Assist to teach the individual to search the internet or select pictures of preferred items, family photos or personal photos of the individual engaged in activities. Although the goal is to build a broad collection of photos, the step-by-step process may need to be presented for reference. The individual may need more assistance through check lists since there are so many variables.

    d. Assist to teach the individual to drag, drop, and/or copy as necessary into predetermined board or program. The written or visual steps will assist in building independence for this hobby.

    e. When finished, close the icon and turn off the computer.

For paper scrapbooking:

4. Assist as necessary for the individual to:

    a. Select the items to collect and the style of scrapbook; preferred items, pictures of preferred items, family photos or personal photos of the individual engaged in activities.

    b. Assist the individual to select the album to put all the items in. Sometimes the books will come with sheets inside. Sometimes the individual my want to select some of the specialty papers for scrapbooking. There are fun stickers and stamps to enhance the paper as well.

    c. Assist as necessary to attach the items to the paper as the individual decides. Note skills that need training.

    d. Leave space for an ongoing project

5. Assist the individual as necessary to stop their work, clean up, and shut down the programs. Scrapbooking is an open-ended project that has no clear ending. Assist the individual by creating an ending, setting a timer, or determining a set amount of items for that day.

Activity Story

Today I will make a scrapbook and put my favorite items or photos on it. A scrapbook is a book or board that can keep my favorite pictures in it.

I will decide what items or photos I like and save them to a special spot. Sometimes I like pictures of _____ (animals, fans). Sometimes I can put in pictures of my friends or family. Sometimes I could put in pictures of me doing fun things.

I will have a special book to look at. Sometimes I can show my friends or family. I will tell my friends or family about my photos or items.

I will add more pictures or items if I want to make my book or board bigger. Sometimes it's hard to get the photos or items into the book or board. I will ask for help if it is hard to get the items in my book.

I will listen carefully when I am told to stop. I can put my book away or turn off the computer. I will work on my book or board another day.

Activity Cards—Physical Activities

Appendix D

BASKETBALL HOOPS

Materials:

- Basketball hoop (adjustable as needed)
- Basketball (size as needed)
- Several of the following:

General Guidelines:

1. The activity story and/or visual sequence provided can offer the key elements of the experience.
2. Decide where you can play hoops; personal home, park or play ground, school
3. Assist the individual as necessary by providing the correct height of hoop and size of ball.
4. Shooting hoops is fun and can be done by oneself or with friends. Simple games with friends could include spelling, not just horse but cat or dog making the game shorter.

Furthermore:

As noted above, there are ways to modify shooting the hoops. Having friends compete like horse, (cat, dog, their name) or marking the backboard with "X"s making the game "hit the X. Depending on the individual's strength they may need more assistance. Instead of a blocking move, change the exchange to be a pushing upward movement. Maybe the individual simply throws toward the hoop and a sound, such as a bell reinforces the effort.

Activity Story

I will play basketball by shooting hoops.

Shooting hoops means to try to throw the basketball into the hoop. The hoop is the round rim with a net on it.

I can shoot hoops by myself or ask a friend to play.

I need to watch the ball because it can come off the hoop and hit me.

Sometimes the basketball goes through the hoop. Sometimes the basketball does not go through the hoop. That's OK, I can try again.

HOPSCOTCH

Materials:
- Hopscotch pattern
- Marker or special token
- Red stop sign (optional)

General Guidelines:
1. The activity story and/or visual sequence provided can offer the key elements of the experience.
2. Model and assist as necessary for the individual to hop on one and then both feet to complete the pattern as given in hopscotch.
3. Model and assist the individual to hop around or over a square with the marker in it.
4. Assist the individual as necessary to place a marker in the increasing squares of the pattern. You may need to assist in placing the marker in each square progressively.
5. A clear finish is when the marker has been in each square all the way up and down. Finish could also be just one way.

Furthermore:
You will need to decide if the original rules should apply. They can be confusing even with the marked and sequential task. With some individuals, it may be okay to say they can put their other foot down and create a game of double footed jumps. Others may need assistance knowing where to place the marker and a buddy could mark the appropriate squares. For some individuals, the markers may not work at all, so suggest jumping in a sequence with friends, playing the game according to the rules or using a picture of a time or person, which could be "put the cat on number 2" or "pick up the cat."

Activity Story
Hopscotch is a game I can play by myself or with friends.

I will hop on one foot or both feet. The pattern of squares on the ground tells me that if there is one square I use one foot. If there are two squares, I use two feet.

I take a marker and put it in a square. I cannot put my foot in a square with a marker. Each turn I put the marker in the next square.

My turn is when I hop down the pattern not putting my foot in the square with a marker. I turn around and hop back.

When I hop back to the beginning, I stop and pick up my marker.

Sometimes, it is hard to pick up the marker. If I am on one foot, I cannot put my other foot down. It is hard to balance.

It is okay if I stumble or fall. I can do better next time.

When I play with friends, I must wait turns. It is my turn, up and back, then they will hop up and back.

A game is over when the marker has been in each square for one turn.

OBSTACLE COURSE

Materials:
- Cardboard or wood box with holes or other bean bag toss target
- Socks filled with pinto beans or bean bags
- Paint sticks or chips and a tin can
- Old ties or sections or string/ribbon
- Playground balls
- Mini trampoline, swing, or activity equipment

General Guidelines:

1. The activity story and/or visual sequence provided can offer the key elements of the experience.

2. Setting up your obstacle course can vary in any way the individual can read concrete clues as to how to go from one obstacle to the other. This may be a presentation in a straight row or masking tape arrows indicating order.

3. Assist the individual as necessary and move through the obstacles. Some individuals may need to practice a station separate of the whole course.

4. A suggestion for setting up the obstacle course might be:
   a. Assist as necessary for the individual to engage using the mini trampoline, swing, or other physical equipment. Some individuals may need a timer, specific number of paint sticks dropped in the tin can (five is a good number), or count the turns on the equipment.
   b. Assist as necessary to retrieve the bean bag next to the physical activity and go to the bean bag toss to use it. When the individual is finished there, have them retrieve the ball next to the bean bag too and move to the ball roll.
   c. Assist as necessary to know when the ball roll is over. Having something to strike or a box to hit can help give them concrete information. Putting tape or tying with a rope can indicate the direction. Rope or ties offers a little resistance for wayward rolls.
   d. Assist as necessary to return to the start. Having another object to drop in a container can keep the sequence consistent. Some individuals will need to know how many turns they will have. Keeping track on a piece of paper, such as one with three lines would indicate three turns and the lines could be crossed off after each turn is completed.

5. Any combination of activities can make an obstacle course. Using outdoor equipment or equipment in a workout room can offer opportunities to sequence participation alone or with friends.

Activity Story

Today, I will do an obstacle course with my friends. An obstacle course is when I do different fun things one after the other. I may throw, kick, jump, or run. I might even crawl through a tunnel. It's a fun game.

Today, I will first jump on a trampoline until I hear it is time to move on.

I will grab the bean bag next to the trampoline and run to the throwing place. I will throw the bean bag at the target.

Next, I will take the ball next to the bean bag toss and run to the lines on the floor. I will roll the ball down the lines on the floor.

I will run back to my seat and wait my turn. My turn to do the obstacle course is when all my friends have done it too.

Sometimes the game may change. I may throw the bean bag first, or I will roll the ball first.

The game will be over when everyone has _____ turns.

RELAYS

Materials:

- Three (or more) bean bags per individual
- Container to hold bean bags
- Masking tape or rope to indicate two rows
- Two pieces of paper with large "X"s on them
- Row of chairs, or other area for two lines

General Guidelines:

1. The activity story and/or visual sequence provided can offer the key elements of the game.
2. Assist as necessary to model or visually explain the pattern of the course, discouraging confused running.
3. Assist as necessary to have the individual; get the bean bag from the container, run to the piece of paper in front of you marked with the X, toss the bean bag, and run back to the line. You made need the runner to yell "Go" or tap the next individual in line so they know it's their turn.
4. Explain that finished is indicated when their container of bean bags is empty.
5. If your individual teams are competitive, you could make the rule that the bean bag must be dropped on the paper, not just tossed.

Furthermore:

There are many ways to vary the race. Some suggestion could be; making more than one task, maybe skipping, jumping your way back and forth, or having to balance the bean bag on your head. Having the individuals decide for the other team what the task might be makes it an interesting competition. Also, modify the game to be more of a relay by having another bean bag found next to the "X" brought back and handed off before the next person takes off.

Activity Story

The game "Relay" is a game to play with friends.

There will be two lines of friends. I will stand or sit behind a friend to wait my turn. I will hold my bean bag in my hand unless there is a hand off.

A turn means, I run as fast as I can to the paper with the "X". I toss the bean bag on the paper.

I will know it's my turn when I see my friend in front of me toss their bean bag on the paper. They will yell "go" or tap my shoulder or hand me the bean bag.

Sometimes I may hop to the paper. Sometimes I might skip. I will listen to know how to go to the paper.

I will run/hop/skip as fast as I can, so my team can finish first.

ROLLER SKATING

Materials:

- Skates (traditional, rollerblades or braking)
- Protective gear (helmet, knee, wrist, and elbow pads)
- Money for a rink (optional)

General Guidelines:

1. The activity story and/or visual sequence provided can offer the key elements of the experience.
2. Assist the individual to put on all protective gear. Some need to understand they must be worn every time so start from the first experience. Providing a visual sequence of steps to put on the gear, with a prompt of no gear-no skating can encourage the individual. Individuals who do not like the sensory experience of the gear, may need to start with light fabric and slowly increase the weight to desensitize. Add ribbing from the fabric store to ankle and knee supports to help in this transition.
3. Assist as necessary to ensure the course of skating is clear. A roller rink provides a circle but neighborhoods may need a flag or cone to indicate the path.
4. Assist the individual's success by increasing or decreasing necessary support. Start with placing your hand on the individual's waist, hold hand, and move the individual further away by using a dowel or pole. Most rinks have a separate space for beginners or practicing.
5. Skating is open ended so the individual will need a concrete prompt to know when skating is over. A watch with an alarm can be helpful.

Furthermore:

Consider where you might be skating. A rink can be noisy and crowded at different times. Check with the rink for the least crowded. Some rinks provide times where even the music is off and a limited number of people are present or sectioned off to minimize crowds. Using headphones can, also, minimize the noise but makes it difficult to hear people skating near the individual.

Activity Story

It's time to go roller skating.

I will put on my knee pads, wrist pads, and helmet. Then I will put my roller skates on. I will ask for help if I need help.

I will roller skate in one direction at the rink or on the sidewalk between the flags.

Sometimes I will fall down. That's OK. It will hurt sometimes and sometimes it won't. When I fall, I can ask for help to get back up or I can get back up by myself.

When it is time to stop I will take my skates off and put them away. I will take all my pads off and put them away.

Activity Cards— Sensory Crafts

CREATING SHAKEABLE MUSIC

Materials:

- Small aluminum cans, such as vegetable or aluminum pie tins
- Beans, rice, plastic poker chips, rock, or any hard object
- Small scooper
- Construction paper-any color
- Duct tape-any color or design

General Guidelines:

1. The activity story and/or visual sequence provided can offer the key elements of the project.
2. Place all items out or in a specific visual sequence.
3. Assist as necessary to choose what items to put in the container for shaking. The individual may need the items put in the can without the top or pie tin. Shaking the items without spilling gives the individual an opportunity for a more accurate choice.
4. Assist as necessary to put paper over the open end. Put duct tape around the paper to adhere it to the can or pie tin.
5. Shake away. See "Furthermore" for band ideas.

Furthermore:

Although the maraca type instrument is typically just shaken and that appears as its only action. However, multiples of containers played by friends can combine into fun activities. Set the individuals in a semi-circle around a selected director. The director selects individuals in the pattern to play their instruments by pointing and an open palm means stop. Individuals can take turns being the director. Another opportunity is to use the containers with favorite music. Starting and stopping as they hear the beat.

Activity Story

Today, I will make a shaker that will make noise. Sometimes the sound will be loud and hard. Sometimes it will be soft.

I will choose a can or a pie tin. I will choose what to put in the can or pie tin. I can choose a loud sound or I can choose a soft sound

I will add an item in the can or pie tin to make a sound. I will listen to my sound. I will add more items if I want it too soft. I will take some items out if I want it louder.

I will put paper over the top of the can or pie tin. I will tape the paper so it will stay.

I can shake and make noise. Sometimes I will shake with friends. Sometimes I will take turns shaking. Sometimes I will wait while my friend shakes their container.

When we are done, I will stop shaking. I will listen and stop shaking my container when shaking time is finished.

CREATING SQUISH ART

Materials:

- Heavy duty, zip lock plastic bag (gallon) doubled
- Duct tape
- Corn syrup, one cup per bag
- Soft items, such as glitter, sequins, cotton balls
- Containers with warm and cold water

General Guidelines:

1. The activity story and/or visual sequence provided can offer the key elements of the experience.
2. Retrieve necessary items and put in a sequenced order or make a visual sequence for directions.
3. Using two bags, one inside of the other, assist as necessary to pour corn syrup into the bags. Most individuals will need help; either to hold bag or pour. Putting the bottom of the bags into a bowl is helpful, also.
4. Assist as necessary to select items for the bag and put them in.
5. Assist as necessary to carefully seal the bags by zipping them up and putting duct tape across the top. Don't have too much air left inside as that can put too much pressure on the seal when squeezing.
6. Allow exploration time for the individual to squish the items around.
7. Assist as necessary to drop the bags into warm water. It may take a few moments to warm. Return to the individual to explore further. Repeat with the cold. The cold would work faster with iced water.
8. With care the bags should last. Check each time they are put away for potential leaks.

Activity Story

Today I will be filling a bag with syrup to make a squishy bag. A squishy bag feels soft and I can push on it with my hands. I will not push hard. I will push soft.

I will pour from a cup the syrup into a bag.

I will choose items to put in with the syrup. This will make it fun to push on the bag.

I will put tape across the top. If I need help, I will ask.

I can softly squish my items in my bag with my hands.

I will put my bag in hot water so it will be warm. I can softly push my items around.

When I am finished, I will put my bag away.

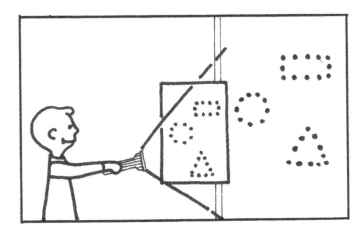

EXPLORING LIGHT AND SHADOW

Materials:
- Heavy paper or cardboard
- Sharp pointed tool or strong scissors
- Glue
- Tissue paper or light fabric, such as netting
- Flashlight or stationary light

General Guidelines:
1. The activity story and/or visual sequence provided can offer the key elements of the experience.
2. Assist as necessary for the individual to draw or trace shapes onto the paper or cardboard. Shapes may be geometric or familiar, such as animals.
3. Assist as necessary or take over the task of cutting out the shapes. The cardboard requires an exact too. The activity works best with a solid background which would be difficult to cut for some individuals.
4. Assist as necessary to cut or tear pieces of tissue or netting. Shape does not matter as long as it's big enough to cover the cut out shapes.
5. Assist as necessary to glue the pieces on so they cover the shapes.
6. Assist as necessary to prop the cardboard on a flat surface facing a wall. Assist the individual to shine light from behind on the wall. Some of the individuals will have difficulty seeing the shapes on the wall from behind the cardboard. This is a good opportunity to use a buddy for assistance. The friends could take turns shinning the light. A table lamp also works well but is very hot and could be a danger to some individuals.

Furthermore:
This is a simple variation to play the old game of making your hands into animals before a light source. The light source will of course make the patterns show as soft or bright. Try putting hands or other objects in front of the screen. For example, animals could dance across a square. Just poking holes in shapes on the board is an alternative to the paper or fabric. The design is harder to be watched with the light but interesting to explore.

Activity Story
I am going to make a pattern on a big piece of paper. I will put different paper over it. I will shine a light on it.

I will decide what shape I want to shine the light on. I will draw or trace the shape on the big paper.

I will cut the shape out. I will ask for help if it is hard to do.

I will choose a color of paper or fabric. I will cut or tear pieces of it to cover my shapes.

I will shine a light behind it and see the pretty colors. I will shine a light in front and see pretty colors on the wall.

I can make the shapes move on the wall. I can find items like plastic and move it in front of the shape. It can dance on the wall with the shape too.

I can make the shape turn off and on or darker with my light.

When I am finished, I will turn off the light and put my big paper away. If I tear my paper I can make another one.

EXPLORING TEXTURES IN BINS

Materials:

- Bed sheet
- Plastic bins with lids
- Variety of textures, such as:
  - Beans
  - Rice
  - Cornmeal
  - Sand
  - Macaroni
  - Corn starch clay or sticky balls
- Variety of utensils to scoop or fill:
  - Spoons
  - Cups, buckets
  - Sifter
  - Funnel
- Trowel
- Spray bottle or watering can

General Guidelines:

1. The activity story and/or visual sequence provided can offer the key elements of the activity.
2. Assist the individual as necessary to spread the sheet on the floor or table if using small bins.
3. Assist as necessary to select a texture item. If individual is only repeatedly picking the same item, select for them. With multiple bins, more than one texture can be chosen.
4. Assist as necessary for the individual to explore in the bins. Add the utensils and allow more exploration time.
5. Assist as necessary to finish by putting the lids on the bins. Anticipating a finish is difficult for some individuals and some resist changing away from the activity. Set a timer, or if using multiple bins, start with closing one bin then the next.
6. Collect the sheet to discard over spill.

Furthermore:

Textiles are fun to explore. If the bins are large enough, say the biggest one is like a holiday storage bin, more than hands could go in. Putting feet in is also fun.

Activity Story

Today I will feel things in a bin. I will feel hard things. I might feel sticky things. I might feel soft things. I can choose the things I want. I will put them in a bin.

I will put my hands into the bins. There might be things to scoop with so I can pour. There might be things I can use to spin things in. I will keep the _____ in the bin.

When I am done, I will put the lid on the bin. I can play another day.

FILLING UP ART PROJECT

Materials:

- Clear acetate paper or contact paper (found at craft stores)
- Safety scissors
- Stapler
- Fillers: colored tissue, feathers, beans, cotton balls, etc.
- Hole punch and yarn

General Guidelines:

1. The activity story and/or visual sequence provided can offer the key elements of the experience.
2. There are two ways to do this project. Please see the "Furthermore" for a second suggestion.
3. Assist as necessary to trace a shape on the acetate. Assist as necessary to cut two of the shapes out. Acetate can tear so it may not always be appropriate for some individuals to attempt without growing frustrated.
4. Assist as necessary to staple around the shape, leaving the top open. Staples should be close enough to prevent the filler from falling out the sides.
5. Assist as necessary for the individual to choose fillers. Placing them on paper plates or containers in front of the individual allows choices. The individual may like to do just a collection of one item or a combination. Some individuals may need the shape to be held for filling or laid on a table secured with tape.
6. Assist as necessary to stuff the items in the shape until the individual decides it is done. Staple shut.
7. Assist as necessary to punch a hole in the center top. String with yarn and hang in an open place to see the stuffed items on both sides.

Furthermore:

An alternative for this project is using contact paper rather than acetate. Cut two shapes out of the contact paper. Peel one and secure to the table. You can turn the edges back to catch on the surface of the table or use masking tape. After allowing the individual to choose what items they want to stuff, assist to place the items on the sticky paper. Some individuals may need only part of the paper peeled back as they cover one area, moving to another. When the individual is done, lay the next cut out shape on top. Working carefully, adhere the top first then slowly pull the paper off a bit at a time. Gently press the contact paper down, sealing the shape. Continue as above, cutting the hole and hanging with a string or yarn. These items should be more secure than the paper ones and can withstand some poking. Consider a game similar to batting a piñata.

Activity Story

Today I will make a pretty shape full of items I like.

I will cut a shape out of a plastic kind of paper. I will cut two of the shapes. Sometimes the cutting is hard. I will ask for help if the cutting is hard for me.

I will use a stapler and staple around my shape. I will not staple the top of my shape. Sometimes stapling is hard. I will ask for help if it is hard for me.

I will choose what I want in my shape. I might choose feathers, cotton, or maybe buttons. There will be many things to choose from.

I will fill the shape (*stick on the items) with the items I chose. I will fill the shape until it is full. *I will not stuff my shape till it pops open. When I am done filling my shape (*I will put the other piece on top. I will softly push the paper on.) I will staple the top shut.

Sometimes stapling is hard. I will ask for help if the stapling is hard.

I will make a hole in the top of my shape. I will put string or yarn in the hole. I will hang my shape with string or yarn.

I will see my shape on both sides when I look at it.

* Changes are for contact paper project.

PLACING OBJECTS ART

Materials:

- Small crumpled pieces of tissue
- Large animal shapes cut out of poster board
- Glue poured into a small flat container like a plate or pie tin

General Guidelines:

1. The activity story and/or visual sequence provided can offer the key elements of the experience.
2. Assist as necessary for the individual to select an animal. Some individuals may want to trace their own from a template. Some could then try cutting them out although the heavy paper may be difficult.
3. Place the items in a sequence; tissue, glue, and cut-out.
4. Assist as necessary for the individual to select a piece of crumpled paper, dip it in the glue, and place it on the cut-out. Repeat as many times as the individual wants to. Some individuals may want to cover the shape or some may want to just add a few.
5. Assist as necessary for the individual to hang their project so they can appreciate their work.

Furthermore:

This activity has many variations. Different items could be used according to the individual's interest. Feathers, beads, scraps of fabric, or other items could be glued on. If the individual is interested in the tissue, the activity could be expanded to include the individual ripping and crumpling themselves. When working with gluing the items, some individuals may need the shape taped down so it is more stable. Another alternative is presenting the shape covered in clear contact paper and slowly peeling it back rather than gluing. Using a variety of shapes can expand the activity further. Shapes, such as the individual's favorite items, animals from the zoo, or a family of animals (mom, dad, and babies)- can expand the activity further.

Activity Story

Today I will make pretty animal shapes. I will use glue and paper.

I will choose small pieces of paper. I will dip it in glue. I will put it on the paper. If I need help, I can ask for help.

I will decide how many pieces of little paper I will put on the animal shape.

When I am finished, I will hang up my animal shape. I will be able to look at my animal when I want.

SHINING MOVEMENT PROJECT

Materials:
- Paint sticks
- Shiny paper, such as Mylar or heavy duty tin foil
- Glue
- Safety Scissors
- Fan or hair dryer with a cool setting

General Guidelines:
1. The activity story and/or visual sequence provided can offer the key elements of the experience.
2. Cut or tear the Mylar or tin foil into pieces that are the width of the paint stick and long as desired.
3. Assist as necessary to glue the width to the paint stick. To make it more sturdy you may wish to wrap it around the paint stick one or two times.
4. Assist as necessary to cut/tear the Mylar/tin foil so there are 2" or 3" strips coming from the glued end
5. Allow exploration time then try putting it in front of the fan or a hair dryer (cool setting). If the individual is interested, they could try flapping it on arms or legs.

Activity Story
Today I will make a flapper. I will shake and flap it. I will make it out of shinny paper.

I will pick the piece of paper I want. Mylar comes in different colors, tin foil doesn't.

I will use a stick and put glue on the stick. I will lay one side on the glue to make it stay on the stick.

I will cut or rip the paper apart in small tears. My paper will now move in the air.

I will try my flapper by shaking it back and forth.

I can put my flapper in front of a fan or hair dryer to make it flap back and forth too.

I will ask for help if my paper tears. I can use more glue and put it on the stick.

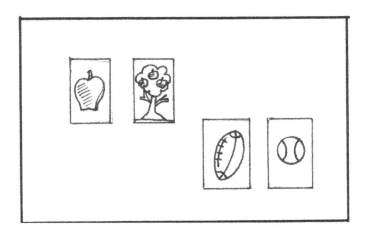

SORTING FUN PICTURES

Materials:

- Catalogs, colored advertisement or brochures of the individual's interests
- An iPad or computer (optional)
- Firm paper, such as poster board
- Glue
- Small baskets or boxes to hold board

General Guidelines:

1. The activity story and/or visual sequence provided can offer the key elements of the activity.
2. Have the poster board cut into sizes that will fit in the baskets or boxes.
3. Assist the individual to find and indicate the item they find in the catalogs, advertisements, or brochures they like.
4. Assist the individual as necessary to cut the item out. Some individuals need to have a black circle around the item to be able to separate it from other items on the page. Accuracy of cutting is not the goal here unless it is a particular goal for the individual to work on.
5. Assist as necessary to glue the pictures on the poster board. The individual may want to add a label or have assistance to label.
6. Set up the boxes or baskets with a sample card or label to sort and add pictures collected. The individual can switch between using the activity to look at the favorite items on cards or work on adding more.
7. This activity has a "natural ending" if using boxes or containers. Sorting or looking is over when the cards go in the container. Other strategies include restrict the access to more items to cut or glue or when all the cards to sort are finished.

Furthermore:

Many individuals like to collect pictures of their favorite items or pictures depicting their favorite activities. The cards might need to be laminated to preserve them. Some individuals enjoy the tactile experience of holding and sorting. Similar pictures may have different points of reference than are immediately recognizable by others, for example, a collection of fan pictures. Since this is a leisure activity it is not necessary to be accurate in sorting either. Beyond the personal enjoyment of the individual to look at or collect pictures there are other ways to use the cards. For example, play the "Go Fish" card game.

Activity Story

I like sorting pictures and thinking about my favorite things. I will keep them to look at. Sometimes it's hard work and confusing but I can ask for help.

I will make the cards by cutting pictures from magazines or the paper. I can also find pictures on the computer.

The pictures will be of things I like to look at. I will use glue to put them on cards. I can look at the card, find more or I will find pictures on the Internet and keep them in my folder.

I can put the pictures in a basket. I can have different pictures in different baskets. I can mix up the cards and put them back in the basket. I can ask a friend to play cards with them.

I can look for more pictures I like. I will keep them safe in the baskets.

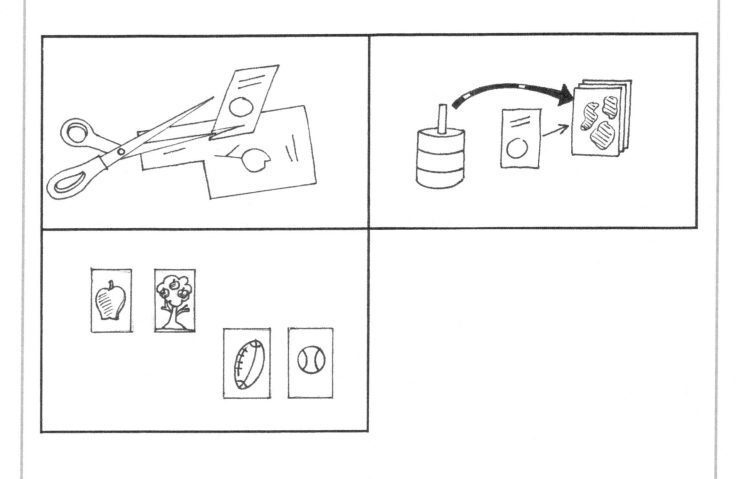

TEXTURE CHOICES

Materials:

- Fabric scraps
- Cardboard cut 8 ½ x 11" with a hole punched in the upper left corner
- Glue
- Metal rings and/or container that will hold cards

General Guidelines:

1. The activity story and/or visual sequence provided can offer the key elements of the experience.
2. Assist the individual to select fabric scraps they prefer from an array presented on the table. Fabric stores may be willing to donate from their discarded fabric.
3. Assist as necessary for the individual to glue the pieces on the card.
4. Assist as necessary to have the individual indicate if they would prefer to store the cards in a container or on rings to make it a book. The goal of the rings is to open with easy access for the individual and be able to add or take away pages.

Furthermore:

Tactile exploration is very important for some individuals with sensory issues. Having an ongoing selection of textures to explore may lead to increasing the textures they resist.

Activity Story

Today I will make a book and put different fabrics or material in it. This kind of book is called my scrapbook. Fabric or materials are both like your clothes or blankets.

Some fabrics will feel soft. Some fabrics will feel rough. I will pick the fabric I like.

I will glue the fabric on a card. If I need help, I will ask.

I will keep my cards in a book (container).

I can take my card out and feel it. I will feel it on my face. I will feel it on my arms. I will not feel it on other places.

When I am done, I will put my book away. I will have it another day.

References

Adams, J. (1995). *Getting people motivated in life and leisure activities, effective motivating techniques.* State College, PA: Venture Publishing.

Aspy, R. & Grossman, B. G. (2007). *The ziggurat model: A framework for designing comprehensive interventions for individuals with high-functioning autism and Asperger syndrome.* Shawnee Mission, KS: Autism Asperger Publishing Co.

Autism Internet Modules. Retrieved on 11/13/2014 from www.autisminternetmodules.org/.

American Psychiatric Association (2013). *Diagnostic and statistical manual of mental disorders, 5th edition* (DSM-5). Washington, DC: Author.

Badia, M., Orgaz, M. B., Verdugo, M. Á. & Ullán, A. M. (2012). Patterns and determinants of leisure participation of youth and adults with developmental disabilities. *Journal of Intellectual Disability Research.*

Badia, M., Orgaz, M. B., Verdugo, M. Á., Ullán, A. M. & Martínez, M. M. (2011). Personal factors and perceived barriers to participation in leisure activities for youth and adults with developmental disabilities. *Research in Developmental Disabilities*, 32(6), 2055–2063.

Baker, M. J. (2000). Incorporating the thematic ritualistic behaviors of children with autism into games: Increasing social play interactions. *Journal of Positive Behavior Interventions*, 2(2), 66.

Bambara, L. M., Spiegel-McGill, P., Shores, R. E. & Fox, J. J. (1984). A comparison of reactive and nonreactive toys on severely handicapped children's manipulative play. *Journal of the Association for Persons with Severe Handicaps*, 9 (2), 142-149.

Baranak, G. T., Little, L. M., Parham, L., Ausduran, K. K. & Sabotos-Devito, M. G. (2013). Sensory features in autism spectrum disorder. In F. Volkmar (Ed), *Encyclopedia of autism spectrum disorders.* New York, NY: Springer.

Blum-Dimaya, A., Reeve, S. A., Reeve, K. F. & Hoch, H. (2010). Teaching children with autism to play a video game using activity schedules and game-embedded simultaneous video modeling. *Education & Treatment of Children* (West Virginia University Press), 351-370.

Boyd, B., Conroy, M. A., Mancil, G. R., Nakao, T. & Alter, P.J. (2007). Effects of circumscribed interests on the social behaviors of children with autism spectrum disorders: Use of structural analysis analogues. *Journal of Autism and Developmental Disorders*, 37 (8), 1550-1561.

Brewster, S. & Coleyshaw, L. (2011). Participation or exclusion? Perspectives of pupils with autistic spectrum disorders on their participation in leisure activities. *British Journal of Learning Disabilities.* 39(4), 284-291.

Burlingame, J. & Blaschko, T. (2010). *Assessment tools for recreational therapy* (4th ed.). Ravendale, WA: Idyll Arbor.

Buron, K. D. (2010). *The social times.* Shawnee Mission, Kan.: Autism Asperger Publishing Company.

Buttimer, J. & Tierney, E. (2005). Patterns of leisure participation among adolescents with a mild intellectual disability. *Journal of Intellectual Disabilities,* 9(1):25-42.

Centers for Disease Control and Prevention. Autism spectrum disorder. Retrieved on 12/13/2014 from http://www.cdc.gov/ncbddd/autism/data.html.

Charlop-Christy, M. H. & Haymes, L. K. (1998). Using objects of obsession as token reinforcers for children with autism. *Journal of Autism and Developmental Disorders,* 28, 189-198.

Chin, H. Y. & Bernard-Opitz, V. (2000). Teaching conversational skills to children with autism: Effects on the development of theory of mind. *Journal of Autism and Developmental Disorders,* 30(6), 569-583.

Coyne P. & Fullerton, A. (2014). *Supporting individuals with autism spectrum disorder in recreation* (2nd ed.). Urbana, IL: Sagamore Publishing.

Coyne P. & Fullerton, A. (2014). Toward a balanced leisure lifestyle for adults with autism spectrum disorder. In M. Tincani & A. Bondy (Eds.). *Autism spectrum disorders in adolescents and adults.* New York, NY: Guilford Press.

Coyne, P. (2011). *Preparing youth with autism spectrum disorder for adulthood.* Portland, OR: Columbia Regional Program. Retrieved 11/15/2014 from http://www.crporegon.org.

Cuhadar, S. & Diken, H. (2011). Effectiveness of instruction performed through activity schedules on leisure skills of children with autism. *Education and Training in Autism and Developmental Disabilities,* 46(3), 386-398.

Dattilo J. (2008) *Leisure Education Program Planning: A Systematic Approach,* (3rd ed.). State College, PA: Venture.

Elementary/Secondary System (ESS) (1993). Specialized Training Program, University of Oregon.

Fox, L., Vaughn, B., Wyatte, M. & Dunlap, G. (2002). 'We Can't Expect Other People to Understand': Family perspectives on problem behavior. *Exceptional Children,* 68(4), 437.

References

Fullerton, A. & Rake, J. (2013). A few perspectives and experiences of individuals with Autism Spectrum Disorder related to recreation. In P. Coyne and A. Fullerton (Eds). *Supporting Individuals with Autism Spectrum Disorder in Recreation* (2nd ed.). Urbana, IL: Sagamore Publishing.

Garruto, M. (2011). The effects of prompt fading and differential reinforcement on selection of novel activities by children with autism. *Dissertation Abstracts International: Section B: The Sciences and Engineering*, 72(4-B), 2426.

Garcia-Villamisar, D. A. & Dattilo, J. (2010). Effects of a leisure programme on quality of life and stress of individuals with ASD. *Journal of intellectual disability research.* 54(7), 611-619.

Gutierrez-Griep, R. (1984). Student preference of sensory reinforcers. *Education and Training of the Mentally Retarded*, 19, 108-113.

Hilton, C. L., Crouch, M. C. & Israel, H (2008). Out-of-school participation patterns in children with high-functioning autism spectrum disorders. *The American Journal of Occupational Therapy*, 62(5), 554-563.

Hochhauser, M. & Engel-Yeger, B. (2010). Sensory processing abilities and their relation to participation in leisure activities among children with high-functioning autism spectrum disorder. *Research in Autism Spectrum Disorders*, 4, 746-754.

Hume, K. & Carnahan, C. (2008). *Overview of structured work systems.* Chapel Hill, NC: National Professional Development Center on Autism Spectrum Disorders, Frank Porter Graham Child Development Institute, The University of North Carolina.

Hutchison S. L., Bland A. D. & Kleiber D. A. (2008). Leisure and stress-coping: implications for therapeutic recreation practice. *Therapeutic Recreation Journal* 42, 9–23.

Kaplan-Reimer, H., Sidener, T. M., Reeve, K. F. & Sidener, D. W. (2011). Using stimulus control procedures to teach indoor rock climbing to children with autism. *Behavioral Interventions*, 26(1), 1-22.

Kreiner, J. & Flexer, R. (2009). Assessment of leisure preferences for students with severe developmental disabilities and communication difficulties. *Education and Training in Developmental Disabilities*, 44(2), 280 – 288.

Lane County, Multimedia Transition Portfolio Guide. Retrieved 10/15/2014 from http://blogs.4j.lane.edu/postsecondarytransitionportfolio.

LeConner, L. (2009). *The socially included child: A parent's guide to successful playdates, recreation, and family events for children with autism.* New York, NY: The Berkley Publishing Group.

Lee, L. C., Harrington, R. A., Louie, B. B. & Newschaffer, C. J. (2008). Children with autism: Quality of life and parental concerns. *Journal of Autism and Developmental Disorders*, 38(6), 1147-1160.

Mazurek, M. O., Shattuck, P. T., Wagner, M. & Cooper, B. P. (2012). Prevalence and correlates of screen-based media use among youths with autism spectrum disorders. *Journal of Autism and Developmental Disorders*, 42(8), 1757-1767.

Mesibov, G. B., Browder, D. M. & Kirkland, C. (2002). Using individualized schedules as a component of positive behavioral support for students with developmental disabilities. *Journal of Positive Behavioral Interventions*, 4, 73 – 79.

Mesibov, G., Shea, V. & Schopler, E. (2005). *The TEACCH® approach to autism spectrum disorders*. New York, NY: Plenum Publishers.

Myles, B. S., Trautman, M. L. & Schelvan, R. S. (2004). *The Hidden Curriculum: Practical solutions for understanding unstated rules in social situations*. Shawnee Mission, KS: Autism Asperger Publishing Company.

National Professional Development Center on Autism Spectrum Disorders (2008). Evidenced-based briefs. Retrieved on 11/15/2014 from http://autismpdc.fpg.unc.edu/content/briefs.

National Professional Development Center for Autism Spectrum Disorder (2014). Evidence-based practices for children, youth, and young adults with autism spectrum disorder. Retrieved on 10/27/2014 from http://autismpdc.fpg.unc.edu/sites/autismpdc.fpg.unc.edu/files/2014-EBP-Report.pdf.

National Professional Development Center on Autism Spectrum Disorders (2014). Evidence-based practices fact sheets. Retrieved on 10/27/2014 from http://autismpdc.fpg.unc.edu/node/727.

Orsmond, G., Krauss, M. & Seltzer, M. (2004). Peer relationships and social and recreational activities among adolescents and adults with autism. *Journal of Autism and Developmental Disorders*, 34, 245-256.

Orsmond, G. I. & Kuo, H. Y. (2011). The daily lives of adolescents with an autism spectrum disorder: discretionary time use and activity partners. *Autism: The International Journal of Research and Practice*, 15(5), 579-599.

Pacer Center (n.d.). Mapping your dreams: recreation. Retrieved on 11/1/2014 from http://www.pacer.org/tatra/resources/MYD/recreation.asp.

Paterson, C. R. & Arco, L. (2008). Using video modeling for general- izing toy play in children with autism. *Behavior Modification*, 31, 660-681.

References

Potvin, M. C., Prelock, P. A., Snider, L. & Savard, L. (2013). Promoting recreational engagement. In F. Volkmar (Ed), *Encyclopedia of autism spectrum disorders*. New York, NY: Springer.

Potvin, M. C., Snider, L., Prelock, P. A., Kehayia, E. & Wood-Dauphinee, S. (2013). Recreational participation of children with high functioning autism. *Journal of Autism and Developmental Disorder*, 43(2), 445-457.

Reid, G. & O'Connor, J. (2003). The autism spectrum disorders: activity selection, assessment, and program organization. *Palaestra*, 19(1), 21.

Reynolds, S., Bendixen, R. M., Lawrence, T. & Lane, S. J. (2011). A pilot study examining activity participation, sensory responsiveness, and competence in children with high functioning autism spectrum disorder *Journal of Autism and Developmental Disorders*, 41, 1496-1508.

Rincover, A., Newson, C., Lovaas, I. O., & Koegel, R. (1977). Some motivational properties of sensory stimulation in psychotic children. *Journal of Experimental Child Psychology*, 24, 312-323.

Roscoe, E. M., Carreau, A., MacDonald, J. & Pence, S. T. (2008). Further evaluation of leisure items in the attention condition of functional analyses. *Journal of Applied Behavior Analysis*. 41(3), 351-364.

Sancho, K., Sidener, T. M., Reeve, S. A. & Sidener, D. W. (2010). A comparison of video priming and simultaneous video modeling to teach play skills to children with autism. *Education and Treatment of Children*, 33, 421-442.

Schleien, S., Rynders, J. & Musstonen, T. (1997). Effects of social play activities on the play behavior of children with autism. *Journal of Leisure Research*, 22(4), 317-329.

Schleien, S., Meyer, L., Heyne, L. & Brandt, B. (Eds.). (1995). *Lifelong leisure skills and lifestyles for persons with developmental disabilities*. Baltimore, MD: Paul H. Brookes.

Schultheis, S. F., Boswell, B. B. & Decker, J. (2000). Successful physical activity programming for students with autism. *Focus on Autism and Other Developmental Disabilities*, 15(3), 159-162.

Solish, A., Perry, A. & Minnes, P. (2010). Participation of children with and without disabilities in social, recreational and leisure activities. *Journal of Applied Research in Intellectual Disabilities*, 23(3), 226-236.

Stumbo, N. J. & Peterson, C. A. (2009). *Therapeutic recreation program design: Principles and procedures* (5th ed.). San Francisco, CA: Pearson Benjamin Cummings. p. 54.

Thompson, D. & Emira, M. (2011). 'They say every child matters, but they don't": An investigation into parental and carer perceptions of access to leisure facilities and respite care for children and young people with autistic spectrum disorder (ASD) or attention deficit, hyperactivity disorder (ADHD). *Disability & Society*, 26(1), 65-78.

Yanardag, M., Akmanoglu N. & Yilmaz I. (2013). The effectiveness of video prompting on teaching aquatic play skills for children with autism. *Disability Rehabilitation*, 35(1), 47-56.

CPSIA information can be obtained
at www.ICGtesting.com
Printed in the USA
BVOW07s1116280316

441584BV00008BA/4/P

9 781941 765036